WHITE-COLLAR AND ORGANIZATIONAL CRIME

New Ideas, Directions, and Perspectives

Edited by
Diana Bociga and Jon Davies

First published in Great Britain in 2025 by

Bristol University Press
University of Bristol
1-9 Old Park Hill
Bristol
BS2 8BB
UK
t: +44 (0)117 374 6645
e: bup-info@bristol.ac.uk

Details of international sales and distribution partners are available at bristoluniversitypress.co.uk

© Diana Bociga and Jon Davies 2025

The digital PDF and ePub versions of this title are available open access and distributed under the terms of the Creative Commons Attribution-NonCommercial-NoDerivatives 4.0 International licence (https://creativecommons.org/licenses/by-nc-nd/4.0/) which permits reproduction and distribution for non-commercial use without further permission provided the original work is attributed.

British Library Cataloguing in Publication Data
A catalogue record for this book is available from the British Library

ISBN 978-1-5292-4712-1 paperback
ISBN 978-1-5292-4713-8 ePub
ISBN 978-1-5292-4714-5 OA PDF

The right of Diana Bociga and Jon Davies to be identified as editors of this work has been asserted by them in accordance with the Copyright, Designs and Patents Act 1988.

All rights reserved: no part of this publication may be reproduced, stored in a retrieval system, or transmitted in any form or by any means, electronic, mechanical, photocopying, recording, or otherwise without the prior permission of Bristol University Press.

Every reasonable effort has been made to obtain permission to reproduce copyrighted material. If, however, anyone knows of an oversight, please contact the publisher.

The statements and opinions contained within this publication are solely those of the editors and contributors and not of the University of Bristol or Bristol University Press. The University of Bristol and Bristol University Press disclaim responsibility for any injury to persons or property resulting from any material published in this publication.

Bristol University Press works to counter discrimination on grounds of gender, race, disability, age and sexuality.

Cover design: Liam Roberts Design
Front cover image: 123RF_mikkyr

Contents

List of Figures and Tables   v
Notes on Contributors   vi

Introduction: Emerging Voices on the Study of White-Collar   1
and Organizational Crime
Diana Bociga and Jon Davies

1. The Diversity Spectrum of Corporate Offending: 8
   A Framework for Research and Practice
   Jelmar J. Meester, Arjan A.J. Blokland, Marieke H.A. Kluin, and Wim Huisman
2. Organizational Culture and Corporate Criminology   23
   Nina Tobsch and Marieke H.A. Kluin
3. Social Control for Leverage: Stakeholders Influencing   41
   Peer Social Control
   Anna Merz
4. A Critical Realist Methodology for Understanding   58
   Noncompliance: From Theory to Practice
   Korry Robert
5. Factorial Survey Research in the Study of White-Collar   78
   and Corporate Crime: Benefits, Applications,
   and Challenges
   Jing Wei
6. Affective Atmosphere and White-Collar Crime: A Case of   97
   Transgressive Thrill in the Art Fair
   Diāna Bērziņa
7. Beyond Mafia: Considerations on Criminal Infiltration in   111
   the Legal Economy
   Giovanni Nicolazzo
8. A Novel Typology of Frauds in Sports: Scripts, Perpetrators,   125
   and Bearers of the Associated Harm
   Sofie Gotelaere and Letizia Paoli

9	White-Collar Crime in Kenyan Agri-Food Markets: Violations of Agri-Food Safety Laws in the Agri-Food Chain *Emmanuel K. Bunei*	153
Index		170

List of Figures and Tables

Figures

1.1	Diversity and occurrence framework	13
4.1	An example of the stratified reality for the NatWest case	71
9.1	The interrelationship between key study observations	163

Tables

2.1	Example of a causal process tracing theory	34
3.1	Mechanisms of leveraging peer social control	47
8.1	Typology of frauds in sports	132
9.1	Profile of key informants	158

Notes on Contributors

Diāna Bērziņa is a researcher on the ERC-funded Trafficking Transformations project at Maastricht University. Her research explores commodities-related crimes and harms, focusing on art and heritage crime. She investigates how object-attuned thinking and ideas around object agency, senses, and atmospheres contribute to our understanding of certain types of crime. Her work examines human–object relationships in spaces not typically seen as criminogenic, such as metal detecting in Russia, the atmosphere of art fairs, and the use of digital spaces to contest the illegality of grey activities. Her work has been published in journals such as *Deviant Behavior, Critical Criminology, Crime, Media, Culture,* and the *European Journal on Criminal Policy and Research*.

Arjan A.J. Blokland is Senior Researcher at the Netherlands Institute for the Study of Crime and Law Enforcement (NSCR) and Professor of Criminology and Criminal Justice at Leiden Law School, Leiden University, the Netherlands. His research, inspired by life-course criminological theory and methods, focuses on the longitudinal patterning of corporate noncompliance and the effects of monitoring and enforcement on corporate criminal careers. He co-authored the chapter 'Life-course criminology and corporate offending' for *The Cambridge Handbook of Compliance*, which explores the merits and challenges of a life-course approach to corporate crime. His other research interests include developmental and life-course criminology, networked criminology, and sexual offending.

Diana Bociga is Research Associate in the Department of Criminology at the University of Manchester. Her research focuses on the UK's approach to combating economic crime, particularly money laundering. Using mixed methods, including social network analysis (SNA), she examines the structure and dynamics of the UK's economic crime governance networks. She has been involved in various research projects, including studies on the regulation and supervision of UK law firms under anti-money laundering (AML) frameworks and the role of artificial intelligence in facilitating and preventing fraud. Her work has been published in *Policing and Society* and the *European*

Journal on Criminal Policy and Research, and she served as a guest editor for a special issue in *Crime, Law & Social Change*. Her broader research interests include economic crime, white-collar crime, illicit finance, public and private responses to economic crime, AML regulations, and security networks.

Emmanuel K. Bunei is Research Fellow at Flinders University, Australia, and Research Associate at the Centre for Rural Criminology, University of New England, Australia. He is an interdisciplinary rural criminologist and social researcher with expertise in rural crime, criminal justice issues, and programme design, implementation, monitoring, and evaluation. Emmanuel holds a PhD in criminology from the University of New England, Australia, and BA and MA degrees in sociology, focusing on rural communities. In 2023, he was awarded the Joseph Donnermeyer Early Research Award for his scholarly excellence and dedication to rural and remote communities. His research has been published in peer-reviewed journals covering topics such as farm crime, compliance with agri-food safety regulations, rural crime, environmental crime, and cultural criminology.

Jon Davies is Lecturer in Criminology at the University of Manchester. His primary research interests focus on white-collar and corporate crimes, especially issues of labour exploitation, food fraud, and governance. He has conducted research across various sectors in the UK, the rest of Europe, and the Middle East. Jon is one of the founding members and the current coordinator of the 'Manchester Organizational Non-Compliance Initiative' (MONI) research group, which specializes in research on white-collar, corporate, and organizational crimes.

Sofie Gotelaere is a PhD candidate in criminology at the University of Leuven's Faculty of Law and Criminology in Belgium. Her research focuses on fraud and money laundering, particularly in the context of sports. She has contributed to multiple research initiatives, including the Prevention of Fraud in Sports (PrOFS) project and a study on mediation in the context of administrative fines. Her work has been published in international journals such as the *European Journal on Criminal Policy* and *Research and Sport in Society*. Her broader research interests include cybercrime, financial and economic crime, white-collar crime, mediation, and the intersection between public (civil, administrative, or criminal) and private (disciplinary) responses to rule violations.

Wim Huisman is Professor of Criminology at the Vrije Universiteit Amsterdam and Head of the Department of Criminology. He is a past president of the Netherlands Society of Criminology and co-Editor-in-Chief of *Crime, Law & Social Change*. He was chair of the Division of White-Collar and Corporate Crime of the American Society of Criminology and is a co-founder and board member of EUROC, the white-collar crime working group of the European Society of Criminology. Huisman is also a member of the Steering Committee of ComplianceNet, an interdisciplinary network on compliance research. His research interests include corporate compliance and white-collar crime, covering fraud, corruption, environmental crime, and corporate involvement in atrocity crimes. His current research adopts a life-course perspective on corporate offending.

Marieke H.A. Kluin is Assistant Professor of Criminology at Leiden Law School, Leiden University, the Netherlands. She is a board member of the European Society of Criminology, co-founder and chair of the Green Criminology European Working Group (GREEN), and co-chair of the Division of Organizational Crime of the Netherlands Society of Criminology. Her research interests include white-collar crime, environmental crime, compliance, and regulatory enforcement. She served as a guest editor for a special issue in *Crime, Law & Social Change* on the multifaceted harms of corporate and white-collar crime and co-authored the chapter 'Life-course criminology and corporate offending' for the Cambridge Handbook of Compliance. She is currently involved in projects applying a life-course criminology perspective to corporate offending and examining the effectiveness of sanctions for environmental crimes.

Jelmar J. Meester is a PhD candidate at the Department of Criminology of the Vrije Universiteit Amsterdam. His research focuses on the development of corporate offending and the applicability of a life-course criminology perspective on corporations. He aims to reveal the interconnectedness of individual-level, corporate-level, and economic-level developments through quantitative and temporal analyses. His other research interests include regulatory enforcement, environmental crime, and violation detection. Meester is co-chair of the Division of Organizational Crime of the Netherlands Society of Criminology.

Anna Merz holds a PhD in criminology from Erasmus University Rotterdam. Her doctoral research focused on peer responses to noncompliance with anti-money laundering (AML) regulations in the Dutch banking industry. Her wider research interests include corporate crime, AML regulation, formal and informal social control of corporate crime, criminological theory, and corporate compliance. She is currently working as a regulator in the Netherlands.

Giovanni Nicolazzo is a PhD candidate in criminology at the Università Cattolica del Sacro Cuore, specializing in the criminal component of the legal economy. His research examines the interaction between criminal practices and financial systems, focusing on organized crime and money laundering. Using qualitative and quantitative methods, he assesses the impact of illicit activities on market dynamics and the effectiveness of current regulatory measures. He has contributed to several research projects providing evidence-based insights into economic crime and policy development. His research aims to identify gaps and propose measures to strengthen financial systems against criminal influence.

Letizia Paoli is Chair of the Department of Criminal Law and Criminology at KU Leuven's Faculty of Law and Criminology and a Life Member of Clare Hall, University of Cambridge. She has published extensively on organized crime, illegal drugs, and sports-related crime and their control policies. With Dr Victoria A. Greenfield (George Mason University), she developed the harm assessment framework to evaluate the harms of crimes and policy interventions. Her latest publication, *Assessing the Harms of Crime: A New Framework for Criminal Policy* (2022, with V.A. Greenfield, Oxford University Press), won the 2023 Book Award from the European Society of Criminology.

Korry Robert is a PhD candidate in criminology at the University of Manchester. Her research focuses on the interpretation and organization of anti-money laundering (AML) compliance within the financial sector, specifically banking and investment institutions in the UK. Using a qualitative methodology with interview and case enforcement data, her work explores how organizational structures and cultures shape (non)compliance behaviours. Her broader research interests include the regulation and organization of white-collar crimes, financial crimes, and illicit financial flows.

Nina Tobsch is a PhD candidate at the University of Amsterdam. Her research focuses on how organizational culture creates and sustains organizational crime, with a particular focus on police misconduct. She is also involved in several other projects, including serving as an editor for *The Cambridge Handbook on Organisational Culture and Misconduct*. Her interests include organizational culture, police departmental culture, organizational crime, and qualitative methods.

Jing Wei is a PhD candidate in criminology at the University of Manchester. Her research examines the deterrence of commercial bribery, exploring which intervention measures or combinations of measures are most effective in preventing misconduct. Using a vignette-based factorial survey and qualitative interviews, her study investigates how different deterrence mechanisms influence corporate decision-making. She holds two master's degrees: one in international business law, where she analyzed causes and mechanisms of corporate bribery by multinational corporations, and another in criminology, where she examined factors influencing public engagement in anti-bribery efforts in China. Her research interests include corruption, corporate and white-collar crime, compliance, and criminal decision-making.

Introduction: Emerging Voices on the Study of White-Collar and Organizational Crime

Diana Bociga and Jon Davies

This edited collection presents cutting-edge research from early-career scholars investigating the complexities of white-collar and organizational crime across the globe. The contributions employ a diverse range of empirical, theoretical, and methodological approaches to illuminate the nature, organization, and control of various forms of white-collar crime, corporate misconduct, and regulatory noncompliance. A key theme of this collection is the focus on advancing innovative methods and approaches to inquiry, guided by criminological perspectives and enriched by insights from various academic disciplines, to enhance our understanding of these evolving and profoundly harmful phenomena.

Central to this collection is the recognition of longstanding debates surrounding the concept of 'white-collar crime'. The term, often seen as an umbrella or sensitizing concept rather than a definitive one, encompasses a wide range of activities that vary in legal, social, and criminological interpretations (Croall, 2001; Levi and Lord, 2023). White-collar crimes involve harmful and exploitative behaviours by ostensibly legitimate actors within business, institutional, or market environments (Levi and Lord, 2023). Edwin Sutherland's famous definition describes it as a crime committed by a person of high social status during their occupation (Sutherland, 1945). However, this definition has been critiqued for its ambiguity and limitations, resulting in a number of more recent and varied definitions associated with white-collar crime (Schrager and Short, 1978; Clinard and Yeager, 1980). Key issues in defining white-collar crime include the challenge of disentangling the crime from the offender's social status, and the broad spectrum of offences it can encompass, including fraud, embezzlement, bribery, insider trading, money laundering, as well as labour-related and environmental crimes. Offender-based and offence-based approaches to understanding these crimes can coexist, as elite positions both provide opportunities for certain offences and help to deter suspicion (M. Benson and Simpson, 2018).

The concept has evolved to cover not only individual offences but also systemic corporate and organizational misconduct. The complexity of corporate operations in various legal and economic contexts increases the diversity of corporate offending behaviour, making traditional frameworks insufficient to address the nuances of these crimes. Chapter 1, by Jelmar J. Meester, Arjan Blokland, Marieke Kluin, and Wim Huisman, addresses these complexities by proposing a novel theoretical framework for analyzing corporate crime. Corporations must navigate varying and sometimes conflicting regulations across different jurisdictions, leading to a spectrum of behaviours ranging from specialized violations tied to specific industries to generalized misconduct across sectors. This chapter argues that, rather than focusing solely on individual corporate offences, research and regulatory practices should explore the root causes of both generalized and specialized patterns of offending.

Understanding why individuals commit white-collar and organizational crimes requires a multi-level analysis that considers not only individual motivations but also the organizational influences and broader social and economic contexts in which these crimes occur (Rorie, 2019). At the individual level, personal gain, the need for status, and self-interest often drive criminal behaviour, while rationalizations and justifications allow offenders to neutralize the guilt or moral dissonance associated with their actions. At the organizational level, corporate hierarchies and cultures play crucial roles in shaping behaviour, with norms, values, and expectations creating an environment that may foster or hinder deviant behaviours. Broader societal and economic factors also exert influence, as market pressures, economic crises, and regulatory environments can create opportunities and incentives for white-collar crimes (M.L. Benson et al, 2016). The dynamic interplay between these levels highlights the complexity of understanding and addressing such crimes (Levi and Lord, 2023).

This collection explores how organizational and broader societal norms shape criminal behaviours within legitimate business settings (M. Benson and Simpson, 2018). The attitudes and behaviours of senior management significantly influence organizational culture. When leadership either implicitly or explicitly condones unethical behaviour, it creates an environment where white-collar crimes are more likely to occur (Shover and Hochstetler, 2006). This 'tone at the top' sets the standard for what is deemed acceptable within the organization (Levi and Lord, 2023). Beyond a singular corporate culture, competing subcultures within an organization may prioritize different values, fostering environments where deviance becomes normalized. Chapter 2, written by Nina Tobsch and Marieke Kluin, explores these issues using the example of police departments to illustrate how organizational culture embeds norms of behaviour and influences whether misconduct is tolerated or discouraged. Furthermore, compliance or noncompliance with legal standards aimed at preventing illicit behaviour – and the adoption of best practices – are influenced by broader societal norms. Chapter 3, by Anna Merz, discusses this topic, exploring how stakeholders such as regulators, policy makers, industry associations, and consultancy firms influence peer social control within the financial industry, particularly in anti-money laundering (AML) practices.

To understand and address white-collar and organizational crimes, it is essential to move beyond surface-level observations and examine the underlying mechanisms and structures that drive such behaviours (Lord and Levi, 2025). Critical realism provides a robust framework for this, as it focuses on the interaction between observable events and the hidden generative mechanisms that shape them (Bhaskar, 2008). Chapter 4, by Korry Robert, illustrates this approach through an analysis of noncompliance with AML regulations, using the NatWest bank in the UK as an example. Systemic issues such as information silos, inadequate governance frameworks, and cultural norms combined to normalize noncompliant behaviours. By adopting a stratified understanding of reality, critical realism enables researchers to identify how structural barriers, such as technological constraints and fragmented communication channels, interact with cultural values, such as trust in relationship managers, to create environments conducive to misconduct.

Building on this foundation, the collection emphasizes the need for innovative methodologies and perspectives that challenge traditional approaches, uncovering the hidden cognitive, sensory, and contextual mechanisms that drive such behaviours. Chapter 5, by Jing Wei, introduces the factorial survey method as a robust tool for exploring the cognitive and organizational drivers of white-collar crimes. This methodology enables researchers to simulate real-world decision-making scenarios, capturing how individual incentives, organizational dynamics, and regulatory pressures interact to shape misconduct. Similarly, Chapter 6, by Diāna Bērziņa, introduces the concept of affective atmospheres, revealing how sensory and atmospheric elements within organizational spaces can subtly yet profoundly influence behaviour and decision-making. Using high-end art fairs as an example, Bērziņa demonstrates how environments engineered with specific sensory cues – such as touch – can foster transgressive behaviours and normalize actions that deviate from societal norms. These chapters collectively highlight the need to examine not only observable events but also the underlying mechanisms driving them, enabling richer and more nuanced explanations of social phenomena.

Understanding these hidden dynamics is particularly relevant when considering the structural and organizational nature of white-collar crime. Sutherland (1945) discussed how white-collar crime can also be seen as a form of organized crime – not in the traditional sense of criminal gangs or mafia-type structures, but through the systematic organization of illegal activities within business frameworks. Building on this foundation, scholars have argued that criminal behaviour can be 'organized' in various ways, whether through formal criminal organizations or corporate networks that facilitate illegal activities such as price-fixing, bribery, or fraud (Nelken, 2012; Levi and Lord, 2023). Corporate criminals often exploit legal structures to carry out financial crimes. Chapter 7, written by Giovanni Nicolazzo, explores how criminals, whether from traditional organized crime or the corporate world, exploit the opportunities presented by the legal economy, blurring the lines between legal and illegal activities, and exploiting vulnerabilities in the legal system for personal gain. This chapter examines the organizational structures, methods, and goals shared by traditional organized crimes and white-collar crimes, illustrating how both types of criminals use legitimate businesses as vehicles for their illegal activities.

This collection also highlights the broad spectrum of behaviours that can be classified as white-collar crimes and the diverse contexts in which these offences occur. The concept of white-collar crime extends beyond traditional corporate settings, encompassing a wide range of sectors and activities that are often overlooked in traditional discussions. Chapter 8, by Sofie Gotelaere and Letizia Paoli, examines the sports sector, discussing the nuances between sports-specific frauds, such as doping and match-fixing, and more generic frauds like tax evasion and embezzlement within sports organizations. Chapter 9, written by Emmanuel K. Bunei, shifts the focus to the Kenyan agri-food sector, where white-collar crime manifests through violations of agri-food safety laws. The chapter illustrates the importance of considering local economic and social dynamics in addressing white-collar crime, particularly in emerging economies where formal regulations may be weakly enforced.

In summary, this collection opens new avenues for exploring white-collar and organizational crime, driven by the innovative research of early-career scholars. By drawing on a wide range of case studies, industries, and global perspectives, the chapters collectively illustrate the complexity of these offences and the challenges associated with regulating and controlling them. The contributions in this volume provide valuable insights into the various forms and contexts of white-collar crime and highlight the crucial interplay between organizational context, structure, culture, and opportunity in explaining these crimes. They provide key frameworks, such as critical realism, and innovative methodologies, such as the use of factorial surveys. Traditional individual-level explanations, such as rational choice theory, are insufficient on their own. Instead, this collection emphasizes the importance of understanding how organizational cultures, political-economic structures, and contextualized theories of rational choice contribute to illegal activities within organizations (M.L. Benson et al, 2016).

Moreover, the collection advocates for a framework that examines the organization of these crimes, identifying the relationships and practices essential for executing criminal enterprises (Levi and Lord, 2023). This includes understanding how motivated offenders recognize and exploit opportunities for financial crime, as well as the skill sets, knowledge, and expertise required to facilitate these illegal activities. Additionally, the conditions that enable this organization – such as access to financial resources, opportunities for crime, and the means to retain illicit gains – are crucial for comprehending how criminal networks are established and sustained within legitimate business structures. As this collection demonstrates, white-collar and organizational crime cannot be fully understood without considering the broader organizational and societal contexts that shape and sustain these behaviours, as well as how these behaviours are organized and perpetuated.

The genesis of this book

White-collar and organizational crimes often extend beyond the traditional focus of criminological studies. However, these offences can cause a wide range of harm, including significant financial, physical, and environmental damage. In recent years, a growing network of researchers across Europe and beyond has dedicated efforts to deepening our understanding of these complex and harmful phenomena. A central hub for this research is EUROC, the European Society of Criminology's Working Group on Organizational Crime. EUROC has expanded considerably over the past five years, now boasting over 190 members worldwide. This network played a vital role in connecting the early-career researchers (ECRs) who contributed to this collection.

The journey of this edited volume began with a workshop hosted at the University of Manchester in July 2023, specifically organized for ECRs studying white-collar and organizational crime. Prior to the workshop, participants were required to submit a 4,000-word essay, which was subsequently shared with senior researchers and peers who served as discussants. During the workshop, ECRs presented their research and received detailed feedback from these discussants. The authors later integrated this feedback into their revised submissions, which form the chapters of this book.

The idea of holding the workshop originated from the Manchester Organisational Non-Compliance Initiative (MONI), a research group based at the University of Manchester. MONI employs empirical and interdisciplinary methodologies to generate insights into the nature, organization, and control of various forms of organizational, corporate, white-collar, and financial crimes. The group aspires to build on the University of Manchester's international reputation in this field, aiming to establish the university as a world-leading research hub for the study of criminal and other illicit behaviours. MONI was founded in 2021 by academic staff and PhD students. All MONI members are also part of EUROC, working collaboratively with European colleagues to advance knowledge on these significant criminological issues.

This collection seeks to showcase cutting-edge research on white-collar and organizational crime, highlighting the contributions of early-career researchers from across the globe. In doing so, it not only advances academic knowledge but also supports the professional development of emerging scholars by expanding their networks and disseminating their research to a broader audience, including academics, students, practitioners, and policy makers. Therefore, the lead author of each chapter is an early-career researcher specializing in topics within the broad fields of white-collar and organizational crime. For the purposes of this book, we define an early-career researcher as either (1) a PhD candidate, or (2) a postdoctoral researcher who completed their PhD within the last five years.

The research presented in this collection expands the traditional study of white-collar and organizational crime in several important ways. For example, it proposes new theoretical frameworks for analyzing corporate crime, addressing the diversity of corporate offending (see Chapter 1 by Meester et al). It broadens the scope of organizational crime research by exploring offences within organizations that are not necessarily motivated by financial gain (see Chapter 2 by Nina Tobsch and Marieke Kluin). It also provides a compelling example of critical realism as a robust framework for understanding white-collar crime (see Chapter 4 by Korry Robert). It also introduces the factorial survey method as an innovative tool for examining the drivers of white-collar crimes (see Chapter 5 by Jing Wei). Furthermore, it investigates how the perception of certain atmospheres contributes to the 'thrill' of white-collar offending (see Chapter 6 by Diāna Bērziņa). Finally, it presents a new typology of fraud in sport, focusing on the individuals, organizations, and institutions affected by these activities (see Chapter 8 by Sofie Gotelaere and Letizia Paoli).

This collection could not have come together without the invaluable support of the MONI group members in Manchester and the contributions from others within the EUROC network. As editors, we extend our sincere thanks to the early career researchers who participated in the Manchester workshop and contributed chapters to this book, as well as to the senior co-authors and academics who provided essential feedback. We are also grateful to the workshop's organizing committee – Peter Duncan, Borja Alvarez, and

Yongyu Zeng – for their efforts in shaping this edited collection. Special thanks go to Nicholas Lord for his advice and guidance throughout the workshop and the development of this volume. Finally, we appreciate the financial support from ESRC-NWSSDTP and Lancaster University, and we are thankful to the publisher for enabling us to share these contributions, fostering the professional development of emerging scholars by disseminating their research to a wider audience.

References

Benson, M.L., Van Slyke, S.R., and Cullen, F.T. (2016) 'Core themes in the study of white-collar crime', in S.R. Van Slyke, M.L. Benson, and F.T. Cullen (eds), *The Oxford Handbook of White-Collar Crime*, Oxford University Press.

Benson, M. and Simpson, S. (2018) *White-Collar Crime: An Opportunity Perspective* (3rd edn), Routledge.

Bhaskar, R. (2008) *A Realist Theory of Science*, Routledge.

Clinard, M. and Yeager, P. (1980) *Corporate Crime*, Free Press.

Croall, H. (2001) *Understanding White Collar Crime* (rev. and updated edn), Open University Press.

Levi, M. and Lord, N. (2023) 'White-collar and corporate crime', in A. Liebling, S. Maruna, and L. McAra (eds), *The Oxford Handbook of Criminology*, Oxford University Press, pp 479–500.

Lord, N. and Levi, M. (2025) *Organising White-Collar and Corporate Crimes*, Routledge.

Nelken, D. (2012) 'White-collar and corporate crime', in M. Maguire, R. Morgan, and R. Reiner (eds), *The Oxford Handbook of Criminology* (5th edn), Oxford University Press, pp 623–59.

Rorie, M.L. (ed) (2019) *The Handbook of White-Collar Crime*, New Jersey: Wiley.

Schrager, L.S. and Short, J.F. (1978) 'Toward a sociology of organizational crime', *Social Problems*, 25(4): 407–19.

Shover, N. and Hochstetler, A. (2006) *Choosing White-Collar Crime*, Cambridge University Press.

Sutherland, E.H. (1945) 'Is "white collar crime" crime?', *American Sociological Review*, 10(2): 132.

1

The Diversity Spectrum of Corporate Offending: A Framework for Research and Practice

*Jelmar J. Meester, Arjan A.J. Blokland,
Marieke H.A. Kluin, and Wim Huisman*

Introduction

Crime is an umbrella concept that is used to refer to very diverse types of human behaviour. Murder is a crime, but so are mortgage fraud, shoplifting, and vandalism. This diversity poses a problem for etiological theories of crime, as they are challenged to aptly explain a wide range of different behaviours. In response, crime theorists have searched for defining features of crime that go beyond the particularities of a certain act. For instance, Gottfredson and Hirschi (1990) see crimes as a subset of acts undertaken in the pursuit of short-term self-interest, while neglecting their direct as well as their long-term negative effects on the self or on others. Wikström (2010), on the other hand, views crimes primarily as actions that breach moral rules that are, in the case of crime, codified in criminal law. Sutherland (1945; 1949/1983) acknowledges two criteria for crime: '[the] legal description of an act as socially injurious, and [the] legal provision of a penalty for the act' (1945, p 132). In other words, crime is defined as harmful and sanctionable. Thus, theories must seek to explain not so much why individuals engage in particular behaviours, but rather why they engage in such behaviour despite their adverse ramifications.

Just like individual crime, corporate crime is distinctly diverse. This diversity is amplified by the fact that corporations, as legal persons, more than natural persons, have to operate within complex and constantly changing legal contexts and increasingly regulated economies that set behavioural boundaries and prescribe corporate action (Smith and Walter, 2006; Pollman, 2021). Depending on their industry or particular operations, different corporations may also have to adhere to different sets of rules (Law and McLaughlin, 2022). As a result, corporate crime can refer to financial reporting violations, environmental crime, occupational health and safety violations, unfair trade agreements, and more. Additionally, violation types can be related or even overlap (see: Sutherland, 1949/1983; Simpson and Schell, 2009; Bartlett et al, 2020; Hunter, 2023). Reflecting this diversity in corporate crime types, corporate crime research, arguably more so than mainstream criminology, is plagued by definitional disagreements (Friedrichs, 2009; Simpson, 2013; 2019). At present, corporate crime is often defined as 'Any act committed by corporations that is punished by the state, regardless of whether it is punished under administrative, civil, or criminal law' (Clinard and Yeager, 1980/2017, p 16).[1] As is the case for individual crime, explanations of corporate crime should focus not on particular corporate acts, but rather on why corporations engage in these acts in the circumstance of their illegality and sanctionability.

In this chapter, we offer a theoretical framework to analyze corporate crime and its causes based on offending diversity. The chapter is organized as follows. First, we will discuss how general and typological theories of crime have tried to explain different patterns of offending. Second, we highlight the difficulties currently faced when searching for explanation(s) of corporate crime. Third, we address the 'diversity of crime' concept and relate this to corporate crime. Fourth, we introduce the occurrence level of offending diversity within the population as a theoretically relevant dimension. Fifth, diversity and occurrence levels are combined in a novel framework aimed at guiding theoretical exploration. We will review the use of this framework and its relevance for theory development and regulatory practice.

General versus typological approaches

Commonalities between criminal acts on the abstract level do not alter the fact that criminal behaviour is found to vary significantly between subjects, not only in its timing and frequency, but also in its seriousness and diversity (Blumstein et al, 1986; 1988). Criminological theories must therefore not only be able to explain a broad array of behaviours, but also accommodate vastly different manifestations of these behaviours within the individual's criminal career from one subject to the next. Broadly speaking, crime theorists have taken one of two approaches to face this etiological dilemma. General theories, on the one hand, assume a single underlying (set of) factor(s) to influence all crime (for example, Gottfredson and Hirschi, 1990), and further assume all dimensions of the individual's criminal career – that is, its timing, frequency, seriousness, and diversity – to be intrinsically linked, so that, for instance, a higher frequency of crime always comes with increased diversity. Typological theories on the other hand, assume multiple causal explanations are needed to explain different manifestations of crime that are characterized by distinct combinations of criminal career dimensions (Paternoster et al, 1997; Piquero et al, 2003). A classic criminological example of a typological approach is Moffitt's dual taxonomy (Moffitt, 1993). This taxonomy provides an explanation for one of the 'brute facts of criminology' (Hirschi and Gottfredson, 1993, p 552): the association between age and crime – a phenomenon first described in 1831 (Quetelet, 1831/1984). Analyses of age and crime in life-course criminology and criminal career research reveal that most delinquent youths desist from crime; persistence in crime is the exception rather than the rule. Additionally, short-lived criminal careers are known to be concentrated in the adolescent life-stage.

Moffitt's taxonomy distinguishes two different manifestations of crime in terms of persistence – the duration of the offending behaviour – and its seriousness. For each of these distinct criminal career types or trajectories, different causal explanations are provided. According to the dual taxonomy, the large majority of offenders show short-lived criminal careers, whereas a small minority show prolonged and more serious criminal careers. As factors constant over age cannot explain behavioural change, Moffitt explains short-lived criminal careers based on dynamic factors, including the changes in legitimate opportunities occurring at the end of adolescence. Persistent criminal careers however, are explained foremost by static, individual factors she refers to as psychosocial deficits (Moffitt, 1993).

Importantly, the theoretical explanations for individual crime offered by the dual taxonomy are guided not only by the nature of the criminal career (short-lived versus prolonged), but also by their prevalence in the community. As short-lived criminal careers are more normative, they need an explanation that holds true for a large part of the population. Given that prolonged criminal careers are exceptional within the population, they should be explained by similarly exceptional circumstances.

Explaining corporate crime

The explanation of corporate crime and the analysis of the corporate criminal careers over the corporate age, comparable to Moffitt's analysis, has been hindered in several ways. First, compared to mainstream criminology, corporate crime research is underdeveloped. As a result, there are no well-established empirical regularities that can be said to constitute the 'brute facts' of corporate crime as of yet. In fact, extant research finds much variation in offending across both corporations and industries (see: Huisman, 2016; Glebovskiy, 2019), making it difficult to conclude what is normative and what is exceptional when it comes to corporate crime. The absence of 'brute facts' therefore offers little guidance to theorists wanting to explain corporate offending in terms of what kinds of causes – common or exceptional – to look for. Second, whereas natural persons progress through life-stages in a sequential manner that is closely linked to biological age, corporate life-stages are currently less well-defined (Simpson, 2019; Blokland et al, 2021; Hunter, 2021). Corporate development may also be more erratic and even cyclical in nature, with corporations moving through developmental stages at a widely varying pace and sequence due to bankruptcies, restarts, mergers, and other corporate-specific developments (Blokland et al, 2021). Finally, longitudinal data of corporate offending is still limited, with very short follow-up periods compared to the potential length of the corporate life-span (Meester et al, 2024). For these reasons, a typological framework for corporate offending based on criminal career *duration*, as in Moffitt's dual taxonomy, is less obvious.

The theoretical framework we now introduce will take these shortcomings into consideration. Rather than offering an explanation for an established empirical regularity, our framework offers theoretical guidance for a diverse set of empirical situations defined by both corporate-level diversity in offending, and the occurrence of corporate-level diversity within the population.

Individual-level diversity

Criminal career research distinguishes various dimensions of the individual's criminal career, diversity being one of them (others are participation, duration, frequency, and seriousness; see Blumstein et al, 1986, 1988; Britt, 1996). Diversity refers to the number of different offending behaviours a single offender is engaged in and the ratio of those different behaviours within the offender's criminal career. Diversity can be seen as a spectrum, with specialized behaviour on the one end and generalized behaviour on the other. Specialized behaviour is the complete absence of diversity. It implies a focused engagement in a specific type of offending over time. Contrastingly, generalized behaviour is the presence of absolute diversity and denotes engagement in a wide variety of offences over time (Nieuwbeerta et al, 2011; Mazerolle and McPhedran, 2018). As a key dimension in criminal career research (Petersilia, 1980; Blumstein et al, 1986; Farrington and Loeber, 2012), diversity has been studied for conventional crime types (Blumstein et al, 1986; Blumstein, 2016; Simpson and Piquero, 2002; Lynam et al, 2004; DeLisi and Piquero, 2011), as well as, be it to a lesser extent, for white-collar crime (Weisburd et al, 2001; Van Onna et al, 2014; Van der Geest et al, 2016), but very little for corporate crime (Wiering et al, 2020). Various studies on offending diversity yield some evidence of specialization, but typically against a background of much diversity (compare: Elliott et al, 2017; Lussier et al, 2017).

Up until now, different corporate offence types, such as environmental, occupational safety, and antitrust violations, have been analyzed as separate behaviours; their interrelations have hardly ever been studied. As a result, researchers have mostly theorized on potential causes for specific types of offences. A more holistic analysis of corporate offending, looking at offending diversity, allows us to consider underlying causes of both generalized and specialized offending. Diversity speaks to the relevance of both general theories of crime, as these would be able to explain generalized offending, and typological theories of crime, as these would be able to explain more specialized offending.

Occurrence of diversity in the population

Although placing individual corporate offending on the diversity spectrum can be informative, additional insights can be gained by simultaneously assessing the prevalence with which different levels of diversity occur within the population. This 'occurrence of diversity' can be viewed as a second spectrum, ranging from low, when high levels of diversity are found only in a single offender or a small minority of offenders, to high, when high levels of diversity are found in most – if not all – offenders within a population. Note that occurrence is different from the level of analysis on which diversity is assessed. To illustrate, consider a population with an equal amount of offenders of type A and of type B. Now consider that offenders of type A only engage in offending of type X, while offenders of type B only engage in offending of type Y. At the population level, offending seems generalized, as offending of types X and Y are both equally prevalent. At the individual level, however, all criminal careers in the population are highly specialized. In this hypothetical population, the occurrence of specialized offending would therefore be high.

Both diversity and the occurrence of diversity within the population provide guidance for criminological theorizing. Generalized offending would support general explanations. Conversely, specialized offending would support the development of typological explanations. Additional knowledge on the occurrence rate would enable differentiation between what is normative and what is exceptional behaviour. This would then allow for the simultaneous appreciation of both common and exceptional causal explanations.

A diversity and occurrence framework

Figure 1.1 shows the intersection of offending diversity and the level of occurrence of diversity within the population. For each quadrant, possible

Figure 1.1: Diversity and occurrence framework

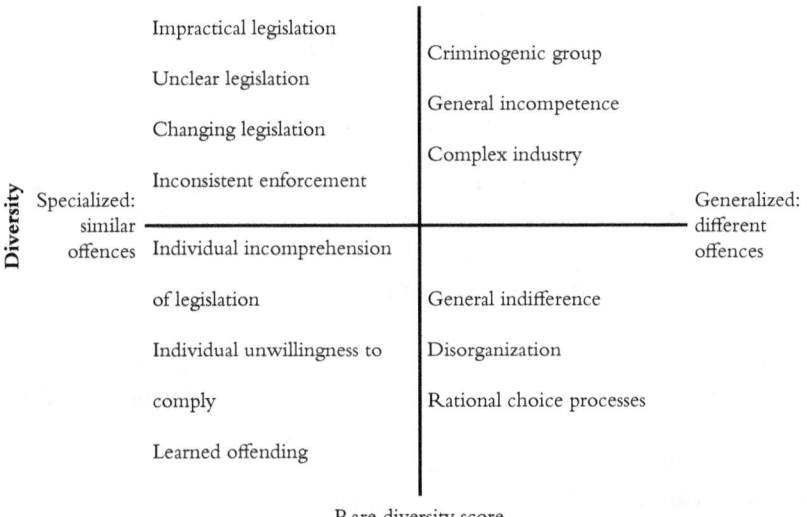

Note: The framework is based on the level of diversity and the occurrence within the analyzed population; potential causal factors are determined for each quadrant.

causal factors are formulated. The diversity spectrum tells us the likely generality of explanations for this behaviour. When offending is highly specialized (diversity is low), causal factors are also likely to be specific, explaining why a particular type of offending is being repeated. When offending is highly generalized (diversity is high), the causal factors invoked should be important to all types of offending behaviour. In other words, when offending is specialized, explanations and interventions should be specific; when offending is generalized, explanations and interventions should be general (Blumstein et al, 1978; Lynam et al, 2004).

The occurrence spectrum tells us something about the prevalence of individual-level offending diversity and, therewith, the commonality of causal factors potentially underlying the observed offending. When the occurrence of a certain level of diversity is high (the behaviour is common), the causal factors implied concern the population as a whole. When the occurrence of a certain level of diversity is low (the observed behavioural pattern is rare), the causal factors underlying this type of offending are likely to pertain to or be present in only a subset of the entire population.

In the top left corner of Figure 1.1 is common-specialized behaviour. This means that a large part of the population showcases a focused engagement in a single or limited set of offending types. This focused behaviour of corporations may indicate industry-wide problems with the application of a specific type of legislation or regulation. In this case, the legislation may be impractical, unclear, or changing, or legislation-specific enforcement by different agencies or within an agency may be inconsistent (Piquero, 2000; Lynam et al, 2004; Mazerolle and McPhedran, 2018; Wiering et al, 2020). In the bottom left is rare-specialized behaviour. Here, a single corporation or a few corporations showcase highly specialized offending. This type of specialized offending may indicate either individual incomprehension of the legislation, unwillingness or inability to comply, or experience-based learned offending. In other words, whereas commonly occurring specialized offending likely points to causal variables that apply to all members of the population (for example, characteristics of the particular legislation), rare-specialized offending would most likely hint at factors that are characteristic of individual corporations (for example, corporations in a particular life-stage, under a certain leadership type or operating a particular corporate culture, or those new to that particular market).

In the top right corner, behaviour is common-generalized, meaning that the majority of the population shows a high variety in offending behaviour. Rather than legislative characteristics, highly prevalent generalized offending behaviour likely indicates industrial characteristics, such as high levels of competitiveness, complexity, or common attitudes or anomie. This could also indicate industry-level financial, practical, or other resource and/or capacity deficits (Black and Baldwin, 2012; Huisman, 2016). Lastly, in the remaining bottom right corner is rare-generalized behaviour. This quadrant pertains to a situation in which only a limited number of corporations show generalized offending. Instead of industry-level characteristics, rare-generalized behaviour is likely to be best explained by general characteristics of the offending corporation, such as a general indifference towards compliance, disorganization, or strategic choice making. These characteristics can be encapsulated within a deviating corporate culture (Huisman, 2001; Van der Berg et al, 2002; Lynam et al, 2004; Goslinga and Denkers, 2009; Nielsen, 2012; Mazerolle and McPhedran, 2018).

Application of the diversity and occurrence framework showcases the potential merits of either a general or typological explanation of corporate offending. When all observed offending in a particular industry clusters within a single quadrant, the applicability of general theories is more obvious. When, however, observed offending falls into (diagonally) opposing quadrants – in other words, when specialized and generalized behaviour co-occur, typological explanations may likely apply. For instance, when the majority of corporations display specialized offending behaviour, but only few display generalized offending, explanations for population-wide specialized offending likely need to be augmented by explanations for the generalized offending observed in a few corporations. Alternatively, it would also be possible to observe generalized offending in most corporations, and specialized offending only in few. However, rather than looking for corporate characteristics that could explain individual-level diversity in offending, in this case researchers may look for factors that protect corporations from engaging in generalized offending, given the overall industry-level conditions conducive of offending. In practice, we expect the scenario in which many corporations show specialized offending, and only few show highly generalized offending more likely.

Implications for regulatory practice

Positioning corporate offending in the quadrants depicted in Figure 1.1, has direct implications for regulatory practice. Although several tools and models are currently used by regulatory agencies to determine what interventions to use – for instance based on the 'Good Regulatory Intervention Design'-matrix (Black and Baldwin, 2012) or on responsive regulation (Ayres and Braithwaite, 1992), the diversity and occurrence framework additionally allows agencies to consider broader, strategic adjustments in oversight and/or prevention. The framework can thus be used for reactive deployment of fitted interventions as well as proactive creation or adjustment of oversight strategies and preventive measures.

Common-specialized offending calls for overarching regulation that accounts for the particularities of the offending behaviour. This entails changes in and/or clarifications of legislation or alignment of enforcement practices between regulatory agencies or officers (Montagnes and Wolton, 2017; Piszcz, 2020). Rare-specialized offending also requires attention to the specific behaviour but with regulation aimed at the minority of corporation(s) that display the specialized offending. Regulatory agencies should keep in mind that the circumstances under which the offending takes place (and thus the risk of violating regulations) can change over time (for better or worse; Black and Baldwin, 2010) and assist corporations in their compliance (Stafford, 2012).

Common-generalized offending can best be met with prevention measures, oversight strategies, and interventions that apply to the industry as a whole and are aimed at the general causes of offending all behaviour. For instance, the permitting practice can be tightened to prevent so-called 'bad apples' (Trevino and Youngblood, 1990) from joining the industry. Additionally, regulatory agencies can address the dominant industry safety culture (Antonsen et al, 2017). Lastly, rare-generalized offending requires measures that are targeted at causes that underly the broad offending behaviour displayed by a minority. These can be targeted inspections, thus influencing the certainty of being caught and punished (Ehren and

Shackleton, 2016). The severity of penalties can also be altered (Earnheart and Friesen, 2023; Friehe et al, 2023). Additionally, repeat offending corporations can be prevented from resuming operations or be assisted to develop an organizational structure that supports compliance.

As stated, multiple (opposing) offending behaviours can co-occur. In these instances, a differentiated approach seems warranted, with the level of diversity observed providing guidance to what type of intervention would best serve what type of corporation.

Discussion

Here, we have proposed a systematic way to evaluate different patterns in the observed diversity of corporate offending, distinguishing the level of diversity observed in the offending behaviour of individual corporations, from the prevalence with which different levels of individual-level offending diversity occur in the population as a whole. These two spectra create a two-dimensional space, with the situation observed in a particular industry falling into one or more quadrants. Common-specialized offending most likely hints at problems with particular legislation, whereas rare-specialized offending suggests dynamic corporate characteristics are most relevant. Contrastingly, common-generalized offending signals industry-level characteristics, whereas rare-generalized offending most likely reflects more or less stable corporate characteristics. The presence of both levels of diversity (that is, specialized and generalized), as has been found in other contexts (compare: Blokland and Nieuwbeerta, 2010; Elliott et al, 2017; Lussier et al, 2017), may furthermore point towards the need for a typological rather than a general approach to theorizing corporate offending, with both behaviours in need of their own explanation.

The proposed framework does not present a new theory. Rather, it is a tool to offer theoretical guidance in the context of corporate offending. The framework can be used alongside previous classifications of either offences (in an offence-based perspective on corporate crime) or offenders (in an offender-based perspective on corporate crime). For example, Friedrichs (2009) introduces two overarching categories of corporate offending: corporate violence – including environment, product, and labour violations – and corporate abuse – including fraud, price-fixing, and exploitation. Such a categorization of offending can be used to assess the level of diversity of a corporation's offending, and the (co-)occurrence of specialized and generalized offending behaviour in the population. A classic example of an offender-based categorization can be found in the work of Kagan and Scholz (1984). They posit that corporations can be viewed as amoral calculators, incompetent corporations, or political citizens, and that interventions should be adapted accordingly. The amoral calculator is money-driven; for this type of corporation, regulatory offences are the outcome of an economic rational choice process. According to Kagan and Scholz, this behaviour should be met with deterrence through legal penalties. In the current framework, and assuming a positive basic ethical standard in the industry under scrutiny, amoral calculating seems to best fit the rare-generalized offending. The incompetent corporation is inclined to comply but cannot. Persuasion is seen as the corresponding intervention. Depending on the level of specialized offending observed in the population, incompetence might explain rare-specialized offending, for example when specialized offending is observed primarily in young corporations, or those new to the industry. Incompetence may also explain common-specialized offending, although in the proposed framework, this 'incompetence' would reflect more on the nature of the legislation than on the competence level of individual corporations. Lastly, the political citizen wants to comply, partly out of self-interest; offending takes place when regulations and self-interest do not align. Such corporations are best dealt with through education. Depending on the level of discrepancy between regulations and self-interest, political citizens are expected to populate the bottom half of Figure 1.1.

Some cautionary notes are also in place. Since the framework aims to offer insight into the possible causal factors underlying corporate offending based on the diversity of that offending, it is important to consider the granularity at which the diversity of offending is operationalized. Is diversity based on different articles of a particular law, where each violated article constitutes a different offence type, or on legislation, where each law violated constitutes an offence type? Or perhaps on certain divisions of law (that is, administrative law and criminal law offending) or on overarching themes (that is, environmental and non-environmental offending)? This decision has important theoretical implications. Too strict or relaxed definitions of offending diversity may result in a bias towards either specialized or generalized behaviour respectively (see: Elliot et al, 2017). Stricter definitions of offending diversity reveal more details on the actual violations. A more relaxed and industry transcendent definition allows for between-industry comparisons.[2]

Relatedly, what level of offending variation is considered 'diverse' may depend on the industry at hand. Offending diversity is contingent on the variety of the applicable legislation: some corporations are governed by a wide set of rules and regulations, while others are not; some rules and regulations include many different offences, while others do not; and some rules and regulations apply to many corporations, while others apply only to a small subset.

Finally, observed offending diversity may also be influenced by the scope of regulatory oversight and intervention practice. Some rules and regulations may receive more attention than others. As such, violations of these rules and regulations might be disproportionally noticed, resulting in biased registrations of corporations' true diversity in offending as well as the level at which this diversity occurs in the population. Alternatively, some rules and regulations may be enforced more harshly than others. If that is the case, these types of violations may be less susceptible to the development of specialized behaviour. Ideally, therefore, when researching diversity in corporate offending, the behaviour of the regulatory agencies should be taken into account.

Conclusion

In this chapter we have outlined how the diversity of offending and its occurrence within the population can aid our understanding of corporate crime. We distinguish four quadrants of offending that can occur in consort, that may each result from different causes, and that may each require different enforcement strategies to successfully prevent future offending and enhance public safety. Future studies should examine how diversity scores are distributed within specific industries and apply the framework to assess its applicability to their specific contexts. Additional causes may be added. Next, the hypothesized causal mechanisms can be researched in more detail and recommendations for regulatory practice can be made. Kagan and Scholz (1984) stated: 'The relevant question ... both from the standpoint of explanatory or predictive theory and from the standpoint of regulatory strategy, is not which theory to use, but when each is likely to be appropriate' (pp 85–6). The framework presented here can be used to answer this question and help determine what type of theory can best be used to explain corporate offending in different industries.

Notes

[1] Contributing to the definitional confusion surrounding corporate crime is that, apart from defining crime, what constitutes a 'corporation' is also a matter of debate. Schrager and Short (1978) speak of *organizational crime* which is defined as 'illegal acts of omission or commission of an individual or group of individuals in a legitimate formal organisation in accordance with the operative goals of the organisation, which have a serious physical or economic impact on employees, consumers or the general public' (Schrager and Short, 1978, pp 411–12). This definition of corporate crime also covers offending behaviour by non-profit organizations.

[2] Measures of offending diversity, be it in the context of individual or corporate offending, are subject to other factors as well: for instance, the time period over which diversity is defined. Say an actor commits three different offence types A, B and C, each three times in a row: A, A, A, B, B, B, C, C, C. Whether this offending pattern is generalized or specialized will depend on the time frame over which diversity is calculated.

References

Antonsen, S., Nilsen, M., and Almklov, P.G. (2017) 'Regulating the intangible: searching for safety culture in the Norwegian petroleum industry', *Safety Science*, 92, 232–40.

Ayres, I. and Braithwaite, J. (1992) *Responsive Regulation: Transcending the Deregulation Debate*, Oxford University Press, pp 33–41.

Black, J. and Baldwin, R. (2010) 'Really responsive risk-based regulation', *Law & Policy*, 32(2): 181–213.

Black, J. and Baldwin, R. (2012) 'When risk-based regulation aims low: a strategic framework', *Regulation & Governance*, 6(2): 131–48.

Blokland, A.A.J. and Nieuwbeerta, P. (2010) 'Considering criminal continuity: testing for heterogeneity and state dependence in the association of past to future offending', *Australian and New Zealand Journal of Criminology*, 43(3): 526–56.

Blokland, A.A.J., Kluin, M.H.A., and Huisman, W. (2021) 'Life-course criminology and corporate offending', in B. van Rooij and D. Sokol (eds), *The Cambridge Handbook of Compliance* (Cambridge Law Handbooks), Cambridge University Press, pp 684–704.

Blumstein, A. (2016) 'From incapacitation to criminal careers', *Journal of Research in Crime and Delinquency*, 53(3): 291–305.

Blumstein, A., Cohen J., and Farrington, D.P. (1988) 'Criminal career research: its value for criminology', *Criminology*, 26(1): 1–35.

Blumstein, A., Cohen, J., and Nagin, D. (1978) *Deterrence and Incapacitation: Estimating the Effects of Criminal Sanctions on Crime Rates*, National Academy of Sciences.

Blumstein, A., Cohen, J., Roth, J.A., and Visher, C.A. (1986) *Criminal Careers and Career Criminals*, Volume 1, National Academy Press.

Britt, C.L. (1996) 'The measurement of specialization and escalation in the criminal career: an alternative modeling strategy', *Journal of Quantitative Criminology*, 12: 193–222.

Clinard, M.B. and Yeager, P.C. (1980/2017) *Corporate Crime* (1st edn), Routledge.

DeLisi, M. and Piquero, A.R. (2011) 'New frontiers in criminal careers research, 2000–2011: a state-of-the-art review', *Journal of Criminal Justice*, 39(4): 289–301.

Earnhart, D. and Friesen, L. (2023) 'Certainty of punishment versus severity of punishment: enforcement of environmental protection laws', *Land Economics*, 99(2): 245–64.

Ehren, M.C. and Shackleton, N. (2016) 'Risk-based school inspections: impact of targeted inspection approaches on Dutch secondary schools', *Educational Assessment, Evaluation and Accountability*, 28(4): 299–321.

Elliott, A., Francis, B., Soothill, K. and Blokland, A.A.J. (2017) 'Changing crime mix patterns of offending over the life course', in A.A.J. Blokland and V.R. van der Geest (eds), *The Routledge International Handbook of Life-Course Criminology*, Routledge, pp 89–111.

Farrington, D.P. and Loeber, R. (2012) 'Two approaches to developmental/life-course theorizing', in F.T. Cullen and P. Wilcox (eds) *The Oxford Handbook of Criminological Theory*, Oxford University Press, pp 226–52.

Friedrichs, D.O. (2009) *Trusted Criminals: White Collar Crime in Contemporary Society* (4th edn), Wadsworth Cengage Learning.

Friehe, T., Langenbach, P., and Mungan, M.C. (2023) 'Does the severity of sanctions influence learning about enforcement policy? Experimental evidence', *The Journal of Legal Studies*, 52(1): 83–106.

Glebovskiy, A. (2019) 'Inherent criminogenesis in business organisations', *Journal of Financial Crime*, 26(2): 432–46.

Goslinga, S. and Denkers, A. (2009) 'Motieven voor regelovertreding: een onderzoek onder ondernemers', *Gedrag & Organisatie*, 22(1): 3–22.

Gottfredson, M.R. and Hirschi, T. (1990) *A General Theory of Crime*, Stanford University Press.

Hirschi, T. and Gottfredson, M. (1993) 'Commentary: testing the general theory of crime', *Journal of Research in Crime and Delinquency*, 30(1): 47–54.

Huisman, W. (2001) *Tussen winst en moraal. Achtergronden van regelnaleving en regelovertreding door ondernemingen* (Dissertation), Boom Juridische Uitgevers.

Huisman, W. (2016) 'Criminogenic organizational properties and dynamics', in S.R. Van Slyke, M.L. Benson, and F.T. Cullen (eds), *The Oxford Handbook of White-Collar Crime*, Oxford University Press, pp 435–62.

Hunter, B.W. (2021) 'Corporate criminal careers: thinking about organizational offending over time', *Journal of Theoretical and Philosophical Criminology*, 13(1): 29–45.

Hunter, B.W. (2023) 'Pinpointing persistent polluters: environmental offending and recidivist companies in England', *Deviant Behavior*, 44(9): 1–16.

Kagan, R.A. and Scholz, J.T. (1984) 'The "criminology of the corporation" and regulatory enforcement strategies', in K. Hawkins and J.M. Thomas (eds), *Enforcing Regulation*, Kluwer-Nijhoff.

Law, M.T. and McLaughlin, P.A. (2022) 'Industry size and regulation: evidence from US states', *Public Choice*, 192(1–2): 1–27.

Lussier, P., McCuish, E., Deslauriers-Varin, N., and Corrado, R. (2017) 'Crime specialization as a dynamic process', in A.A.J. Blokland and V.R. van der Geest (eds), *The Routledge International Handbook of Life-Course Criminology*, Routledge, pp 112–39.

Lynam, D.R., Piquero, A.R., and Moffitt, T.E. (2004) 'Specialization and the propensity to violence: support from self-reports but not official records', *Journal of Contemporary Criminal Justice*, 20(2): 215–28.

Mazerolle, P. and McPhedran, S. (2018) 'Specialization and versatility in offending', in D.P. Farrington, L. Kazemian, and A.R. Piquero (eds), *The Oxford Handbook of Developmental and Life-Course Criminology*, Oxford University Press, pp 49–69.

Meester, J.J., Kluin, M.H.A., Blokland, A.A.J., Huisman, W., Schuur, M.C.M., and Wassenburg, S.I. (2024) 'Corporate offending in Dutch inland shipping: a trajectory analysis', *European Journal of Criminology*, 22(1): 76–105.

Moffitt, T.E. (1993) 'Adolescence-limited and life-course-persistent antisocial behavior: a developmental taxonomy', *Psychological Review*, 100(4): 674–701.

Montagnes, B.P. and Wolton, S. (2017) 'Rule versus discretion: regulatory uncertainty, firm investment, and bureaucratic organization', *The Journal of Politics*, 79(2): 457–72.

Nielsen, V.L. (2012) 'Mixed motives: economic, social, and normative motivations in business compliance', *Law and Policy*, 34(4): 428–62.

Nieuwbeerta, P., Blokland, A.A.J., Piquero, A.R., and Sweeten, G. (2011) 'A life-course analysis of offense specialization across age: introducing a new method for studying individual specialization over the life course', *Crime & Delinquency*, 57(1): 3–28.

Paternoster, R., Dean, C., Piquero, A., Mazerolle, P., and Brame, R. (1997) 'Generality, continuity and change in offending careers', *Journal of Quantitative Criminology*, 13(3): 231–66.

Petersilia, J. (1980) 'Criminal career research: A review of recent evidence', *Crime and Justice: An Annual Review of Research*, 2: 321–79.

Piquero, A.R. (2000) 'Frequency, specialization, and violence in offending careers', *Journal of Research in Crime and Delinquency*, 37(4): 392–418.

Piquero, A.R., Farrington, D.P., and Blumstein, A. (2003) 'The criminal career paradigm', in M. Tonry (ed), *Crime and Justice: A Review of Research*, Vol. 30, University of Chicago Press, pp 359–506.

Piszcz, A. (2020) 'Anything new under the sun? Legal clarifications as a Polish new tool for interpreting business law', *International Journal for the Semiotics of Law*, 33(2): 601–16.

Pollman, E. (2021) 'The supreme court and the pro-business paradox', *Harvard Law Review*, 135(1): 220–66.

Quetelet, A. (1831/1984) *Research on the Propensity for Crime at Different Ages* (S.F. Sylvester, trans.), Anderson.

Schrager, L.S. and Short, J.F. (1978) 'Toward a sociology of organizational crime', *Social Problems*, 25(4): 407–19.

Simpson, S.S. (2013) 'White-collar crime: a review of recent developments and promising directions for future research', *Annual Review of Sociology*, 39(1): 309–31.

Simpson, S.S. (2019) 'Reimagining Sutherland 80 years after *White-Collar Crime*', *Criminology*, 57(2): 189–207.

Simpson, S.S. and Piquero, N.L. (2002) 'Low self-control, organizational theory, and corporate crime', *Law & Society Review*, 36(3): 509–47.

Simpson, S.S. and Schell, N. (2009) 'Persistent heterogeneity or state dependence? An analysis of occupational safety and health act violations', in S.S. Simpson and D. Weisburd (eds), *The Criminology of White-Collar Crime*, Springer, pp 63–78.

Smith, R.C. and Walter, I. (2006) *Governing the Modern Corporation: Capital Markets, Corporate Control, and Economic Performance*, Oxford University Press.

Stafford, S. (2012) 'Do carrots work? Examining the effectiveness of EPA's compliance assistance program', *Journal of Policy Analysis and Management*, 31(3): 533–55.

Sutherland, E.H. (1945) 'Is "white collar crime" crime?', *American Sociological Review*, 10(2): 132.

Sutherland, E.H. (1949/1983) *White Collar Crime: The Uncut Version*, Yale University Press.

Trevino, L.K. and Youngblood, S.A. (1990) 'Bad apples in bad barrels: a causal analysis of ethical decision-making behavior', *Journal of Applied Psychology*, 75(4): 378–85.

Van der Berg, E.A.I.M., Aidala, R., and Beenakkers, E.M. (2002) *Organisatiecriminaliteit*, Wetenschappelijke Onderzoeks-en Documentatie Centrum.

Van der Geest, V.R., Weisburd, D., and Blokland, A.A.J. (2016) 'Developmental trajectories of offenders convicted of fraud: a follow-up to age 50 in a Dutch conviction cohort', *European Journal of Criminology*, 14(5): 543–65.

Van Onna, J.H.R., Van der Geest, V.R., Huisman, W., and Denkers, A.J. (2014) 'Criminal trajectories of white-collar offenders', *Journal of Research in Crime and Delinquency*, 51(6): 759–784.

Weisburd, D., Waring, E., and Chayet, E.F. (2001) 'Dimensions of official criminal careers', in D. Weisburd, E. Waring, and E. F. Chayet (eds), *White-Collar Crime and Criminal Careers*, Cambridge University Press, pp 27–50.

Wiering, E., Kluin, M.H.A., Peeters, M.P., Blokland, A.A.J., and Huisman, W. (2020) 'Diversiteit van regelovertreding in de chemische industrie: specialisten of generalisten?', *Tijdschrift voor Toezicht*, 11(2): 72–85.

Wikström, P.-O. (2010) 'Explaining crime as moral action', in S. Hitlin and S. Vaysey (eds), *Handbook of the Sociology of Morality*, Springer, pp 211–39.

2

Organizational Culture and Corporate Criminology

Nina Tobsch and Marieke H.A. Kluin

Introduction

Organizational culture, defined as 'a pattern of shared basic assumptions learned by a group as it solved its problems of external adaptation and internal integration, which has worked well enough to be considered valid and, therefore, to be taught to new members as the correct way to perceive, think, and feel in relation to those problems' (Schein, 2010, p 18), has drawn substantial attention for its influence on various organizational outcomes, including performance, satisfaction, and notably, organizational misconduct (Belias and Koustelios, 2014; van Rooij and Fine, 2018; Akpa et al, 2021). Organizational misconduct refers broadly to unethical behaviour and violations of legal and social norms by individuals within an organization (MacLean, 2008), and can have serious implications for both the organization as well as society (Hald et al, 2021). The study of organizational culture as an explanatory variable for organizational misconduct lies in its role in shaping behaviour, as it sets implicit norms and expectations for employees that guide perceptions of acceptable conduct (Hofstede et al, 2010; Schein, 2010). In this context, macro-level processes, like economic pressures, regulatory environments, and political ideologies can also influence what are considered acceptable attitudes and practices within an organization, thereby (indirectly) impacting the organizational culture. Increasingly, organizations recognize the importance of culture and are investing in efforts to assess and improve it (Schein, 2010). Concurrently, academic research has also intensified, examining organizational culture's impact on behavioural outcomes such as misconduct (van Rooij and Fine, 2018), while regulatory institutions have begun incorporating cultural assessments into their oversight functions (Zwetsloot et al, 2020).

The study of the relationship between organizational culture and misconduct is fragmented across disciplines, including management and business science, anthropology, and sociology. Corporate criminology, although addressing how the organizational context can relate to crime, has not been the primary lens for examining this link. This might be because organizational sciences tend to use terms like 'unethical' or 'rule-violating' rather than 'crime'. Nevertheless, perspectives from corporate criminology can offer valuable theoretical frameworks and empirical methods that can deepen our understanding of organizational misconduct (Clinard and Yeager, 2006). Indeed, the notion of corporate crime, as defined by van Erp and Huisman (2017), encompasses 'illegal or harmful acts, committed by legitimate organizations or their members, primarily for the benefit of these organizations' (p 248), which aligns with definitions of organizational misconduct that refer to behaviours judged as transgressing legal, ethical, or social norms (Greve et al, 2010, p 56). On the other hand, organizational studies significantly contribute to our understanding of organizational crime and its prevention (van Erp, 2018). Insights from organizational studies are essential for explaining organizational dysfunctional and antisocial behaviour, misconduct and crime, which is known as the 'dark side of organizations' (Vaughan, 1999; Greve et al, 2010; Linstead, et al, 2014).

Therefore, this chapter argues that further incorporation of studying organizational culture and its link with misconduct in corporate criminology is both necessary and beneficial. This chapter first shows the current status and empirical limitations of our understanding of the relationship between organizational culture and crime. Subsequently, it will present a methodological approach that might help corporate criminologists come to a rich understanding of organizational culture and crime, illustrated by an example of how we can use this method to understand misconduct within a public organization, namely the police institution.

Organizational culture and organizational misconduct

Since Sutherland's (1949) seminal work on white-collar offending, the focus on this new area of criminal behaviour to study is not one without obstacles, and as such it has garnered widespread criticism and confusion concerning the definition and scope of behaviours to include (Jordanoska and Schoultz, 2019). In early empirical research, explanations of rule-violating behaviour within organizations were often reduced to individual motivations, pathologies, and human nature during this time (Hirschi and Gottfredson, 1988); as such, the field still lacked theories on white-collar offenders and corporate offending specifically. The call for a closer examination of organizational aspects and their relationship to rule-violating behaviour in an organization was partly due to dissatisfaction with this earlier research (Simpson, 1993). Using an organizational level of analysis, as opposed to an individual one, would allow researchers to identify, explore, and examine organizational factors such as organizational culture to gain a better understanding of organizational deviance and misconduct (Kramer, 1982). Moving to this organizational level of analysis, the central idea at first was that organizations violate rules to remain in business or stay competitive when profitability is vulnerable, but the support for this hypothesis turned out to be mixed (Clinard and Yeager, 1980; Barnett, 1986; Simpson, 1986; 1987; Wang & Holtfreter, 2012). Other organizational characteristics (such as size, type of organization, competition, or industry pressure) showed similar mixed empirical results (Simpson, 2013). Therefore, scholars increasingly underscored the added value in studying the causes of organizational misconduct and rule-violating behaviour in a more a multidimensional approach (Clinard and Yeager, 1980).

There is much we can learn about organizational crime from organizational science, as it developed in business and management science and organizational psychology and sociology (van Rooij and Fine, 2018). According to organizational studies, key elements in any organizational design are organizational strategy, structure, and culture (Morgan, 2006). Shafritz and Ott (1987) describe organizational culture as the 'basic assumptions and beliefs that are shared' (p 384) by members of the organization 'that operate unconsciously and that define in a basic taken-for-granted fashion an organization's view of itself and its environment'. Organizational culture is seen as an essential factor that explains organizational behaviour generally and organizational misconduct specifically (Shafritz and Ott, 1987). Assumptions and beliefs of the organizational culture are learned responses to organizational problems of 'survival in its external environment and its problems of internal integration' (Shafritz and Ott, 1987, p 384).

Members of an organization learn values, norms, beliefs, assumptions, and required behaviours that give them opportunities to participate (Ott, 1989). When new members enter an organization, they are socialized into the organizational culture. This organizational socialization can provide new members with the knowledge and tools they need to participate or even survive in the organizational environment (Ott, 1989). Ott (1989) states that members within an organization are 'rewarded or punished for correct or incorrect actions' (p 90). This further enhances the existing organizational culture and can be seen as a symbolic message of cultural expectations that also provides a warning signal on deviance from organizational culture to the members who remain (Ott, 1989). Hofstede (1980) conceives culture in the workplace as 'a collective programming of the mind which distinguishes one group from another' (p 25). He views these collective programmes, or cultures, as containing values that 'direct our feelings of good and evil' (Hofstede, 1985, p 347). As such, new members learn the desired attitudes and behaviour through interactions with those who already know how to behave in their own roles (van Maanen and Schein, 1977; Ashfort et al, 2007). When these desired practices include unwanted behaviour, the organizational culture can thus lead to the sustaining or creating of organizational misconduct.

Starting with Sutherland (1949) and later taken up by Geis (1967) and Vaughan (1983), deviant cultures and subcultures (Zey-Ferrell et al, 1979; Zey-Ferrell anfd Ferrell, 1982) are implicated as agents of criminal socialization. However, only limited criminological work has focused on studying organizational culture in relation to crime. Vaughan (1983) proposes that deviant cultures arise in organizations when employees experience pressure to achieve defined goals because the legitimate means to compete are limited, restricted, and/or unsuccessful. Benson (1985, 2012) studied a sample of convicted white-collar offenders and explained how their involvement in criminal activities is deeply connected to the social organization of the rule violation. He states that, on the one hand, their statements were related to techniques of neutralization (Sykes and Matza, 1957) to relieve themselves of the duty to behave according to social norms, and on the other hand they were related to the organizational context, the type of offence committed and its mechanisms. Sonnenfeld and Lawrence (1978) concluded that the 'culture of the business' is an important cause for differential participation in price-fixing behaviour of organizations, and even suggested that this price-fixing became a 'way of life' (p 149). Keane (1995) indicates that relative autonomous subunits might have cultures that differ from that of the parent organization, and Huisman (2016) states that these subcultures within organizations can define certain activities as acceptable due to their isolation, even if these actions are condemned by society as a whole. Shover and Hochstetler (2002) showed the existence of inter- and intra-organizational cultures, although they state that most research on organizational culture starts from a monolithic bias. Therefore, they observed that most of the earlier research concentrates on variables that describe or characterize organizations in their entirety. Shover and Hochstetler (2002) conclude that this approach neglects the complexity of organizational culture. Cohen (1995) and van Rooij and Fine (2018) set out to assess the characteristics of toxic elements within a corporate culture. Van Rooij and Fine (2018) demonstrated that toxic cultures exist at BP, Wells Fargo, and Volkswagen at the levels of structures, values, and practices; organizational misconduct was not the result of a single act or actor, but the result of several core processes within the organization's culture.

Methods and limitations of studying organizational culture

While the influence of organizational culture on individual behaviour is assumed to be significant (Hofstede et al, 2010; Schein, 2010), the concept is complex and multidimensional, and its ambiguous nature paired with the challenges in measuring the construct pose difficulties in fully understanding its impact. This has led to several gaps in our knowledge regarding the relationship. One limitation in the literature is the enigmatic nature of the concept of organizational culture itself. Different scholars and researchers have offered various definitions and perspectives on organizational culture, leading to a lack of consensus regarding its exact meaning. In his historical overview on the development of the organizational culture construct, Ott (1989) identified over 70 different ways of defining organizational culture, and in their systematic review on the measurement of the construct, Jung et al (2009) identified around the same number of instruments used to study organizational culture. As a result, it becomes challenging to establish a unified understanding of the concept and synthesize findings across different disciplines. One reason for this is that the different conceptualizations and definitions have led to conflicting understandings of how a culture is to be classified. Generally, there are two approaches: typological and dimensional (Jung et al, 2009). Typological instruments distinguish between different *types* of organizational culture. For example, Cameron and Quinn (2005) differentiate between four types – clan, adhocracy, hierarchy, and market – to develop their now widely-used Organizational Cultural Assessment Instrument. Conversely, the dimensional approach studies the extent to which certain cultural *elements* are present in an organization. For instance, Kaptein (2008) developed his Corporate Ethical Virtues Model based on how 'ethical' a culture within an organization is believed to be. These different understandings on how to classify organizational culture contribute to confusion and make it difficult to establish a comprehensive understanding of how organizational culture influences individual behaviour.

As mentioned in the introduction, Schein (2010) provides one of the most widely-used definitions and operationalizations of organizational culture. His work is not typological or dimensional, but rather provides an operationalization of the elements and antecedents of what an organizational culture consists of. In line with earlier studies like Shafritz and Ott (1987), his work shows clearly that organizational culture has three levels. The first consists of what he refers to as 'artifacts'. These are the concrete aspects of an organization's culture which consist of the 'visible and feelable structures and processes' as well as of 'observed behavior' (Schein 2010, p 23). Artifacts are at the surface of an organization's culture, and are visible products of how the organization manifests its culture (this can include architecture, style, published documents, and organizational charts). The second level are what Schein refers to as 'the espoused beliefs and values', which encompass shared ideals, goals, values, and aspirations between individuals within an organization. The third level of an organizational culture are the 'basic underlying assumptions'. These are embedded within the organization and operate non-visibly and unconsciously through organization members. They concern taken-for-granted beliefs and values that can 'determine behavior perception, thought and feeling' (Schein 2010, p 24).

A second limitation in the literature is the difficulty in measuring the culture of an organization. As disussed, culture in general is an intangible construct that is deeply embedded in the beliefs, values, and behaviours of individuals. It exists on different levels of depth: for instance, some cultural values shape behaviour because they are communicated clearly and directly, whereas other values have become so ingrained that they steer conduct implicitly (Huisman, 2001; van Rooij and Fine, 2018). Because of this complexity, it is crucial to understand the organizational culture in various dimensions and levels of depth. Ideally, studying organizational culture would be done inductively with a focus on the causal processes that link this culture to behaviour. However, the majority of studies in the organizational science literature rely on self-report measures and interviews to assess employees' own perceptions of the organizational context and characteristics; these self-reports are subjective and may be influenced by factors such as social desirability, individual interpretations, or individual biases (Ouchi and Wilkins, 1985; Krosnick, 1999). Furthermore, whereas it is generally the norm in organizational science studies to focus on one aspect of the culture, for example its ethicality, it is questionable whether this provides a sufficient representation of the cultural influence on behaviour.

Empirical research on the relationship of organizational culture and organizational crime according to Huisman (2016) is not empirically strong. As is often the case when studying corporate offending, case studies (Verhage, 2009) are used that post hoc reconstruct explanatory variables and how they shed light on exceptional rule-violating behaviour. Those case studies are often high-profile landmark cases and are interpreted in the context of the scandal (Shover and Hochstetler, 2002). While there is a distinct tradition of conducting such case-study research in the broader examination of corporate criminology, specifically studying organizational culture in a qualitative manner remains less common. For instance, in her review of the Challenger space shuttle disaster, Vaughan (1996) argued that the process of cultural normalization of rule-breaking and risky behaviour within the organization was one of the most influential causes that led to the explosion of the space shuttle. In a similar vein, in his analysis of several financial misconduct cases, van de Bunt (2010) stated that an organizational environment that fosters a 'code of silence' stimulates and sustains misbehaviour among employees. While these studies have shown the importance of organizational cultural factors in explaining organizational crime, they ultimately did not set out to measure or examine the organizational culture as such, and therefore do not offer a systematic and in-depth analysis of this culture.

Organizational culture and misconduct: the case of police misuse of force

Due to their unique role and responsibilities, police departments are often not perceived as typical organizations. Unlike private organizations that focus on profit, or public organizations that deliver services, police departments prioritize law enforcement, public safety, and social order. This role and the critical nature of the work are relatively unique to the policing profession, and can influence their operational procedures, public interactions, attitudes, and occupational culture (Loftus, 2010). However, police departments share significant similarities with more 'traditional' organizations. Structurally, they have formal and informal hierarchical frameworks, clear chains of command, and well-defined roles and responsibilities (King, 2005; Davis, 2018). Like private and public organizations, they engage in strategic planning, resource management, and performance evaluations to achieve their goals (Farmer, 2013; Cordner, 2023). Furthermore, they face similar challenges, including resource scarcity, employee training, and the need to adapt to societal demands and changes (Blumberg et al, 2019; Dunham et al, 2021). Including police departments in corporate criminology can thus be highly valuable, as the insights from this discpline into the relationship between organizational culture and employee behaviour might offer new insights into our understanding of police misbehaviour. Corporate crime literature has, for the most part, neglected the police as an organization to study. An exception is a chapter on the Los Angeles Police Department (LAPD) that was published in a landmark book on corporate crime (Ermann and Lundman, 2000). The Rampart Division Scandal of the LAPD showed outrageous misconduct, including allegations of corruption, brutality, and due process abuses, and organizational culture was presumed to play a major role in sustaining these behaviours, because of officer's shared willingness to 'participate in, or condone, misconduct' (Kaplan, 2009, p 64).

One severe type of police misbehaviour is the misuse of force, also known as excessive use of force or police brutality. The use of excessive or unnecessary force by law enforcement officers may result in physical injury, psychological trauma, or even death (Prenzler et al, 2013; McLeod et al, 2020); this type of misconduct is a significant issue that has garnered widespread attention and concern over the past several decades. Numerous studies have been conducted to examine the factors contributing to police misuse of force, particularly in relation to individual characteristics of officers, individual characteristics of civilians, situational characteristics, and organizational characteristics such as police culture (Friedrich, 1980; Lersch and Mieczkowski, 2005; Eitle et al, 2014).

The concept of 'police culture' is commonly seen as being associated with police (mis)behaviour (Coady et al, 2001; Cockroft, 2012). In the second half of the last century, scholars started noting that police officers develop a distinct set of norms, values, and behaviours that set them apart from other professions and influence their day-to-day activities. This shared notion of the occupational context became known as police culture (Cockroft, 2012). Recently, scholars have made great advancements in the understanding and studying of police culture, namely on the environments, prescriptions, and outcomes, and have established a strong empirical link between cultural attitudes and officers' behaviours (Ingram et al, 2018). However, as with corporate criminology, to date minimal work has attempted to incorporate the theoretical foundations of organizational culture into this framework (for a theoretical exception, see Armacost, 2003). Furthermore, researchers have not fully studied the concept as collective and shared, instead studying the attitudes of individual officers (see, for example, Ingram et al, 2018). In doing so, culture is assessed based on individual perceptions, mainly using surveys and interviews, but not studied within the shared context of the department (although there have been recent efforts to incorporate the shared nature of the concept of culture in policing surveys, see for example Paesen et al, 2019). Here, we again see overlap with the broader research on organizational culture and its link with organizational misconduct; as we discussed earlier, those studies also often rely on individual-level measurements to come to an understanding of the shared culture.

In sum, the general literature on organizational culture, as well as the literatures on organizational culture and crime and police culture struggle with similar limitations, namely the confusion on what constitutes a culture that is 'criminogenic', how a culture can be identified, and how best to measure the construct so that it becomes clear how culture exerts its influence on behaviour (Shover & Hochstetler, 2002; Trahan, 2011). Further academic work is needed for two main reasons: (1) to create a theoretical framework of organizational culture that can be used to study its relationship with organizational crime, and (2) to identify and develop an adequate methodological approach to study organizational culture in relation to organizational crime. In other work (Tobsch et al, 2024), we explore how we can operationalize such a theoretical framework based on the definition provided by Schein (2010) discussed earlier. In the remainder of this chapter, we discuss how corporate criminology can study such an understanding of cultural aspects that lead to dysfunctional behaviour using a method that can capture more shared aspects of an organizational culture, namely the causal process tracing method.

An alternative approach to studying organizational culture and crime

As we have described, general social science studies have shown us the multifaceted and complex nature of organizational culture, existing at different dimensions and levels of depth. However, most studies rely on survey measures, which only measure individual perceptions of organizational values, often focusing on one dimension of culture. On the other hand, criminological work does employ case studies. However, a deeper understanding and focus on the culture construct remains largely absent. Studies focus on elements of the organization that could be considered part of an organizational culture, like the use of neutralization techniques or silencing within organizations (van de Bunt, 2010; Schoultz and Flyghed, 2020), but do not set out to study a full understanding of an organizational culture in specific cases.

Remaining in the tradition of using a case-study design, we propose the use of the causal process tracing method to gain a more systematic understanding of the relationship between organizational culture and crime. Causal process tracing, defined as 'a research method for tracing causal mechanisms using detailed, within-case empirical analysis of how a causal process plays out in an actual case' (Beach, 2017, p 1), is a methodological approach employed in anthropology and social sciences to analyze and understand the causal mechanisms behind complex real-world phenomena through individual case studies (Beach and Pedersen, 2019). A case study is 'a research approach that is used to generate an in-depth, multifaceted understanding of a complex issue in its real-life context' (Crowe et al, 2011, p 1). In a case study, the researcher carefully analyzes *how* things played out in a real-world case, therefore allowing them to answer questions such as 'how did X come to influence Y?'. The process tracing method gained prominence as researchers sought to move beyond simply establishing correlation between variables, and instead focused on unraveling the intricate causal relationships at play (the 'how'). Over time, scholars recognized the limitations of traditional statistical methods in capturing these complex dynamics, leading to the development of more nuanced and qualitative approaches such as process tracing (Blatter and Haverland, 2014). In corporate criminology specifically, this 'mechanism-focused' approach is increasingly being developed and applied to the study of organizational crime (see, for example, Lord and Levi, 2025).

In terms of research design, causal process tracing should involve a systematic and iterative process (Beach and Pedersen, 2019). Researchers should start by developing an initial theoretical framework that outlines the expected causal mechanisms and their key parts. They should then select a small number of cases that are most suitable for investigating these mechanisms, often using purposive sampling based on theoretical relevance or empirical variation. The next step is the detailed examination of sources and evidence, including archival records, interviews, and organizational documents, to reconstruct the causal processes at play in each case. This involves tracing the causal chains and identifying the mechanisms, contexts, and intervening factors that link causes to outcomes. Weighing the empirical evidence and evaluating its plausibility and strength are essential components of causal process tracing. Posing critical questions to the evidence to assess its credibility, the researcher assesses questions about the sufficiency, consistency, and specificity of the evidence, as well as considerations of rival explanations and potential bias. By subjecting the evidence to these systematic and rigorous evaluations, researchers can enhance the reliability and validity of their findings. To make inferences about the gathered data, researchers use Bayesian logic, which offers a structured way to update and adjust how confident we are in different hypotheses as new evidence emerges. This method supports a more detailed and flexible understanding of how causal mechanisms work by considering both what we expect theoretically and what the actual data shows (Beach and Pedersen, 2019).

Using this methodological approach fills several gaps in the literature as discussed thus far. First, by combining evidence from different sources, we can study the effect of different aspects and levels of depth of culture on corporate crime. Whereas interviews and surveys mainly measure internal perceptions on organizational values, the evidential record used in this approach allows the researcher to also look at the external level of culture (that is, what the organization communicates to the outside world in regard to its culture), and offers the possibility of studying practices and structures more deeply. Furthermore, by studying *how* an organizational culture leads to corporate crime, we can come to a more integrated and holistic theoretical framework of this relationship, for example by identifying certain 'risk factors' or 'toxic elements' within the culture of an organization, which can in turn inform larger studies. Lastly, this approach does not demand to 'identify' a culture as a whole; rather, it aims to identify criminogenic cultural processes (Apel and Paternoster, 2009).

Oakland Police Department as an illustration

To illustrate the methodological approach and its benefits, this chapter will briefly examine the Oakland Police Department (OPD), a policing agency of a midsize city in California. Investigating the events related to organizational culture and misconduct within the OPD offers a preliminary step before data collection and analysis, allowing for an assessment of the suitability and feasibility of conducting an in-depth case study using causal process tracing. It is important to note, however, that the discussion below is purely exploratory and intended to support the claims regarding the usability of causal process tracing: no systematic analysis using causal process tracing has been conducted on this case as of yet.

The OPD has faced numerous cases of police brutality and violence. Incidents have involved excessive use of force, racial profiling, and administrative misconduct (Winston and BondGraham, 2023). One high-profile case involved the shooting of Oscar Grant in 2009, which sparked public outrage and protests (Ferrer, 2009). Another notable case was the investigation into the 'Riders' scandal in the early 2000s, in which a group of officers were accused of framing and abusing residents. The department has also faced criticism for its handling of protests, including the use of tear gas and rubber bullets (Winston and BondGraham, 2023). One of the identified causes for this issue were the department's high arrest targets, which may have contributed to a culture that prioritizes aggressive tactics over community-oriented policing (Winston and BondGraham, 2023). In the early 2000s, the department introduced arrest targets double the arrest record set a decade prior, in order to efficiently and significantly reduce the city's crime rates. Through a system of evaluation and promotion, OPD officers were incentivized to use hard policing tactics, such as proactive policing, to meet these targets. To justify their use of force to make arrests, OPD officers relied on the elevated crime rates and brutal offenders as their rationale for violent behaviour.

Following Schein's (2010) levels of organizational culture, this example can be seen as an inherent cultural value as well as a shared practice; the organization values the targets it sets, influencing the organization-wide practices by promoting officers that met the targets and evaluating new recruits on the basis of the arrests they made, therefore also influencing individual behaviour of members of that organization. From earlier case-study research, we know that the goal-seeking aspect within an organization can make it more prone to misconduct (van Rooij and Fine, 2018). Applying the causal process tracing method, and based on strain theory (Agnew and White, 1992; Agnew, 2006), we can propose that: when the organizational context includes targets (and when organizational values support such targets), but is structured in a way that organizational members cannot attain these, this will make those members engage in harmful conduct.

Table 2.1 shows such a mechanism, as well as the data we would need to identify in the evidential record to support our hypothesized mechanism and its parts. The former shows how theoretical insights from organizational sciences and criminology can be combined, whereas the latter highlights the various sources that can be utilized to come to a deeper understanding of an organization's culture.

Conclusion

In this chapter, we have argued that the study of organizational culture as a cause for organizational crime is crucial for corporate criminology. Organizational culture, including the complex interaction of shared values, structures, and practices, has been shown to influence employee

Table 2.1: Example of a causal process tracing theory

Cause	Part 1	Part 2	Part 3	Part 4	Outcome
The police department sets high arrest targets as part of a tough-on-crime strategy	Through the enforcement of incentives and formal/social norms and values, the organization *communicates* the high value of these targets to organizational members	Organizational members are *unable to meet* these high targets due to lack of resources, including time, technical equipment or abilities, knowledge, and finances	Not being able to meet these targets with the legitimate resources provided by the organization *creates negative emotions* among organizational members	Motivated by the need to meet targets (for example, in order to keep job, get more resources, and so on), organizational members *engage in illegitimate ways*	Police misconduct, including the use of excessive force to secure arrests
Traceable in the informal organizational targets	Traceable in evaluation systems linking targets to rewards and promotions, as well as in leadership messages	Traceable by looking at what is needed to meet these targets and whether that is available, whether any member in this or a similar organization meets these targets, or what the existing average accomplishment is on these targets	Traceable in complaints/whistleblowing documents, existing interviews with organizational members, memoirs of organizational members indicating the stress of their jobs linked to the targets	Traceable by looking at key instances of deviant or damaging behaviour and looking at whether any such behaviour was reported as being done to attain organizational targets	

misbehaviour within organizational studies, but systematic examinations of such organizational cultures remain largely absent in the field of corporate criminology. A renewed and systematic focus on organizational culture can be valuable as it shifts the lens from individual rule-violators to the broader organizational environment that creates, enables, and sustains such behaviour, which corresponds with the idea that corporate crime is often the result of systemic issues rather than of isolated incidents or individual behaviour.

The causal process tracing method might be particularly suitable for studying organizational culture due to its comprehensive approach to analyzing complex real-world processes. Unlike traditional methods that may either oversimplify the relationship between culture and misconduct, like surveys, or be too costly, like ethnographical methods, causal process tracing allows for an in-depth study of how specific cultural elements contribute to organizational crime within an organization. This method's systematic nature and the use of diverse sources enable researchers to construct detailed case studies that capture the complex nature of organizational culture and its impact on behaviour. By identifying and tracing these causal processes, scholars might be better equipped to understand the conditions and 'risk factors' under which organizational culture comes to stimulate or sustain corporate crime.

Future research should expand both empirically and theoretically in several key areas. Empirically, case studies using causal process tracing should be conducted across different industries and organizational contexts in order to build a wide body of evidence on how organizational culture influences misconduct. Additionally, comparative studies can help identify common patterns and unique cultural dynamics in various organizational settings and sectors, contributing to a more comprehensive understanding of the influence of the concept.

Theoretically, there is a need for developing integrated frameworks that combine insights from organizational studies and (corporate) criminology. These frameworks should articulate the specific mechanisms through which culture influences behaviour, drawing on theories such as the earlier mentioned differential association, subcultural theory, and strain theory, but also the wider rich body of theories used in corporate criminology. By bridging these disciplinary perspectives, researchers can develop a more holistic understanding of organizational culture and its role in creating, enabling, and sustaining misconduct.

In conclusion, understanding organizational culture as a cause for organizational crime is essential for both theoretical advancement and practical application in corporate criminology. This integration and the method proposed here offer a powerful way for uncovering the mechanisms through which culture shapes behaviour, which enhances our understanding of the risk factors within organizations.

References

Agnew, R. (2006) *Pressured into Crime: An Overview of General Strain Theory*, Oxford University Press.

Agnew, R. and White, H.R. (1992) 'An empirical test of general strain theory', *Criminology*, 30(4): 475–500.

Akpa, V.O., Asikhia, O.U., and Nneji, N.E. (2021) 'Organizational culture and organizational performance: a review of literature', *International Journal of Advances in Engineering and Management*, 3(1): 361–72.

Apel, R. and Paternoster, R. (2009) 'Understanding "criminogenic" corporate culture: what white-collar crime researchers can learn from studies of the adolescent employment–crime relationship', in S.S. Simpson and D. Weisburd (eds), *The Criminology of White-Collar Crime*, Springer New York, pp 15–33.

Armacost, B.E. (2003) 'Organizational culture and police misconduct', *George Washington Law Review*, 72(3): 453–546.

Ashforth, B.E., Sluss, D.M., and Harrison, S.H. (2007) 'Socialization in organizational contexts', in G.P. Hodgkinson and J.K. Ford (eds), *International Review of Industrial and Organizational Psychology*, John Wiley & Sons, pp 1–70.

Barnett, H.C. (1986) 'Industry culture and industry economy: correlates of tax noncompliance in Sweden', *Criminology*, 24(3): 553–74.

Beach, D. (2017) 'Process-tracing methods in social science', in *Oxford Research Encyclopedia of Politics*, Oxford University Press.

Beach, D. and Pedersen, R.B. (2019) *Process-tracing Methods: Foundations and guidelines* (2nd edn), University of Michigan Press.

Belias, D. and Koustelios, A. (2014) 'Organizational culture and job satisfaction: a review', *International Review of Management and Marketing*, 4(2): 132–49.

Benson, M.L. (1985) 'Denying the guilty mind: accounting for involvement in a white-collar crime', *Criminology*, 23(4): 583–607.

Benson, M.L. (2012) 'Denying the guilty mind', in D.A. Dabney (ed), *Crime Types: A Text/Reader*, Aspen Publishing, pp 393–406.

Blatter, J. and Haverland, M. (2014) 'Case studies and (causal-) process tracing', in I. Engeli and C. Rothmayr Allison (eds), *Comparative Policy Studies: Conceptual and Methodological Challenges*, Palgrave Macmillan, pp 59–83.

Blumberg, D.M., Schlosser, M.D., Papazoglou, K., Creighton, S., and Kaye, C.C. (2019) 'New directions in police academy training: a call to action', *International Journal of Environmental Research and Public Health*, 16(24): 4941–54.

Cameron, K.S. and Quinn, R.E. (2005) *Diagnosing and Changing Organizational Culture: Based on the Competing Values Framework*, John Wiley & Sons.

Clinard, M. and Yeager, P. (1980) *Corporate Crime*, Free Press.

Clinard, M. and Yeager, P. (2006) *Corporate Crime* (2nd edn), Transaction Publishers.

Coady, C., James, S., Miller, S., and O'Keefe, M. (2001) *Violence and Police Culture*, Melbourne University Press.

Cockcroft, T. (2012) *Police Culture: Themes and Concepts*, Routledge.

Cohen, D.V. (1995) 'Ethics and crime in business firms: organizational culture and the impact of anomie', in F. Adler and W. S. Laufer (eds), *The Legacy of Anomie Theory*, Transaction Publishers, pp 183–206.

Cordner, G.W. (2023) *Police Administration* (11th edn), Routledge.

Crowe, S., Cresswell, K., Robertson, A., Huby, G., Avery, A., and Sheikh, A. (2011) 'The case study approach', *BMC Medical Research Methodology*, 11(1): 1–9.

Davis, C. (2018) 'Rank matters: police leadership and the authority of rank', *Policing and Society*, 30(4): 446–61.

Dunham, R.G., Alpert, G.P., and McLean, K.D. (2021) *Critical Issues in Policing: Contemporary Readings*, Waveland Press.

Eitle, D., D'Alessio, S.J., and Stolzenberg, L. (2014) 'The effect of organizational and environmental factors on police misconduct', *Police Quarterly*, 17(2): 103–26.

Ermann, M.D. and Lundman, R. J. (2000) *Corporate and Governmental Deviance: Problems of Organizational Behavior in Contemporary Society*, Oxford University Press.

Farmer, D.J. (2013) *Crime Control: The Use and Misuse of Police Resources*, Springer Science & Business Media.

Ferrer, C.J. (2009) 'The Art of Protest: The Oscar Grant Memorial Arts Project', *Race, Poverty & the Environment*, 16(1): 40–3.

Friedrich, R.J. (1980) 'Police use of force: individuals, situations, and organizations', *The Annals of the American Academy of Political and Social Science*, 452(1): 82–97.

Geis, G. (1967) 'The heavy electrical equipment antitrust cases of 1961', in M. Clinard and R. Quinney (eds), *Criminal Behavior Systems*, Rinehart & Winston, pp 139–50.

Greve, H.R., Palmer, D., and Pozner, J. (2010) 'Organizations gone wild: the causes, processes, and consequences of organizational misconduct', *The Academy of Management Annals*, 4(1): 53–107.

Hald, E.J., Gillespie, A., and Reader, T.W. (2021) 'Causal and corrective organisational culture: a systematic review of case studies of institutional failure', *Journal of Business Ethics*, 174(2): 457–83.

Hirschi, T. and Gottfredson, M. (1988) 'Towards a general theory of crime', in W. Buikhuisen and S.A. Mednick (eds), *Explaining Criminal Behaviour*, Brill, pp 8–26.

Hofstede, G. (1980) *Culture's Consequences: International Differences in Work-related Values*, Sage.

Hofstede, G. (1985), 'The interaction between national and organizational value systems', *Journal of Management Studies*, 22(4): 347–57.

Hofstede, G., Hofstede, G.J., and Minkov, M. (2010) *Cultures and Organizations: Software of the Mind* (3rd edn), McGraw-Hill Professional.

Huisman, W. (2001) *Tussen winst en moraal. Achtergronden van regelnaleving en regelovertreding door ondernemingen*, VU Amsterdam.

Huisman, W. (2016) 'Criminogenic organizational properties and dynamics', in S.R. Van Slyke, M.L. Benson, and F.T. Cullen (eds), *The Oxford Handbook of White-Collar Crime*, Oxford University Press, pp 435–62.

Ingram, J.R., Terrill, W., and Paoline III, E.A. (2018) 'Police culture and officer behavior: application of a multilevel framework', *Criminology*, 56(4): 780–811.

Jordanoska, A. and Schoultz, I. (2019) 'The "discovery" of white-collar crime: the legacy of Edwin Sutherland', in M. L. Rorie (ed), *The Handbook of White-Collar Crime*, Wiley-Blackwell, pp 1–15.

Jung, T., Scott, T., Davies, H.T., Bower, P., Whalley, D., McNally, R., and Mannion, R. (2009) 'Instruments for exploring organizational culture: a review of the literature', *Public Administration Review*, 69(6): 1087–96.

Kaplan, P.J. (2009) 'Looking through the gaps: a critical approach to the LAPD's rampart scandal', *Social Justice*, 36(1): 61–81.

Kaptein, M. (2008) 'Developing and testing a measure for the ethical culture of organizations: the corporate ethical virtues model', *Journal of Organizational Behavior*, 29(7): 923–947.

Keane, C. (1995) 'Loosely coupled systems and unlawful behavior: organization theory and corporate crime', in F. Pearce and L. Snider (eds), *Corporate Crime: Contemporary Debates*, University of Toronto Press, pp 168–81.

King, W.R. (2005) 'Toward a better understanding of the hierarchical nature of police organizations: conception and measurement', *Journal of Criminal Justice*, 33(1): 97–109.

Kramer, R.C. (1982) 'Corporate crime: an organizational perspective', in P. Wickman and T. Dailey (ed), *White-Collar and Economic Crime: Multidisciplinary and Cross-National Perspectives*, Lexington Books, pp 75–95.

Krosnick, J.A. (1999) 'Survey research', *Annual Review of Psychology*, 50(1): 537–67.

Lersch, K.M. and Mieczkowski, T. (2005) 'Violent police behavior: past, present, and future research directions', *Aggression and Violent Behavior*, 10(5): 552–68.

Linstead, S., Garance, M., and Griffin, R.W. (2014) 'Theorizing and researching the dark side of organization', *Organization Studies*, 35(2): 165–88.

Loftus, B. (2010) 'Police occupational culture: classic themes, altered times', *Policing and Society*, 20(1): 1–20.

Lord, N. and Levi, M. (2025) *Organising White-Collar and Corporate Crimes*, Routledge.

MacLean, T.L. (2008) 'Framing and organizational misconduct: a symbolic interactionist study', *Journal of Business Ethics*, 78(1–2): 3–16.

McLeod, M.N., Heller, D., Manze, M.G., and Echeverria, S.E. (2020) 'Police interactions and the mental health of Black Americans: a systematic review', *Journal of Racial and Ethnic Health Disparities*, 7(1): 10–27.

Morgan, G. (2006) *Images of Organization*, Sage.

Ott, J.S. (1989) *The Organizational Culture Perspective*, Dorsey Press.

Ouchi, W.G. and Wilkins, A.L. (1985) 'Organizational culture', *Annual Review of Sociology*, 11(1): 457–83.

Paesen, H., Maesschalck, J., and Loyens, K. (2019) 'Beyond police culture: a quantitative study of the organisational culture in 64 local police forces in Belgium', *Policing: An International Journal*, 42(5): 814–31.

Prenzler, T., Porter, L., and Alpert, G.P. (2013) 'Reducing police use of force: case studies and prospects', *Aggression and Violent Behavior*, 18(2): 343–56.

Schein, E.H. (2010) *Organizational Culture and Leadership* (4th edn), John Wiley & Sons.

Schoultz, I. and Flyghed, J. (2020) 'From "we didn't do it" to "we've learned our lesson": development of a typology of neutralizations of corporate crime', *Critical Criminology*, 28(4): 739–57.

Shafritz, J.M. and Ott, J.S. (1987) *Classics of Organization Theory*, Brooks/Cole Publishing Company.

Shover, N. and Hochstetler, A. (2002) 'Cultural explanation and organizational crime', *Crime, law and social change*, 37: 1–8.

Simpson, S.S. (1986) 'The decomposition of antitrust: testing a multi-level, longitudinal model of profit-squeeze', *American Sociological Review*, 51(6): 859–75.

Simpson, S.S. (1987) 'Cycles of illegality: antitrust violations in corporate America', *Social Forces*, 65(4): 943–63.

Simpson, S.S. (1993) 'Strategy, structure, and corporate crime: the historical context of anticompetitive behavior', in F. Adler and W.S. Laufer (eds), *New Directions in Criminological Theory*, Transaction Publishers, pp 71–93.

Simpson, S.S. (2013) 'White-collar crime: a review of recent developments and promising directions for future research', *Annual Review of Sociology*, 39(1): 309–31.

Sonnenfeld, J. and Lawrence, P.R. (1978) 'Why do companies succumb to price fixing?', *Harvard Business Review*, 56(4): 145–57.

Sutherland, E.H. (1949) *White Collar Crime*, Dryden Press.

Sykes, G. and Matza, D. (1957) 'Techniques of neutralization: a theory of delinquency', *American Sociological Review*, 22(6): 667–70.

Tobsch, N., Lyne, S., and van Rooij, B. (2024) 'Can organizational culture predict major wrongdoing? A review of existing survey measures' [Manuscript submitted for publication], University of Amsterdam, Department of Jurisprudence.

Trahan, A. (2011) 'Filling in the gaps in culture-based theories of organizational crime', *Journal of Theoretical & Philosophical Criminology*, 3(1): 89–109.
van De Bunt, H. (2010) 'Walls of secrecy and silence: the Madoff case and cartels in the construction industry', *Criminology & Public Policy*, 9(3): 435–53.
van Erp, J. (2018) 'The organization of corporate crime', *Administrative Sciences*, 8(3): 36–48.
van Erp, J. and Huisman, W. (2017) 'Corporate crime', in A. Brisman, E. Carrabine and N. South (eds), *Routledge Companion to Criminological Theory and Concepts*, Routledge.
van Maanen, J.E. and Schein, E.H. (1977) *Toward a Theory of Organizational Socialization*, Massachusetts Institute of Technology.
van Rooij, B. and Fine, A. (2018) 'Toxic corporate culture: assessing organizational processes of deviancy', *Administrative Sciences*, 8(3): 23–60.
Vaughan, D. (1983) *Controlling Unlawful Organizational Behavior: Social Structure and Organizational Misconduct*, University of Chicago Press.
Vaughan, D. (1996) *The Challenger Launch Decision: Risky Technology, Culture, and Deviance at NASA*, University of Chicago Press.
Vaughan, D. (1999) 'The dark side of organizations: mistake, misconduct, and disaster', *Annual Review of Sociology*, 25: 271–305.
Verhage, A. (2009) 'Corporations as a blind spot in research: explanations for a criminological tunnel vision', in M. Cools, S. De Kimpe, B. De Ruyver, M. Easton, L. Pauwels, P. Ponsaers et al (eds), *Contemporary Issues in the Empirical Study of Crime*, Governance of Security Research Papers Series I, Maklu.
Wang, X. and Holtfreter, K. (2012) 'The effects of corporation-and industry-level strain and opportunity on corporate crime', *Journal of Research in Crime and Delinquency*, 49(2): 151–85.
Winston, A. and BondGraham, D. (2023) *The Riders Come Out at Night: Brutality, Corruption, and Cover-up in Oakland*, Simon and Schuster.
Zey-Ferrell, M.K., Weaver, M., and Ferrell, O.C. (1979) 'Predicting unethical behavior among marketing practitioners', *Human Relations*, 32(7): 557–69.
Zey-Ferrel, M.K. and Ferrel, O.C. (1982) 'Role set configuration and opportunity as predictors of unethical behavior in organizations', *Human Relations*, 35(7): 587–604.
Zwetsloot, G.I., van Middelaar, J., and Van der Beek, D. (2020) 'Repeated assessment of process safety culture in major hazard industries in the Rotterdam region (Netherlands)', *Journal of Cleaner Production*, 257: 1–11.

3

Social Control for Leverage: Stakeholders Influencing Peer Social Control

Anna Merz

Introduction

In the last three decades, the social control of corporations and their behaviour has shifted from the state being the only sheriff in town (Abbott and Snidal, 2009, p 87) to a more diverse group of control agents, including corporations, civil society, investors, consumers, and local communities (Garland, 1996; Black, 2001; Lobel, 2004; Nielsen and Parker, 2008; Grabosky, 2013; van Wingerde and Bisschop, 2022).

The responsibilization of banks as gatekeepers under anti-money laundering (AML) and counter-terrorist financing (CTF) regulations is an example of the decentralization of control. As illicit money moves through banks' accounts, they are able to detect suspicious transactions or clients in their systems. In the Netherlands, which is the scope of this chapter, noncompliance with AML regulations has become a top priority on the political and regulatory agenda since 2018. In September 2018, the largest bank of the Netherlands, ING Bank, settled investigations into shortcomings for €775 million. Since then, the two other systemic banks[1] have either settled criminal investigations (ABN AMRO for €480 million) or are still being investigated (Rabobank). Given the shared responsibility as gatekeepers, AML noncompliance has become an industry problem, prompting other banks to respond to violations in the industry (Merz, 2023). Such peer responses by other banks can take different forms, ranging from solidarity and cooperation to disapproval of noncompliant practices and closing ranks as an industry (Merz, 2023).

Besides banks, a range of stakeholders (for example, regulators, policy makers, the Financial Action Task Force, the Financial Intelligence Unit, compliance certification professionals, consultancy firms, and industry associations) have a (direct) role and interest in the anti-money laundering (AML) regime. These stakeholders also engage in (or shape) debates on money laundering in the financial industry. This has resulted in a regime in which 'many interests (and thereby profits) are involved' (Verhage, 2009a, p 29).

This chapter takes a novel perspective on the governance of organizational crime, examining how different stakeholders can act as levers to get the behaviour they want from corporations.[2] The chapter aims to answer how and for what purpose stakeholders influence peer social control between corporations.

First, an overview of what we already know on stakeholder influence and what we are still lacking is presented. Four stakeholder groups who cultivate direct interactions with banks and, therefore, (directly) interfere with AML in the financial industry were selected: regulators, policy makers, industry stakeholders, and consultancy firms. The chapter draws on interviews with ten stakeholders and content analysis of publicly available information (for example, media coverage, guidance reports, parliamentary debates) to identify different mechanisms and purposes of leveraging peer effects. After introducing the methods and four stakeholder groups, mechanisms and purposes of stakeholders leveraging peer effects are presented. Through the leverage of peer effects, banks have been responsibilized as social control agents of each other's behaviour by stakeholders. As for now, the leverage of peer pressure seems to work, as banks fear sanctions and reputational damage and are uncertain on whether and when measures taken are sufficient (see van Wingerde and Hofman, 2022, p 107; Merz, 2023). The chapter ends with a recap of the benefits and risks of leveraging peer social control.

What we do (not) know about stakeholder influence and leverage

Numerous studies have explored the involvement of third parties in the governance of organizational crime and its benefits for compliance (Gunningham et al, 1999; Nielsen and Parker, 2008; Grabosky, 2013).

Gunningham et al (2003) identify three stakeholder groups influencing corporate behaviour: economic stakeholders (investors, shareholders, customers), legal/regulatory stakeholders (regulators, government, citizens), and social stakeholders (neighbours, civil society, public). Each has different roles, monitors compliance differently (Gunningham et al, 2003, pp 35–40; Nielsen and Parker, 2008, p 312), and potentially has distinct interests. Social stakeholders rely on shame and publicity, economic stakeholders focus on share prices, investments, and loans, while regulatory stakeholders use inspections, legal action, and moral persuasion (Gunningham et al, 2003, p 377). Civil society and local communities are well-studied as third-party actors in addressing organizational crime (Bartley, 2007). Nielsen and Parker (2008) find that while third-party reactions by customers, shareholders, employees, business partners matter to businesses, they do not impact business behaviour. Therefore, this chapter explores how stakeholder groups directly involved in the AML regime leverage peer social control, shedding light on their differing interests. Existing research that focuses on indirect influence mostly sheds light on the power of public pressure and negative publicity (Fisse and Braithwaite, 1983; Braithwaite, 1989; Gunningham et al, 2003; van Erp, 2008).

The inclusion of (relevant) third parties in regulation, next to the state and the corporation, is widely known as 'tripartism' (Ayres and Braithwaite, 1992) or 'regulatory pluralism' (Gunningham and Sinclair, 1999). Tripartism or regulatory pluralism entail including interest groups, NGOs (non-governmental organizations), local residents, and citizens by giving them access to regulatory information, roles in decision-making on supervision and enforcement, and even the capacity to enforce if necessary (Ayres and Braithwaite, 1992; Nielsen and Parker, 2009). Ayres and Braithwaite (1992) introduced tripartism to mitigate regulatory capture, which can occur when regulators overidentify with or are influenced by the regulated business, resulting in a neglect of public interests. Decentralizing control offers several advantages. It enables authorities to manage limited resources in tackling organizational and white-collar crime (Garland, 1996; van Wingerde and Bisschop, 2022: 64). Third parties can hold the state accountable and pinpoint authorities' failure to enforce (Ayres and Braithwaite, 1992; Bartley, 2007; van Erp, 2008). Also, private actors, with better access to data, resources, or proximity to violations, may more effectively detect and prevent certain crimes (see Nielsen and Parker, 2008). However, tripartism can create conflicts of interest among actors (Mascini and van Erp, 2014).

In the existing literature, third parties are predominantly seen as holding auxiliary roles or performing 'surrogate regulatory functions' (Gunningham et al, 1999, p 212). They have been given a role in the promotion of compliance with regulation (Gunningham et al, 2003; Gunningham and Sinclair, 2017). In other words, we think of leverage foremost as promoting compliance. Yet, little literature covers other stakeholder roles or gives insights into how stakeholders indirectly use their leverage. Leverage describes a process in which a small input is used to enhance the potential return. In the leverage of peer effects (or peer social control),[3] the small input is influencing or triggering these peer effects to amplify stakeholders' objectives.

Stakeholder groups may use peer social control for purposes beyond promoting compliance. Van Erp's (2018) study on short films created by regulators in four countries to combat cartels identified four regulatory objectives. The first anti-cartel film, presented by the Dutch competition authority at an international conference, inspired similar efforts by other regulators (van Erp, 2018, p 230). While compliance was the common ultimate goal, regulators employed different approaches: dissuasive (encouraging informal social control among cartel members), educational (providing compliance information), punitive (deterring through fear of punishment), and normative (highlighting the immorality of cartels) (van Erp, 2018). These objectives, reflecting varied interests, are transferable to other stakeholders and purposes beyond compliance. They serve as the foundation for examining how stakeholders leverage peer effects in this chapter.

Shedding light on stakeholders' leverage of peer social control

The study utilized semi-structured interviews with ten stakeholders and a content analysis of publicly available sources. The data was gathered as part of the author's doctoral dissertation, focused on peer responses to corporate crime. Due to the small sample size, the stakeholder interviews are exploratory and not representative of their groups.

Four stakeholder groups were selected for their direct involvement with banks and AML. Regulatory stakeholders, including the Dutch financial regulators *Autoriteit Financiële Markten* (AFM) and *De Nederlandsche Bank* (DNB), monitor compliance with AML regulators and sanction noncompliance. Policy makers influence legislation, safeguard societal and client interests, and participate in AML partnerships as financiers. Industry stakeholders, such as expertise groups and the banking association, share AML-related knowledge, advocate for banks, and coordinate public-private cooperation. Commercial stakeholders, like consultancy firms, support banks' compliance programmes (for example, remediation programmes) and partnerships.

Respondents were selected based on their affiliation with AML in the Dutch financial industry. Eight were recruited from the author's network, one via online search, and another through 'snowballing' (asking respondents to refer others). Recruitment was conducted via email and phone. The sample included three industry stakeholders, three regulators, two consultants, and two policy makers. Conducting interviews with professionals at the final stage of my doctoral research allowed me to leverage a thorough understanding of the AML regime. This minimized the risk of being challenged by respondents. However, in some interviews, it was challenging to stay in charge and on topic as respondents occasionally strayed from the core subject.

Interviews, conducted between January and December 2022, averaged 54 minutes and covered stakeholder interactions, peer effects, and leveraging peer dynamics. Six interviews were held via videoconference, one by phone, and three in-person. All participants gave informed consent,[4] ensuring anonymity, voluntary participation, and full disclosure of the research purpose (Davies, 2006). Interviews were recorded, transcribed, and analyzed using Atlas.ti. The research combined online and offline interviews, which both resulted in in-depth information on the leverage of social control. Most respondents preferred being interviewed online, as these were easier to schedule and less time-consuming. Online interviews tended to get straight to the topic, with little room for informal interactions.

Secondary data, published by or referring to (one of) the stakeholder groups from the period of September 2018 (the time of the first settlement case for AML shortcomings in the Netherlands) to December 2022, included 25 Dutch parliamentary debates,[5] policy documents, media coverage, and supervisory reports on AML noncompliance at banks. The analysis focused on content (what was said) and discourse (how it was said). Data analysis involved coding and memo functions in Atlas.ti. Some codes were literature-driven (for example, leverage objectives by van Erp, 2018), while others, such as a monetary objective, emerged inductively. Code groups addressed stakeholder-bank relations, peer dynamics awareness, and three leverage mechanisms: comparing, threatening, and connecting.

How stakeholders leverage peer social control

To identify how stakeholders leverage peer social control, we must first define what constitutes as indirect influence mechanisms through leverage. A distinction between direct and indirect influence is not always clear-cut. Sanctioning a corporation in itself is a direct influence mechanism by regulators or law enforcement that targets one noncompliant corporation. When this sanction is published, this direct influence is complemented by an indirect influence mechanism as the publication of the sanction may impact other industry members. Stakeholders often (implicitly) trigger or aim at peer effects when they take social control to the public sphere. The public status threatens peers (reputationally) as it increases the risk of comparisons and contagion (Lang and Stulz, 1992; Jong and Van der Linde, 2022; Merz, 2023). Mechanisms that target the industry likewise entail a peer element as they rely on either peer pressure or learning and, thus, are indirect influence mechanisms through leveraging peer social control. This does not imply that all public or industry actions entail peer effects. Rather, they increase the likelihood of leveraging peer effects.

Another difficulty is distinguishing between deliberate and unintentional influence of peer effects. Only when stakeholders have formalized the use of peer social control in policies can we know for sure that they deliberately use peer effects. Regulators were the only stakeholder group with formulated policies regarding (1) the publication of sanctions, and (2) the sharing of good practices. For the other stakeholder groups and mechanisms, the availability of other means of influence is a good indicator for deliberate leverage. Using peer effects is more likely to be deliberate for stakeholders who have other means of influence, as they do not rely on peer social control to get their way.

Table 3.1 gives an overview of three mechanisms (comparing, threatening, and connecting) for leveraging peer social control identified in this study. Connecting banks is the only mechanism that uses learning effects between peers by stimulating exchange in roundtables or through the sharing of good practices. The other two mechanisms rely on peer pressure in which peers (are forced to) adapt their practices because they, for example, do not want to be the worst performer in the industry (Verhage, 2011).

Different stakeholders shared that the leverage of peer pressure was pivotal as banks will only move when other industry members do. Relying on peer pressure also has a downside, as shared by a regulatory respondent: it functions as an extrinsic motivation for banks. Then banks adapt their practices not because they have internalized the benefit or underlying norm, but because they fear reputational damage. In the respondent's view, intrinsically motivated changes are preferable as they are more sustainable.

The sharing of good practices was named by all stakeholders and often was the first thing that came up when asked about ways of influencing social control between banks. Sharing good practices happens anonymously, without naming the corporation. It targets the industry and is mostly done publicly in (research) reports, roundtables, guidance documents or personal meetings. One respondent working for a regulator shared that their organization deliberately publishes good examples that they encounter in their supervision:

> We make use of that effect [peer pressure between banks]. We publish good practices. These are examples that we have seen as solutions to a problem in supervision and regard as good. We never call them best practice on purpose. It's not necessarily the best way, but it's a good way to comply. These good practices are not tied to specific institutions. But they are published. This creates an idea of 'apparently that works, because other institutions did it and we can't fall short of this'. Banks certainly look at each other, especially when it comes to new solutions because if another bank has a solution to a problem and you don't, you run the risk of being told off by the regulator.

While comparing was used by all stakeholders, the other two mechanisms are specific to one (or two) stakeholder groups. The second mechanism, threatening, is limited to regulators (and other formal control agencies) who have the authority to enforce and, thus, put their threats into practice. Threatening was found in the publication of sanctions, which creates a reputational threat not only to the sanctioned party but also to other (peer)

Table 3.1: Mechanisms of leveraging peer social control

Mechanism	Examples	Peer effect	Stakeholder group	Stakeholder's objectives
Comparing	• Sharing good practices • Organization of roundtables • Publication of research projects • Recommendations in reports • Parliamentary debates	Peer pressure	Regulators Policy makers Consultancy firms	Normative Monetary Informative
Threatening	• Media appearance • Publication of sanctions	Peer pressure	Regulators	Normative Punitive
Connecting	• Sharing good practices • Organization of roundtables	Peer learning	Industry stakeholders Consultancy firms	Informative

banks, and in media appearances of regulators using threatening language. For instance, in 2021, the current director of financial regulator DNB expressed the regulator's frustration with banks' efforts on AML compliance in an interview with the Dutch financial newspaper *Het Financieele Dagblad* (Betlem, 2021).He criticized the fact that banks (still) have extensive and persistent problems with AML compliance, calling their efforts still insufficient (Betlem, 2021).

The third mechanism, connecting, is mainly used by industry stakeholders to encourage knowledge sharing and learning between banks. Consultants also shared that they aim to connect banks so as to amplify learning circles. To them, learning is particularly interesting when peers learn about other banks' practices, which has been set-up with the help of consultancy firms. Rather than making use of peer pressure, connecting is achieved by leveraging peer learning. Peer learning exemplifies Sutherland's (1983) differential association. According to differential association, people learn values, attitudes, motives, or techniques of deviant or compliant behaviour in association with intimate, personal groups. Peers are an example of such intimate, personal groups. Connecting banks triggers the learning of compliant behaviour – in form of good practices or lessons learned from mistakes.

Interestingly, policy makers negated the use of peer effects, stating that they lack influential power. One respondent responded that 'in practice we can't really do anything except having an opinion on something … and change legislation and policy, but mostly it's having an opinion on an issue'. It is striking that policy stakeholders seem unaware of their influence, although they have the position and power to inquire on and draw attention to AML cases. In parliamentary debates, which are publicly available, parliamentary members regularly draw comparisons between banks (noncompliance). Moreover, an opinion by policy makers is not just any opinion, as they ultimately have the capacity to make and change the laws on AML (compliance). In 2019, the Money Laundering Action Plan (*Plan van aanpak witwassen*) was introduced in the Netherlands as a response to the ING settlement. The Money Laundering Action Plan includes the set-up of public-private partnerships, the intensification of investigations and prosecution of noncompliance, and a commitment towards increasing punishments for AML noncompliance for banks and their directors.

Like policy makers, industry stakeholders did not consider themselves to have the position or power to influence peer social control, a point shared by two respondents. Unlike policy (and other) stakeholders, their leverage is limited given their vertical relation and interest in sharing knowledge, offering support, and connecting banks. Industry stakeholders have an interest in keeping good relations with private parties, or even a role in supporting them, which makes the leverage of social control less appealing.

Why stakeholders leverage peer social control

Having shed light on *how* stakeholders leverage peer social control, this section discusses their underlying objectives. Objectives refer to the goals, both short-term and long-term, that stakeholders aim to achieve using peer social control.

Three objectives – normative, punitive, and informative (similar to the four objectives in van Erp's (2018) research on anti-cartel enforcement) – were found among the stakeholder groups. Additionally, a monetary objective, focused on profit-making, emerged from the interviews with consultancy firms. Some objectives are specific to certain stakeholders, such as the monetary objective to consultancy firms and the informative objective to industry stakeholders, while others are pursued by multiple stakeholders, such as the normative objective. The mechanisms of comparing and threatening are linked to multiple objectives, while connecting peers serves an informative objective.

Normative objective: norm confirmation and benchmark setting

Leveraging peer effects for normative objectives aims at confirming the (latest) norms and pursuing their implementation with the help of peer pressure. This was commonly done with the sharing of good practices, which was used by all stakeholder groups.
While not all stakeholders aim for normative objectives with their sharing of good practices, these good practices ultimately become the new benchmarks for compliance as regulators have an interest in enforcing good practices. This results in banks being confronted with the best and the worst practices of their peers. Sharing good practices leads to a peremptory race to the top, with ever higher standards for AML compliance that might even exceed legal requirements, as suggested by a respondent working at a consultancy firm: 'In a way, especially when we talk about recommendations and best practices, consultancy firms also set a certain standard. And often that standard is higher than the rules.' In van Erp (2018), the normative objective focuses on communicating a moral message: the wrongfulness of cartels. In the present study, respondents criticized the fact that internalization of the moral wrongfulness of money laundering was still lacking in the banking industry.

Punitive objective: hoping for deterrence

The punitive objective was found in mechanisms of leverage by regulatory stakeholders, for instance in publishing sanctions. It aims at deterrence by triggering a fear of punishment and reputational damage, as shared by a regulatory respondent:

Take fines. There are three factors that play a role when deciding for or against this measure: severity, culpability, and compliance orientation ... The decision also considers the general preventive effect of fines, especially with the publication options that we now have. The publication aims at a deterrent effect for the individual institutions. Banks don't want to appear on the regulator's website like this, but it also has a broader preventive effect. At least that's the assumption, whether this has been evaluated, I don't know.

Deterrence inherently links to the leverage of peer pressure. Research by van Wingerde (2012), however, shows that deterrence hardly forms a direct threatening effect on business compliance. Rather, organizations comply due to indirect deterrence from negative publicity or reputational damage related to sanctions (Fisse and Braithwaite, 1983; van Wingerde, 2012). Publicity serves as an implicit reminder of compliance duties and as a reassurance of regulatory consequences for industry members (Thornton et al, 2005).

Informative objective

The informative objective aims at sharing knowledge and guidance and creating learning circles among banks and in partnerships. It is mainly pursued by industry stakeholders and fits their profile of supporting banks in AML compliance. At first sight, the informative objective seems to resemble the educational objective of raising awareness of competition regulation to stimulate compliance found by van Erp (2018, p 237). The informative objective in this research, however, is not educative, as leveraging peer learning does not convey a normative message of stimulating compliance or setting a standard, but merely serves as guidelines. It is limited to support and the facilitation of learning.

For industry stakeholders, however, leveraging peer effects for informative objectives is not necessary as (1) they can connect banks without the use of leverage by direct forms of influence, and (2) in any case, banks examine peer practices to compare and learn from these for image guarding (Verhage, 2009b, p 386; Merz, 2023).

Monetary objective: social control as a business model

Lastly, leveraging peer social control forms a business model for commercial stakeholders, who use it to achieve their monetary objective of profit-making. In her research on the AML complex, Verhage (2009a, pp 16, 29) demonstrates that external advisors 'stimulate the demand for advice', becoming an integral part of tackling AML. The open norms and persistent attention to AML shortcomings have turned AML into a goldmine for consultancy firms. In order to retain their position in the AML regime, consultancy firms need to sell their tools and services to as many banks (and other gatekeepers) as possible. The prioritization and criminalization of AML in the Netherlands since the ING settlement in September 2018 has urged many banks to complete remediation programmes. Consultancy firms are commonly hired to assist in this by offering workforce, identifying gaps, or working on solutions. This support in remediation can be self-initiated by or imposed by regulatory stakeholders; often, it is consultancy firms' ticket to selling more far-reaching services to banks: 'In the past three years, banks come with a problem, [say] a backlog: they can no longer handle alerts. Depending on the trust you have built, once you know the client [the bank], you can share your expertise and try to start a conversation [on other solutions].' While consultancy firms see themselves as independent, they ultimately are guided by profit-making and try to manifest themselves as an integral part of money laundering prevention to keep on selling their products and services.

What are the risks and benefits of leveraging peer social control?

This last section summarizes the risks and benefits of leveraging peer social control. Sharing good practices, for instance, itself poses a risk to maintaining a risk-based approach to money laundering. Adopted in 2005, the risk-based approach replaced the rule-based system, where banks followed predefined rules for suspicious transactions or clients regardless of actual risks. The risk-based method (theoretically) offers banks flexibility to identify, assess, and mitigate money laundering risks. However, research shows that shared industry practices often become norms enforced across the sector. While initially risk-based, peer pressure can transform these practices into standardized rules, effectively reverting to a rule-based system. As good practices become the norm upon which authorities act, not implementing these new standards becomes a risky business. The Dutch financial regulator has reiterated its commitment to risk-based compliance and supervision (DNB, 2022). This reiteration might seem superfluous at first sight, given the long history of the risk-based approach. However, it highlights the persistent challenge of avoiding the rigidity of a rule-based approach, emphasizing the need for risk-based practices moving forward.

This study also raises further questions on what Verhage (2009b, p 387) has described as a dramatization of risks by the compliance industry almost 15 years ago. Verhage (2009b, p 386) observed that authorities oblige banks to use tools and services developed by the compliance industry, including consultancy firms. The fact that it is hard to determine what works on AML compliance is exploited by commercial stakeholders, as stated by Pol

(2020, p 77): 'Many stakeholders also have strong incentives to repeat (or not openly question), rather than rigorously test, the official narrative. Hundreds of thousands of businesses and professionals comprise a business ecosystem dependent on the current paradigm'. The study indicates that consultancy firms have even further appropriated AML, turning it into a successful business model. Banks and authorities should be aware of this dramatization.

Such an awareness is even more important as consultancy services are not only sold to the banking industry, but also to other stakeholders, such as policy makers. In an evaluation of the implementation of AMLD4 by consultancy firm EY on behalf of the Ministry of Finance, EY concluded that small financial institutions are less aware of AML/CTF guidelines and face difficulties complying with these (EY, 2021). While they raise an important point, EY (or the Ministry of Finance) did not reflect on the consultancy firm's role in raising benchmarks leading to small institutions' difficulties with adhering to these. Consultancy firms have established widespread networks and filled the vacuum that the delegation of tasks by the state has created. Mazzucato and Collington (2023) criticize the fact that the dependence on consultancy firms prevents the public sector – and in this case private parties as well as the banking industry – from developing in-house capabilities. While insights and services by consultants can be beneficial and help the industry in strengthening their AML frameworks, it is important to remain critical towards the need for their services, as their ultimate goal is profit-making.

The position of consultancy firms links to another risk regarding the accountability of organizational behaviour. Bovens (1998) criticized the fact that often accountability clashes with 'the problem of many hands'. Many hands are involved in AML, in and beyond the financial industry, but accountability is mainly restricted to banks. Despite their involvement, consultancy firms, for example, do not bear the risks or costs of their decisions – and are thus not held accountable, as these are transferred back to banks (Mazzucato and Collington, 2023). Stakeholders should likewise be responsible for their actions and their leverage of peer effects.

This study shows that banks are also increasingly responsibilized as social control agents by stakeholders who want to profit from effects of peer pressure. The leverage of peer effects is an example of this. This development is in line with enforced self-regulation (Braithwaite, 1982), of which the responsibilization of banks is an example. The banking industry is responsible for the creation, monitoring, and reporting of compliant policies and norms. External, formal pressure by authorities ensures that self-regulation occurs, as noncompliance will lead to sanctions or increased supervision. Enforced self-regulation, however, requires mutual trust, room for dialogue, and regulators having sufficient knowledge and understanding of the management system and procedures at corporations (van Wingerde, 2012, pp 329–32).

This study indicates that regulators have limited knowledge on peer effects, raising the question of how well they know banks' systems and procedures. Rather, regulators presume that stimulating peer social control contributes to reaching their objectives. While for consultancy firms this seems to pay off, as they succeed so as to manifest themselves as an integrated part of AML in (and beyond) the financial industry, authorities can be less sure whether their efforts actually lead to more compliance. Merz (2023) shows that the responsibilization of banks through criminalization has led to front-forming and defiance by banks against regulators. Consequently, the esteemed deterrence through the publication of sanctions by regulators (and other official control agencies) often does not work as peers embrace each other.

The leverage of peer social control can also have benefits if it is used with consideration. First, leveraging peer effects is a comparably cheap tool for regulators to get their way. In the words of a regulatory respondent: 'compliance of their own accord is a lot cheaper than the compliance that we have to enforce'. Utilizing peer effects takes comparably little effort, as regulators can make use of existing dynamics between peers or trigger new ones. This allows them to bypass or delay (costly) enforcement measures. Second, informal social control, for example by peers, can be more powerful than formal control (Simpson, 2002, p 107; Gunningham and Sinclair, 2017, p 134). Braithwaite's (1989) work on reintegrative shaming emphasized that peers play a crucial role in influencing the behaviour and perceptions of deviant corporations. Just like people or groups, corporations respond to and interact with each other rather than operating in isolation. Research by Verhage (2011, pp 82–83), for example, shows that peer pressure plays a role in defining compliance benchmarks within financial institutions. Consequently, stakeholders can profit from the power of peer social control by leveraging these. And third, stakeholders might lack the authority or legal ground to enforce their interests and therefore rely on the leverage of peer pressure or other peer dynamics. This is, for instance, the case for the enforcement of soft law. Also, some stakeholder groups are simply not in positions to enforce. Leveraging peer social control enables them to act nonetheless.

Conclusion

This chapter has aimed to shed light on the question of how and for what purpose stakeholders influence informal social control mechanisms between corporations. Most existing research focuses on stakeholder involvement for the promotion of compliance and direct mechanisms of influence (Gunningham et al, 1999; Nielsen and Parker, 2008; Grabosky, 2013). This study, on the contrary, discusses indirect influence mechanisms through leveraging peer effects.

Interviews with ten stakeholders from four stakeholder groups (regulators, policy makers, industry stakeholders, and consultancy firms) and content analysis of publicly available information by and on stakeholders (for example, reports, parliamentary debates) were used to answer that question. All four stakeholder groups leveraged peer social control, but their leverage differed in mechanisms, intensity, formalization, and objectives. Stakeholders' objectives were either informative (industry stakeholders), normative (regulators and policy makers), punitive (regulators) or monetary (consultancy firms). To reach these interests, stakeholders mainly relied on stimulating comparisons, and thus peer pressure, between banks.

Peer social control has potential for regulatory governance of organizational crime but must be integrated accordingly in existing frameworks. As private parties are increasingly responsibilized in the fight against money laundering, and more generally in a landscape of manifested regulatory pluralism, activating this potential can be fruitful for governance.

This requires that authorities dare to step back from stricter sanctions and think of ways to use criminalization to stimulate peer social control. One possibility is to make better use of the spectrum of responsive regulation (Ayres and Braithwaite, 1992). While financial regulators already use other instruments in supervision, the past years have focused on escalations up the regulatory pyramid and fines. Such an approach should stimulate banks' moral responsibility for fighting illicit money flows.

We need more research that examines the diverse interests and direct and indirect influence mechanisms of the manifold stakeholders that participate in and beyond regulation. It would, for example, be interesting to learn more about how peer social control shapes regulation or stakeholder interests and vice versa.

Notes

[1] Systemic banks are financial institutions whose failure could disrupt the financial system and economy, making them 'too big to fail'.

[2] This chapter is a modified version of the chapter 'Social control for leverage: stakeholders leveraging peer social control' from the author's unpublished doctoral dissertation *Peers as social control: An empirical study into peer responses to corporate crime*.

[3] In this chapter, 'peer social control' and 'peer effects' are used interchangeably.

[4] The research was not evaluated by the Ethical Commission of the Erasmus School of Law (Erasmus University Rotterdam, The Netherlands), which was only installed after fieldwork had started. The research was discussed with the privacy officer of Erasmus School of Law who approved the informed consent form and the project's Data Management Plan. The research was subjected to a Data Protection Impact Assessment (ID 1231).

[5] In total, a search on 'bank' and 'money laundering' resulted in 158 debates. Debates that did not primarily focus on anti-money laundering violations at Dutch banks such as debates on derisking, sanctions, underground banking, fraud cases or cryptocurrencies were excluded.

References

Abbott, K.W. and Snidal, D. (2009) 'The governance triangle: regulatory standards institutions and the shadow of the state', in W. Maatli and N. Woords (eds), *The Politics of Global Regulation*, Princeton University Press, pp 44–88.

Ayres, I. and Braithwaite, J. (1992) *Responsive Regulation: Transcending the Deregulation Debate*, Oxford University Press.

Bartley, T. (2007) 'Institutional emergence in an era of globalization: the rise of transnational private regulation of labor and environmental conditions', *American Journal of Sociology*, 113(2): 297–351.

Betlem, R. (2021) 'Opvallend harde kritiek DNB op witwasaanpak banken', *Het Financieele Dagblad*, [Online] 7 December. Available from: https://fd.nl/financiele-markten/1422476/opvallend-harde-kritiek-dnb-op-witwasaanpak-banken-ncb2ca3n7ouO

Black, J. (2001) 'Decentring regulation: understanding the role of regulation and self-regulation in a "post-regulatory" world', *Current Legal Problems*, 54(1): 103–46.

Bovens, M.A.P. (1998) *The Quest for Responsibility: Accountability and Citizenship in Complex Organisations*, Cambridge University Press.

Braithwaite, J. (1982) 'Enforced self-regulation: a new strategy for corporate crime control', *Michigan Law Review*, 80(7): 1466–1507.

Braithwaite, J. (1989) *Crime, Shame, and Reintegration*, Cambridge University Press.

Davies, P. (2006) 'Informed consent', in V. Jupp (ed.), *The Sage Dictionary of Social Research Methods*, Sage, pp 150–55.

DNB (2022) 'From recovery to balance', [Online] Available from: https://www.dnb.nl/media/mdgafi3a/from-recovery-to-balance.pdf

EY (2021) 'Onderzoek effecten Wwft – De effecten van de Implementatiewet vierde anti-witwasrichtlijn op Wwft-instellingen', [Online] Available from: https://open.overheid.nl/documenten/ronl-8cebb1a48ab31f51a11ccc45c2b6a558406f1ac0/pdf

Fisse, B. and Braithwaite, J. (1983) *Impact of Publicity on Corporate Offenders*, State University of New York Press.

Garland, D. (1996) 'The limits of the sovereign state: strategies of crime control in contemporary society', *The British Journal of Criminology*, 36(4): 445–71.

Grabosky, P. (2013) 'Beyond responsive regulation: the expanding role of non-state actors in the regulatory process', *Regulation and Governance*, 7(1): 114–23.

Gunningham, N. and Sinclair, D. (1999) 'Regulatory pluralism: designing policy mixes for environmental protection', *Law & Policy*, 21(1): 49–76.

Gunningham, N. and Sinclair, D. (2017) 'Smart regulation', in P. Drahos (ed), *Regulatory Theory: Foundations and Applications*, ANU Press, pp 133–48.

Gunningham, N., Phillipson, M., and Grabosky, P. (1999) 'Harnessing third parties as surrogate regulators: achieving environmental outcomes by alternative means', *Business Strategy and the Environment*, 8(4): 211–24.

Gunningham, N., Kagan, R.A., and Thornton, D. (2003) *Shades of Green: Business, Regulation, and Environment*, Stanford University Press.

Jong, W. and van der Linde, V. (2022) 'Clean diesel and dirty scandal: the echo of Volkswagen's dieselgate in an intra-industry setting', *Public Relations Review*, 48(1): 1–7.

Lang, L.H. and Stulz, R. (1992) 'Contagion and competitive intra-industry effects of bankruptcy announcements: an empirical analysis', *Journal of Financial Economics*, 32(1): 45–60.

Lobel, O. (2004) 'The renew deal: the fall of regulation and the rise of governance in contemporary legal thought', *Minnesota Law Review*, 89: 262–390.

Mascini, P. and van Erp, J. (2014) 'Regulatory governance: experimenting with new roles and instruments', *Recht Der Werkelijkheid*, 35(3): 3–11.

Mazzucato, M. and Collington, R. (2023) *The Big Con: How the Consulting Industry Weakens Our Businesses, Infantilizes Our Governments, and Warps Our Economies*, Penguin.

Merz, A. (2023) '"It could have been us": peer responses to money-laundering violations in the Dutch banking industry', *Crime, Law and Social Change* [Preprint], 1–20.

Nielsen, V.L. and Parker, C. (2008) 'To what extent do third parties influence business compliance?', *Journal of Law and Society*, 35(3): 309–40.

Nielsen, V.L. and Parker, C. (2009) 'Testing responsive regulation in regulatory enforcement', *Regulation & Governance*, 3(4): 376–99.

Pol, R.F. (2020) 'Anti-money laundering: the world's least effective policy experiment? Together, we can fix it', *Policy Design and Practice*, 3(1): 73–94.

Schell-Busey, N., Simpson, S.S., Rorie, M., and Alper, M. (2016) 'What works? A systematic review of corporate crime deterrence', *Criminology and Public Policy*, 15(2): 387–416.

Simpson, S.S. (2002) *Corporate Crime, Law, and Social Control*, Cambridge University Press.

Sutherland, E.H. (1983) *White Collar Crime: The Uncut Version*, Yale University Press.

Thornton, D., Gunningham, N., and Kagan, R. (2005) 'General deterrence and corporate behaviour', *Law and Policy*, 27(2): 262–88.

van Erp, J. (2008) 'Reputational sanctions in private and public regulation', *Erasmus Law Review*, 1(5): 145–62.

van Erp, J. (2018) 'Anti-cartel thrillers as a new film genre: how regulator-produced films portray and problematize cartels and communicate deterrence', *Crime, Media, Culture*, 14(2): 229–46.

van Wingerde, K. (2012) 'De afschrikking voorbij: Een empirische studie naar afschrikking, generale preventie en regelnaleving in de Nederlandse afvalbranche', doctoral dissertation, Erasmus University Rotterdam.

van Wingerde, K. and Bisschop, L. (2022) 'Measuring compliance in the age of governance: how the governance turn has impacted compliance measurement by the state', in M. Rorie and B. Van Rooij (eds), *Measuring Compliance*, Cambridge University Press, pp 55–70.

van Wingerde, K. and Hofman, C. (2022) 'Wachters aan het woord: dilemma's van accountants, advocaten, belastingadviseurs en notarissen in hun rol als poortwachter', policy report, Erasmus University Rotterdam, Available from: https://www.politieenwetenschap.nl/publicatie/politiekunde/2022/wachters-aan-het-woord-376/#files

Verhage, A. (2009a) 'Between the hammer and the anvil? The anti-money laundering-complex and its interactions with the compliance industry', *Crime, Law and Social Change*, 52(1): 9–32.

Verhage, A. (2009b) 'Supply and demand: anti-money laundering by the compliance industry', *Journal of Money Laundering Control*, 12(4): 371–91.

Verhage, A. (2011) *The Anti Money Laundering Complex and the Compliance Industry*, Routledge.

4

A Critical Realist Methodology for Understanding Noncompliance: From Theory to Practice

Korry Robert

Introduction

In the past few decades, critical realism has become an influential philosophical framework for empirical research. Despite its popularity, relatively few studies discuss how it can be applied as a methodology, particularly for understanding white-collar and organizational crimes (Ackroyd and Karlsson, 2014; Fletcher, 2017). This chapter adds to this methodological discussion by providing an accessible account of how critical realism can be used for understanding noncompliance with anti-money laundering (AML) laws. A critical realist approach contends that there is an independent and multi-layered reality, where behaviours and events are driven by 'real' mechanisms that are often unobservable (Danermark, 2019). Identifying these mechanisms is key to understanding how illicit and licit behaviours can be explained and addressed. This is particularly useful for understanding white-collar and organizational crimes, including AML noncompliance, where harmful behaviours are embedded within legitimate professional settings and are shaped by less observable structures and cultures (van Erp, 2018).

Since this chapter is inspired by my own journey of how to best understand and apply critical realism principles for my doctoral project, I draw upon some of my findings surrounding the drivers and inhibitors of AML compliance behaviours. However, the focus of this chapter remains on the application of critical realism as a philosophical framework, rather than providing a comprehensive causal explanation for noncompliance. The National Westminster Bank Plc's (NatWest) AML case based in the

UK is used to frame the analysis. The case is significant as it illustrates how noncompliance is rarely the result of a singular event or individual deviancy. The violations emerged from an interplay of individual actions, governance, and information structures, as well as the prevailing cultural values and assumptions within the organization. The chapter presents critical realism as an innovative approach for identifying influential 'real' factors and theorizing how they come together to produce organizational misconduct.

The chapter begins with a brief overview of the NatWest case used to frame this analysis. The following section then provides some background to critical realism, including key concepts of structure and agency. I consider how this interacts with traditional criminological scholarship, and how a critical realism framework can facilitate a more contextualized theoretical explanation for how the noncompliant behaviours unfolded. Following this, the four-stage process used to develop a critical realist informed study is outlined. This includes a brief discussion about developing a research question and data collection, before moving on to discuss the analytical process undertaken. Throughout this chapter, I include practical examples and some reflections to show how critical realist concepts can be systematically applied for researching and understanding the multi-layered nature of how such crimes unfold.

NatWest as an illustrative case study

The case begins with Fowler Oldfield, a family gold dealer and jewellery business based in Bradford, UK. In 2011, they opened an account with NatWest, a subsidiary of NatWest Group Plc, one of the largest British holdings offering retail and commercial banking in the UK (R (FCA) v National Westminster Bank Plc Agreed Statement of Facts, 2021, henceforth referred to as 'NatWest Agreed Statement').[1] At this point, the directors of Fowler Oldfield presented their company as a gold dealer with a projected annual turnover of £15 million. However, between 2012 and 2016, a total of £365 million was deposited into their NatWest account, a sum far above their expected business activity. In actuality, Fowler Oldfield was involved in an extensive laundering scheme, where the funds deposited were used to buy gold and then exported overseas (Croft, 2022; Piercy, 2022). Under Money Laundering Regulations (2017) (as amended),[2] financial firms in the UK, including banks like NatWest, must carry out due diligence on their clients, monitor their activities, and report any suspicious transactions to the Financial Conduct Authority (FCA).[3] This forms part of the UK's overall strategy to prevent and deter money laundering and counter-terrorist financing (HM Treasury and Home Office, 2020). Failures to monitor and recognize suspicious activity, which occurred in this case, can result in financial penalties or criminal prosecutions (Proceeds of Crime Act, 2002, Part 7).

What is clear now is that concerns were raised internally, but a full inquiry into Fowler Oldfield's banking history only arose after West Yorkshire Police contacted NatWest about their investigations into Fowler Oldfield in 2016. The bank's internal investigation found several key issues that contributed to why the activities of Fowler Oldfield persisted for years. During this period, bank staff across the country raised several internal money-laundering suspicious activity alerts about the large amounts of cash deposited (NatWest Agreed Statement, pp 32–6). At times deposits reached £1.8 million in a single day and filled the storage rooms of local branches. News reports afterwards would frequently cite the 'prominent, musty smell' and how deposits brought in in large bin liners tore under the weight of the cash (BBC News, 2021; Venkataramakrishnan and Croft, 2021; Withers, 2021).

Other alerts were also generated by NatWest's automated transaction monitoring systems. The bulk of these reports were closed, based on assurances from the relationship manager. This meant that Fowler Oldfield's activities were not disclosed to law enforcement. Over time, the analysts reviewing these reports also made assessments based on previous decisions not to disclose. The internal investigations also found concerns regarding their automated transaction monitoring systems. This included how Fowler Oldfield's risk rating was erroneously downgraded to low risk after a bank-wide remediation programme before it was eventually manually rectified in 2016 by the relationship manager. There were also broader issues which affected the bank as a whole. This included how cash deposits were misclassified as cheques by their automated systems. This meant that the deposits and Fowler Oldfield's transactions in general were subject to lower monitoring measures. At first glance, this suggests that, similar to other white-collar and organizational crimes like corruption and fraud, the organizational context provided the means, opportunity, and motives for these behaviours to occur (Punch, 2014). Therefore, understanding and addressing these offences require an appreciation of how the broader systemic weaknesses within the organization's structures contributed to the failure to comply.

These findings were self-reported to the FCA and, in 2021, the FCA filed the first criminal prosecution against a UK bank for these monitoring failures under the Money Laundering Regulations (2017). The case proved successful, as NatWest pleaded guilty to three criminal charges related to failures to comply with their money-laundering requirements and they were fined £264.8 million (R (FCA) v National Westminster Bank Plc Sentencing Remarks, 2021, henceforth referred to as NatWest Sentencing Remarks).[4]

Foundations of critical realism

The foundation of critical realism begins with the initial works of Roy Bhaskar (Bhaskar, 1989, 2008 originally published in 1975), which was later developed by a number of scholars (Collier, 1994; Archer, 1995, 1998; Lawson, 1998; Norrie, 2010; Sayer, 2010; Danermark, 2019; Elder-Vass, 2021). It emerged as an alternative methodological framework to positivist and interpretivist approaches (Elder-Vass, 2021). Critical realism attempts to overcome the 'epistemic fallacy' of positivist approaches which reduce reality to what is observable (Bhaskar, 2008, p 20), and interpretivist assumptions that consider reality as a product of human interaction and experiences. Critical realism adopts a middle-ground by accepting that reality exists independent of individual perceptions and experiences (O'Mahoney and Vincent, 2014). However, how we understand and experience this real world is socially mediated. While the production of knowledge is 'a social activity', it is possible to develop plausible and practical knowledge about reality through empirical research (Sayer, 2010, p 11). The chapter later discusses how this is developed through an abstraction, abduction, and retroduction process.

In critical realist ontology, reality exists as an 'open system' that is 'stratified' into three domains (Bhaskar, 2008: 107). These three levels (empirical, actual, and real) capture the complexity of reality. The 'empirical domain' is the surface level of reality. This represents all events that are measurable and observable. In a research project, what we know about the empirical domain is based on how we experience, collect, and interpret this data. In the NatWest case, empirical events observed can include which units made internal suspicious activity reports, and which units did not. At the next level, the 'actual domain' consists of all events that occur, regardless of whether these events are observed. For example, a staff member may discuss their suspicions with other employees but decide not to make a report. These discussions, unless documented, occurred but are not observable to others external to this conversation. Other more intangible actual events may be the decision-making process an individual undertakes after these discussions which leads to a decision not to file. Finally, all events observable or not can be understood as emerging from the interactions between the deeper underlying structures and generative mechanisms that exist in the 'real domain' (Bhaskar, 2008) The structures at the real domain level have capacities, powers or 'mechanisms' capable of affecting other structures. By structures, I mean 'internally related objects or practices' that can be observable or unobservable (Danermark et al, 2019, p 80). For example, structures can have material forms but may also be socially constructed. The concept of money, for instance, is a structure which governs how we exchange goods and services. Physical currency is a tangible part of this structure, but it is the unobservable collective assumptions and beliefs about the note as a form of payment that makes it money (Elder-Vass, 2021). The visible monetary instrument, coupled with our shared assumptions, allows us to purchase and sell goods. Similarly, AML processes and procedures dictated by NatWest policies are observable structures. These structures impose specific compliance-related responsibilities onto NatWest employees. In contrast, the less observable cultural norms which govern business operations also shape how employees comply with their responsibilities.

Structure and agency

The interaction between structure (that is, a set of related objects or practices that makes something what it is) and human agency (that is, individual capacity to act) is key to understanding how these events are produced (Archer, 1995; Sayer, 2010, p 63). The nature of this relationship is conceptualized in varying ways (see Bhaskar, 1993; Parker, 2000; Manicas, 2006); however, Archer's analytical dualism proposition is convincing (Archer, 1995, 2017). She proposes that while structures can enable and constrain human agency, it is also reproduced and transformed by human activity over time. For example, the concepts of money and banking systems are enduring structures that influence how monetary transactions are executed. Yet, in the past few decades, the development of handheld devices, accessible internet coverage, and globalization spurred by human actions has created rapid changes in how we interact with banking institutions and think about money. It is possible to create an electronic bank account within a few minutes and move money, in different forms, across borders almost instantly. In the same vein, how banks monitor customer activity has evolved, where the use of automated systems has become an expected norm for large banks dealing with millions of online and offline transactions. Here, we see how pre-existing social structures provide the context in which individuals exercise their agency, and how this interaction can transform these structures.

In addition to structure and agency, organizational cultures reflected in employees' norms and practices are also fundamental for understanding compliance (Hutter and Gilad, 2011; Parker and Gilad, 2011). Broadly, (non) compliance can be understood as emerging from the interaction between 'formal systems for compliance management, the perceptions, motivations and strategies of individuals' and 'the local norms and habituated practices that mediate between corporate structures and individual agency' (Parker and Gilad, 2011, p 172). Organizational culture literature demonstrates how shared underlying assumptions (that is, assumptions about their organizations), values (that is, employee beliefs about their work and work behaviours), and norms (that is, routine work practices based on these assumptions and values) affect employee behaviours (Campbell and Göritz, 2014; Schein and Schein, 2016). Research into corporate misconduct also identifies how certain practices, such as using corrupt means to achieve organizational targets, can be rationalized and institutionalized based on shared organizational cultures, particularly when incentivized or tolerated by individuals in leadership positions (Shover and Hochstetler, 2002, 2006; Campbell and Göritz, 2014).

The plurality factors involved mean that an 'organizational' analytical framework is needed to unpack how these social, cultural, and contextual factors come together to produce harmful behaviours (Lord and Levi, 2025). Critical realism's focus on both structure and agency provides a framework for exploring how the organizational setting influences individual capacities, and how these interactions can lead to noncompliant behaviours. The ontological and epistemological underpinnings of critical realism encouraged me to think about what were the (observable and unobservable) events that occurred, how each occurred, why it happened, and '*under which conditions*' (Danermark et al, 2019, pp 201–2, emphasis in original). This meant moving from surface level observations to consider how events unfold within its wider context (O'Mahoney and Vincent, 2014; Elder-Vass, 2021). Thinking in this way helped structure how I went about building a more contextualized explanatory model for the noncompliant behaviours observed.

Developing a critical realist project

At the start of my initial foray into the critical realism sphere, I quickly realized that although critical realism has been used for empirical research (see Irfan and Wilkinson, 2020; Goodall, 2022), material on how to apply it as a framework has been particularly absent within criminology and legal scholarship. This meant I had to draw upon literature from various other disciplines such as sociology, education, information systems, and healthcare to inform my research (Bygstad et al, 2016; Fletcher, 2017; Haigh et al, 2019; Hastings, 2021; Lawani, 2021; Fryer, 2022). In this section, I build upon this body of knowledge by describing how critical realist concepts were used to frame the analysis. This is presented in a four-stage process. Stages one and two relate to the development of the research project and data collection. This draws upon my general experience related to my doctoral research. Stages three and four focus on the analytical process. Even though many researchers do not necessarily use these terms, the analysis process can be categorized into an empirical analysis and a theoretical analysis stage, as suggested by Hastings (2021). The final section discusses some of the conclusions and future directions for research.

Stage one: developing the research project and research questions

The first step of any research method usually begins with developing the scope of a research project, including its research question and methods. There are no presumed research methods required for a critical realist project. Instead, critical realism acts as a meta-theory or an 'under-labourer' by providing a framework to guide the empirical work (Frauley and Pearce, 2007; Locke (1959) cited in Bhaskar, 2008, p xxxi). It encourages a focus on developing answers to causal questions but is open to how this is done. In line with traditional methodological guidance, the nature of the research study and the research question tend to determine the methods (Wilkinson et al, 2022). This means it is a useful framework for integrating different methodological approaches (Haigh et al, 2019). It can act as a convergent point for interdisciplinary research, especially since white-collar crimes are complex social phenomena involving a diverse range of behaviours, actors, motivations, and contexts (see Pontell, 2016; Friedrichs, 2019).

Since critical realism research is orientated towards identifying a multi-level explanation for the research phenomena under study, the research questions posed in my doctoral study evolved to include questions focused on identifying the mechanisms, structures, and conditions that enable or constrain behaviours. Drawing on this experience, this chapter works through a similar research question grounded in the NatWest context. Through this chapter, I aim to consider what structures and mechanisms produced the recurrent compliance issues in the NatWest case. The research question provides the scope to consider the broader social, organizational, and individual factors relevant to understanding noncompliant behaviours. Accordingly, a qualitative approach was selected to obtain rich and detailed data needed for theorizing about the nature of the structures and conditions in place (Sayer, 2010; Danermark, 2019).

Stage two: data collection

As indicated, the purpose of utilizing this case study is to provide an example for applying a critical realism framework, rather than developing a comprehensive explanatory model for why the behaviours described occurred. Therefore, the data used for this chapter is predominantly drawn from publicly available data collected for a larger body of work investigating (non)compliance behaviours in financial firms for my doctoral project. The data used consisted of media reports relating to the case and the court transcripts. The court transcripts included the sentencing remarks and an agreed statement of facts, jointly composed by the FCA and NatWest. This provided the most detail about how the events unfolded. However, since these documents reflect the perceptions of state actors and NatWest, this can limit what is observable and the theoretical propositions developed, as it may not be possible to identify all potential factors that contributed to these failures. For future works, including other data sources – such as internal organizational documents and interview data from the regulatory actors and NatWest employees if accessible – would be beneficial for developing a more robust explanatory analysis.

Stage three: descriptive empirical analysis

For this case study, a reflective thematic analysis (Braun and Clarke, 2019) using an adaptive approach is used (Layder, 1998). The adaptive approach involves using a flexible approach, where the analysis is informed by key literature and revised accordingly based on ongoing engagement with the empirical data. This approach is particularly compatible with the critical realism framework as it provides flexibility to incorporate existing knowledge, such as critical realist presumptions about the role of structures and agency, while iteratively refining the analytical process in response to new insights.

The first step in this analysis, as suggested by Hastings (2021), is descriptive in nature and focused predominantly on the empirical realm. The main aim is to provide a holistic view of what can be observed. To do this the data transcripts were coded through NVivo software using semantic codes that intended to capture the explicit 'surface' meaning of the data (Braun and Clarke, 2019). This allowed me to map out a detailed picture of who and what processes were involved in this case. Several questions guided this analysis. The first question focused on how NatWest's compliance procedures and processes were structured. This involved identifying what type of systems were in place (that is, manual due diligence and monitoring procedures, automated monitoring systems), and how these systems were organized (that is, which teams are responsible for which procedures). Second, I attempted to deconstruct the nature of these AML violations by identifying which actors, actions, or omissions were involved.

I found it useful at the beginning of the analysis to keep track of this using dedicated 'Structures', 'Agents', 'Events', and 'Omissions' nodes. For example, sub-codes under the 'Events' heading included 'provision of adequate training', 'practice of relying on the relationship manager', and 'reporting suspicion'. At this stage, I began to realize that many actors, internal and external to NatWest, contributed in some way or form to the failures described and the eventual conviction. This included inter-organizational actors, such as the branches and cash centres which received bulk deposits, the relationship management team overseeing Fowler Oldfield's activities, and the analysts who reviewed the reports. Actors external to NatWest included West Yorkshire Police, who triggered the internal review, and NatWest's subsequent self-reporting of their failures to the FCA. Accordingly, the knowledge gathered here provided a foundation for unpacking how these different actors and behaviours came together to result in the prosecution in the next stage.

Stage four: theoretical analysis
Abstraction and demi-regularities
The theoretical analysis phase involves an abstraction, abduction, and retroduction process (Danermark, 2019; Hastings, 2021). Abstraction

involved isolating key components of the observed phenomena. Abduction attempts to understand these observations through existing theoretical knowledge, and retroduction asks what conditions and mechanisms must exist to explain the observed events. Although discussed sequentially, this process is often interrelated and overlapping. It is through this process that we can identify the potential unobservable structures and mechanisms operating in the real domain.

The first step in the abstraction process begins by attempting to isolate the fundamental components or influences involved (Sayer, 2010). In other words, which objects, structures, or relationships are present or absent thereby allowing the observed behaviours to flourish (Norrie, 2010). In order to do this, I identified any noticeable recurring trends or patterns in the data, particularly related to how the bank interacted with Fowler Oldfield. This is usually referred to as 'demi-regularities' (Lawson, 1998, p 149; Fletcher, 2017). The presence of demi-regularities suggests that there are 'systematic and identifiable mechanisms' that that can be uncovered through theoretical analysis (Lawson, 1998, p 152).

One demi-regularity identified early on in the analysis related to how staff tended to rely on the relationship manager for information about Fowler Oldfield's activities. The relationship manager provided assurances that the gold dealer's transactions were in line with their proposed business activity, when in fact they were not. The analysts at the Borehamwood office, who investigated the suspicious activity reports, would frequently close the report based on this assurance.[5] This practice was not restricted to analysts located at Borehamwood, as even a financial crime manager in the Commercial and Private Banking Business Control division felt 'satisfied' by the explanations provided by the relationship manager (NatWest Agreed Statement, p 35). In this case, some fundamental components governing these interactions included:

- the organizational roles of relationship managers, analysts and other staff;
- NatWest's communication structures, which allowed staff across the country to communicate with each other;
- the motivations and skill capacities of the actors involved; and
- underlying assumptions, values, and routine norms which govern these interactions.

Analysis of this demi-regularity also included an absence of one key component – a cohesive information structure. The Borehamwood analysts, in many instances, did not have complete access to all client information held with the bank. One of the systems used by relationship managers, containing information about client management and risk ratings, remained inaccessible to the analysts until around 2015. I considered that these components may be relevant for explaining why NatWest employees tended to request client information from relationship managers and to rely on the responses received.

At this point of the coding process, I began to recode the initial semantic codes using broader sub-headings. According to Fletcher's (2017) suggestion, parent codes that aimed to identify the potential structures underlining the empirical observations were used. Some of the observations from the demi-regularity were coded into 'Structures – occupational responsibilities', and 'Culture – deference to relationship managers'. The codes used were also expanded, deleted, and refined throughout the theoretical analysis process.

Abduction

Abductive reasoning is then used to understand these events through theoretical concepts. The demi-regularities are redescribed using existing knowledge to theorize about why these events occur (Danermark et al, 2019). Using the example outlined in the previous section, surface-level explanations could understand the deference to the relationship manager as a simple exercise of human agency. However, the repeated nature of the event implies the existence of deeper mechanisms at play. An alternative proposition could be made using rational choice theories, where the analysts at Borehamwood considered that the benefits of achieving their targets outweighed the risks of being punished for failing to investigate the reports properly (Cornish and Clarke, 2014). The perceived risk of being punished may have gradually decreased as more reports were routinely closed without any observable consequences. While this is one potential explanation, critical realist reasoning encourages understanding these observed events in relation to more 'real' factors.

As discussed earlier, compliance and criminological scholarship also suggest that there are additional factors that bound or influence individual agency (Parker and Gilad, 2011; Huisman, 2016). Concepts of organizational structures and culture were more convincing theoretical constructs for understanding these observed behaviours. Taking this approach, I theorized that the relationship managers, analysts, and managers are all occupants of a governance structure within NatWest. This governance structure imposes specific roles and expectations onto the NatWest employees. In particular, relationship managers are responsible for managing client relationships, while analysts typically do not interact with clients. This is seen through how relationship managers can influence client onboarding based on their assessments. Initially, the team that approves the onboarding of high-risk customers declined to onboard Fowler Oldfield due to the high-risk nature of its gold dealing business. However, the relationship manager was given the opportunity to pursue an application. This was subject to two conditions. The relationship manager had to collect detailed information about the company's AML and know your customer procedures and the regional director had to be 'happy to bank the business' (NatWest Agreed Statement, p 22). Fowler Oldfield's relationship manager pursued this opportunity, and Fowler Oldfield was onboarded under the condition that the relationship manager should undertake a close overview of the account and conduct a review after six months. Unfortunately, there is no documentary evidence confirming if the review took place. Nonetheless, it is evident that there are clear structural constraints governing client interactions and the agency of NatWest employees (that is, high-risk relationships must be approved, and conditions attached to the approval). These structures also provide a certain level of autonomy to relationship managers (that is, to pursue the onboarding of a customer, and to monitor client activities).

These structures and continued staff interactions also imply the existence of cultural values and norms related to client relationships and between employees. As the point of contact for clients, relationship managers are assumed capable of making normative and business decisions regarding client behaviours based on their occupational role. NatWest staff then share expectations that they can trust in these assessments. This is especially pertinent in light of structural barriers which limited the Borehamwood analysts' access to internally held information. This is not to say that they should not have pursued other alternatives, but it becomes plausible to contend that the limitation of the information structures further reinforced the norms of relying on relationship managers. This was further compounded by the relative inexperience of the staff at Borehamwood. Multiple concerns were raised about the lack of financial crime expertise within Borehamwood and the lack of support from the more experienced staff in the Edinburgh office. There were also indications of a pressured environment within the Borehamwood office, where staff operated under a heavy workload. This pressure to meet unrealistic targets led to 'a drive for speed over quality' norms (NatWest Agreed Statement, pp 58–9).

So, an alternative theoretical proposition may be that these behaviours are a form of normalized deviance which emerges from the combination of the structural and individual characteristics present in the case (Vaughan, 1998; Shover and Hochstetler, 2002). The NatWest staff learn to rely on relationship managers' client assessments and the high levels of cash deposits increasingly become an accepted business activity with each closed report. This normalization occurs through repeated staff interactions alongside the present and absent organizational structures in NatWest. It becomes plausible to reinterpret these events and consider that the financial analysts may not have considered their behaviours as noncompliant, but rather in line with the expected practices and norms.

Another closely linked demi-regularity observed is how some NatWest employees, particularly from Basingstoke and Washington cash centres, remained suspicious of Fowler Oldfield's activities.[6] A highly 'experienced' risks and controls manager at the Basingstoke cash centre remained unconvinced by the relationship manager's assurances. The volume of cash involved was the most he had ever encountered from a single customer. Since the cash centres handled the deposits directly, cash centre employees had unique insight into the 'extraordinary' and 'sheer' scale of cash involved (NatWest Agreed Statement, pp 35–6). Specific training about money-laundering issues was undertaken by NatWest employees, including cash centre staff who as part of their roles could identify suspicious activity. This included examples of cash deposits that are indicative of money laundering (such as unusually large deposits or Scottish or English notes being deposited where they would not be normally used). This knowledge and firsthand experience may have provided the context for why some cash centre employees retained their suspicions.

However, some cash centres and branches, despite the fact that they had training and direct contact with the scale of the deposits, did not raise suspicious activity alerts. Several branches contacted the relationship management team about their difficulties in dealing with the incoming levels of cash or raised alerts about 'the security of the physical bags of cash' (NatWest Agreed Statement, p 36). Their concerns related to the operational capacity for processing the cash, not the origins of the cash. It became plausible to identify that there were competing cultural values which influenced how individuals engaged with the 'sheer' size of incoming deposits. For some, the predominant priority remained on ensuring the operations of the businesses, while others had internalized the responsibility to be alert to activity indicative of money laundering. The staff with suspicions, nonetheless, faced extreme difficulty in escalating their concerns, since the responsibility for escalating and investigating suspicion remained with Borehamwood and subsequent financial crime units. The autonomy of the cash centre agents was constrained by the roles they occupied.

Retroduction

Building on this abductive thought process, 'retroduction' is an inferential mode of reasoning focused on identifying the conditions and mechanisms that lead to the events observed (Sayer, 2010). The demi-regularities unpacked in the previous sections are two examples among other trends observed. It therefore becomes crucial to consider these behaviours holistically. This involves asking:

- What must exist for the events observed to occur?
- How do these structures or mechanisms identified interact to produce noncompliant behaviours?
- Under which conditions and combinations do these behaviours occur?
- What is the most plausible explanation for why a behaviour occurred?

There is not enough room in this chapter to fully expand on all the potential mechanisms and structures at play. However, the analysis of this case shows there were multiple issues occurring at various levels within NatWest. Figure 4.1 illustrates what the stratified reality may look like in the NatWest case, based on the analytical process undertaken. In this case it is possible to identify the significance of organizational structures, including culture, and individual capacities in producing noncompliant behaviours as seen through the demi-regularities discussed. This reflects broader patterns observed in research related to organizational misconduct, where cultural and structural weaknesses within organizations can foster an environment conducive to misconduct and unethical behaviours (see Vaughan, 1998; Huisman, 2016; Van Rooij and Fine, 2018). First, NatWest's governance structures provided an essential context for enabling and constraining agent behaviours. The structural component of NatWest allocates certain roles and responsibilities to its staff. Second, as employees act within these structures, shared values of trust and expectations arise. These cultural values act as a mechanism which influences routine practices. Individuals were more resistant or receptive to these shared values, depending on their experiences and occupational roles. This is observed through how some staff showed greater alignment with their compliance responsibilities, which may have been influenced by their previous experiences and firsthand knowledge. In contrast, the Borehamwood team suffered from a critical skills gap while under operational pressure to meet targets. This was further compounded by material constraints of the information and technological silos. The interaction of these structural barriers led to norms of relying on the relationship manager and closing reports based on previous assessments for the analysts involved, while the governance structures hindered cash centre staff's ability to escalate and prevent further suspicious activity. The combination of these structures and their mechanisms in this case created a normalization of deviance. In this environment, large deposits became accepted practices and Fowler Oldfield's money-laundering involvement remained unidentified and unreported. Ultimately, these activities form the basis of NatWest's noncompliance conviction.

Stage five: consolidating findings

The final step of any research project is to consolidate the empirical findings in response to the research question. From a critical realist perspective, the purpose is to develop a conceptually coherent and plausible explanation. The explanation offered here suggests that the observable events are driven by an interaction human agency and deeper organizational structures and cultures (see Figure 4.1). While this takes a context-based approach, part of the consolidation process involves thinking about the wider implications of the findings. One notable implication from this analysis is the importance

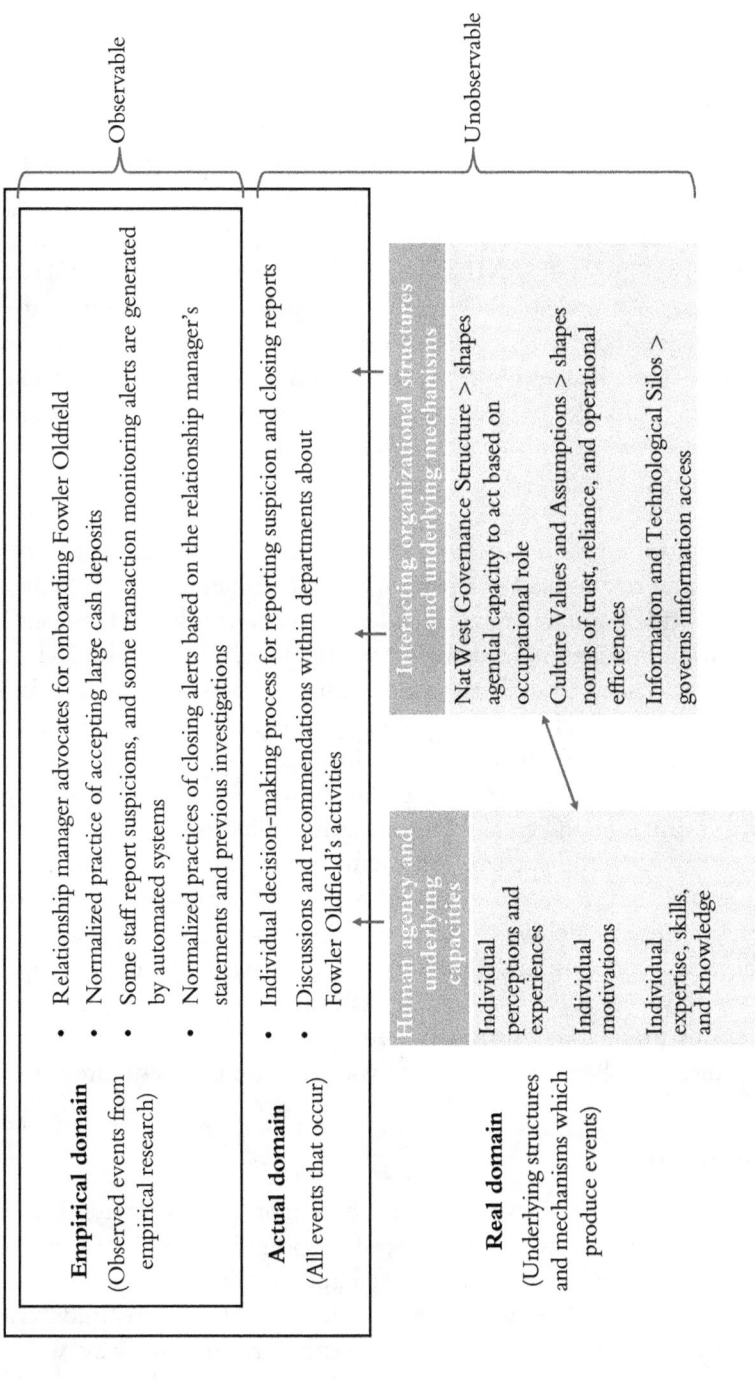

Figure 4.1: An example of the stratified reality for the NatWest case

of understanding compliance failures holistically rather than as isolated incidents. Instead of attributing compliance failures to simply negligence or 'bad actors', we should consider how the underlying structures come together to collectively create environments that are conducive to noncompliance. Analyzing behaviours in this way can capture how 'specific white-collar offences are shaped by various mechanisms and factors' which come together in particular contexts and time (Lord and Levi, 2025, p 83). Critical realism, as shown, provides a robust framework for developing this knowledge base.

In the aftermath of these failures, NatWest committed to making several changes to improve its AML controls (see NatWest Group, 2021; NatWest Sentencing Remarks). This included implementing measures to ensure that repeated reports are escalated for further review and to emphasize the importance of challenging explanations provided by relationship managers. From a critical realist perspective, achieving these changes requires sustained commitment as organizational structures are enduring and shared cultural norms are developed through continuous social activity. This requires addressing the observable barriers (that is, the lack of structured escalation routes) and the unobservable counteracting mechanisms (that is, norms of reliance and operational efficiency). Since the operations of a bank as large as NatWest is facilitated by a clear demarcation of roles and responsibilities, relationship managers are likely to have the most contact with clients. From the data available, it is difficult to ascertain the motivations of the relationship manager. However, his depiction and championing of Fowler Oldfield was a key driving force in initiating and maintaining the client relationship. From this, we can infer that key changes in how the relationship management teams continue to interact and monitor their clients, in addition to the other commitments outlined, may be useful intervention points for improving compliance controls. Since critical realism advocates refining knowledge through further fieldwork, this explanatory account remains open to elaboration and critique. Integrating the experiences and perceptions of the employees involved, as well as examining the interactions between the structures present in the broader financial and regulatory landscape and those discussed here, would be one way of refining this theoretical analysis.

Conclusion

The analysis of the NatWest case in this chapter demonstrates how critical realism can be used as a framework for conducting criminological research about potentially harmful white-collar and organizational crimes that occur within professional settings. Using critical realism as an 'under-labourer' influences the questions we seek to answer, and the way we critique and develop theoretical knowledge. In particular, the ontological and epistemological standpoint of a critical realist philosophy enables researchers to move beyond surface level observations to explore the observable as well as unobservable structures and conditions that produce organizational misconduct. It encourages thinking not only about what happened, but why it happened in order to develop richer and more nuanced explanations of social events. This is particularly useful when there are recurring incidents involving various individuals across a large and complex organization which occur alongside legitimate organizational activities.

The analysis presented in this chapter also shows how a qualitative approach can be used to build causal explanatory accounts. A qualitative approach was valuable for capturing the depth and detail needed to abstract the underlying structures and mechanisms involved. The barriers arising from the governance structures, cultural values, and information and technological silos contributed to normalizing certain business practices, which allowed Fowler Oldfield's banking activities to persist. Failing to prevent these banking activities meant that NatWest was noncompliant with their AML obligations. The flexibility of a critical realist approach means this explanatory account can be refined by integrating further empirical data and methods. There are many ways that critical realism can be employed across various disciplines. The process discussed in this chapter is one of many. It is drawn from my own journey and reflections on what it means to be a critical realist researcher. In line with other researchers who discuss the value of applying a critical realism framework, I also hope that this chapter offers a starting point and some inspiration for how we can conceptualize and operationalize critical realism concepts.

Notes

[1] https://www.fca.org.uk/publication/corporate/agreed-statement-facts-fca-national-westminster-bank.pdf
[2] The Money Laundering, Terrorist Financing and Transfer of Funds (Information on the Payer) Regulations 2017, https://www.legislation.gov.uk/uksi/2017/692
[3] The FCA is the supervisory body for financial service providers responsible for monitoring and enforcing compliance with Money Laundering Regulations (FCA, 2019).
[4] https://www.fca.org.uk/publication/corporate/agreed-statement-facts-fca-national-westminster-bank.pdf
[5] The Borehamwood office was responsible for investigating alerts related to non-retail customers and reviewed most of the alerts related to Fowler Oldfield.
[6] Cash centres process and distribute cash. At the time, Fowler Oldfield made several direct deposits to various cash centres across England.

References

Ackroyd, S. and Karlsson, J.Ch. (2014) 'Critical realism, research techniques, and research designs', in P.K. Edwards, J. O'Mahoney, and S. Vincent (eds), *Studying Organizations Using Critical Realism: A Practical Guide*, Oxford University Press, pp 21–45.

Archer, M.S. (1995) *Realist Social Theory: The Morphogenetic Approach*, Cambridge University Press.

Archer, M.S. (ed) (1998) *Critical Realism: Essential Readings* (Critical realism: interventions), Routledge.

Archer, M.S. (ed) (2017) *Morphogenesis and Human Flourishing*, Springer International Publishing (Social Morphogenesis).

BBC News (2021) 'NatWest fined £265m after bin bags of cash laundered', *BBC News*, Business [Online], 13 December. Available from: https://www.bbc.com/news/business-59629711

Bhaskar, R. (1989) *The Possibility of Naturalism: A Philosophical Critique of Contemporary Human Sciences* (2nd edn), Harvester Wheatsheaf.

Bhaskar, R. (1993) *Dialectic: The Pulse of Freedom*, Verso.

Bhaskar, R. (2008) *A Realist Theory of Science*, Routledge.

Braun, V. and Clarke, V. (2019) 'Reflecting on reflexive thematic analysis', *Qualitative Research in Sport, Exercise and Health*, 11(4): 589–97.

Bygstad, B., Munkvold, B.E., and Volkoff, O. (2016) 'Identifying generative mechanisms through affordances: a framework for critical realist data analysis', *Journal of Information Technology*, 31(1): 83–96.

Campbell, J.-L. and Göritz, A.S. (2014) 'Culture corrupts! A qualitative study of organizational culture in corrupt organizations', *Journal of Business Ethics*, 120(3): 291–311.

Collier, A. (1994) *Critical Realism: An Introduction to Roy Bhaskar's Philosophy*, Verso.

Cornish, D.B. and Clarke, R.V.G. (eds) (2014) *The Reasoning Criminal: Rational Choice Perspectives on Offending*, Transaction Publishers.

Croft, J. (2022) 'Yorkshire dealer used illegal cash to export gold to Dubai, court told', *Financial Times* Money laundering [Online], 4 May. Available from: https://www.ft.com/content/2e375209-40db-4950-9f33-357f22d1098f

Danermark, B. (2019) *Explaining Society: Critical Realism in the Social Sciences* (2nd edn), Routledge.

Danermark, B., Ekström, M., and Karlsson, J.C. (2019) *Explaining Society: Critical Realism in the Social Sciences* (2nd edn), Routledge.

Elder-Vass, D. (2021) 'Critical realism', in G. Delanty and S.P. Turner (eds), *Routledge International Handbook of Contemporary Social and Political Theory* (2nd edn), Routledge, pp 241–49.

FCA (2019) *FCA Mission: Approach to Supervision*, [Online] Available from: https://www.fca.org.uk/publication/corporate/our-approach-supervision-final-report-feedback-statement.pdf

Fletcher, A.J. (2017) 'Applying critical realism in qualitative research: methodology meets method', *International Journal of Social Research Methodology*, 20(2): 181–94.

Frauley, J. and Pearce, F. (2007) 'Critical realism and the social sciences: methodological and epistemological preliminaries', in J. Frauley and F. Pearce (eds), *Critical Realism and the Social Sciences*, University of Toronto Press, pp 3–29.

Friedrichs, D.O. (2019) 'White collar crime: definitional debates and the case for a typological approach', in M. Rorie (ed), *The Handbook of White-Collar Crime*, John Wiley & Sons, pp 16–31.

Fryer, T. (2022) 'A critical realist approach to thematic analysis: producing causal explanations', *Journal of Critical Realism*, 21(4): 365–84.

Goodall, O. (2022) 'Rural criminal collaborations and the food crimes of the countryside: realist social relations theory of illicit venison production', *Crime, Law and Social Change*, 78(5): 483–505.

Haigh, F., Kemp, L., Bazeley, P., and Haigh, N. (2019) 'Developing a critical realist informed framework to explain how the human rights and social determinants of health relationship works', *BMC Public Health*, 19(1): 1571.

Hastings, C. (2021) 'A critical realist methodology in empirical research: foundations, process, and payoffs', *Journal of Critical Realism*, 20(5): 458–73.

HM Treasury and Home Office (2020) *National Risk Assessment of Money Laundering and Terrorist Financing 2020*, HM Treasury and Home Office, [Online] Available from: https://assets.publishing.service.gov.uk/governm ent/uploads/system/uploads/attachment_data/file/945411/NRA_2020_v1.2_FOR_PUBLICATION.pdf

Huisman, W. (2016) 'Criminogenic organizational properties and dynamics', in S. Van Slyke, M.L. Benson, and F.T. Cullen (eds), *The Oxford Handbook of White-Collar Crime*, Oxford University Press, pp 435–62.

Hutter, B.M. (2011) 'Negotiating social, economic and political environments: compliance with regulation within and beyond the state', in C. Parker and L.N. Vibeke (eds) *Explaining Compliance: Business Responses to Regulation*, Edward Elgar Publishing, pp 305–21.

Irfan, L. and Wilkinson, M. (2020) 'The ontology of the Muslim male offender: a critical realist framework', *Journal of Critical Realism*, Routledge, 19(5): 481–99.

Lawani, A. (2021) 'Critical realism: what you should know and how to apply it', *Qualitative Research Journal*, 21(3): 320–33.

Lawson, T. (1998) 'Economic science without experimentation', in M. Archer, R. Bhaskar, A. Collier, T. Lawson, and A. Norrie (eds), *Critical Realism*, Routledge, pp 144–69.

Layder, D. (1998) *Sociological Practice*, Sage.

Lord, N. and Levi, M. (2025) *Organising White-Collar and Corporate Crimes*, Taylor & Francis Group.

Manicas, P.T. (2006) *A Realist Philosophy of Social Science: Explanation and Understanding*, Cambridge University Press.

Money Laundering Regulations (2017) 'Money laundering, terrorist financing and transfer of funds (information on the payer) regulations', [Online] Available from: https://www.legislation.gov.uk/uksi/2017/692

NatWest Group (2021) 'National Westminster Bank Plc fined £264.8m for breaches of Regulations', NatWest Group [Online] Available from: https://www.natwestgroup.com/news-and-insights/news-room/press-releases/our-updates/2021/dec/national-westminster-bank-plc-fined-p264-8m-for-breaches-of-regu.html

Norrie, A.W. (2010) *Dialectic and Difference: Dialectical Critical Realism and the Grounds of Justice*, Routledge.

O'Mahoney, J. and Vincent, S. (2014) 'Critical realism as an empirical project: a beginner's guide', in P.K. Edwards, J. O'Mahoney, and S. Vincent (eds), *Studying Organizations Using Critical Realism: A Practical Guide*, Oxford University Press, pp 1–20.

Parker, J. (2000) *Structuration*, Open University Press.

Parker, C. and Gilad, S. (2011) 'Internal corporate compliance management systems', in C. Parker and L.N. Vibeke (eds), *Explaining Compliance: Business Responses to Regulation*, Edward Elgar Publishing, pp 170–98.

Piercy, E. (2022) 'Nick Johnson KC secures acquittal of chartered accountant in one of the largest money laundering trials in British legal history', Exchange Chambers, [Online] Available from: https://www.exchangechambers.co.uk/nick-johnson-kc-secures-acquittal-of-chartered-accountant-in-one-of-the-largest-money-laundering-trials-in-british-legal-history/

Pontell, H.N. (2016) 'Theoretical, empirical, and policy implications of alternative definitions of "white-collar crime": "trivializing the lunatic crime rate"', in S. Van Slyke, M.L. Benson, and F.T. Cullen (eds), *The Oxford Handbook of White-Collar Crime*, Oxford University Press, pp 39–59.

Proceeds of Crime Act (2002) [Online] Available from: https://www.legislation.gov.uk/ukpga/2002/29/contents

Punch, M. (2014) 'The organizational component in corporate crime', in J.J. Gobert and A.-M. Pascal (eds), *European Developments in Corporate Criminal Liability*, Routledge, pp 101–13.

Sayer, R.A. (2010) *Method in Social Science: A Realist Approach* (2nd edn), Routledge.

Schein, E.H. and Schein, P.A. (2016) *Organizational Culture and Leadership*, John Wiley & Sons.

Shover, N. and Hochstetler, A. (2002) 'Cultural explanation and organizational crime', *Crime, Law and Social Change*, 37(1): 1–18.

Shover, N. and Hochstetler, A. (2006) *Choosing White-Collar Crime*, Cambridge University Press.

van Erp, J. (2018) 'The organization of corporate crime: introduction to special issue of administrative sciences', *Administrative Sciences*, 8(3): 36.

Van Rooij, B. and Fine, A. (2018) 'Toxic corporate culture: assessing organizational processes of deviancy', *Administrative Sciences*, Multidisciplinary Digital Publishing Institute, 8(3): 23.

Vaughan, D. (1998) 'Rational choice, situated action, and the social control of organizations', *Law & Society Review*, 32(1): 23–62.

Venkataramakrishnan, S. and Croft, J. (2021) 'NatWest's anti-money laundering failures laid bare in gold dealer case', *Financial Times*, NatWest Group [Online] 16 December. Available from: https://www.ft.com/content/4cd6c43e-e727-4792-b2c0-083694bd51ce

Wilkinson, M., Quraishi, M., Irfan, L. and Schneuwly Purdie, M. (2022) 'Building on the shoulders of Bhaskar and Matthews: a critical realist criminology', *Journal of Critical Realism*, 21(2): 123–44.

Withers, I. (2021) 'Bin bags of cash: NatWest fined for dirty money breaches', *Reuters*, Finance [Online] 13 December. Available from: https://www.reuters.com/business/finance/around-50-natwest-branches-involved-money-laundering-case-fca-2021-12-13/

5

Factorial Survey Research in the Study of White-Collar and Corporate Crime: Benefits, Applications, and Challenges

Jing Wei

Introduction

White-collar and corporate crime are among the least understood yet most impactful types of crime, with evident harm to individuals, organizations, and society as a whole (Benson et al, 2009; Simpson, 2013; Yeager, 2016). Despite their undeniable significance, the study of white-collar and corporate crime faces a range of challenges. These arise not only from the inherent complexity of such offences and the ambiguity in their definitions, but also from the lack of systematic and comprehensive data to support research (Simpson et al, 2014). Likewise, key individuals within corporations, such as executives, are often difficult to access or approach (Piquero et al, 2021).

Some studies in this field rely on official data (Eitle, 2000; Karpoff et al, 2008). However, such data only reflect offences recorded by law enforcement agencies and fail to capture crimes that remain undetected or unreported to authorities. Equally significant is the fact that official data provide limited insight into how individuals within organizations make decisions to engage in criminal behaviour, or how these decisions are shaped by factors at the organizational, industry, or broader societal levels (Simpson et al, 2013; Rorie, 2022). Some research adopts qualitative approaches, such as post hoc analyses of high-profile case studies, to explore violations within specific contexts (Brickey, 2006; Van De Bunt, 2010). However, the findings from such studies often lack generalizability to broader contexts or populations. Despite these data and methodological limitations, scholars have advanced the study of white-collar and corporate crime through innovative data collection techniques. Among these, the factorial survey method has gained particular attention due to its ability to combine the strengths of experimental and survey research. This method addresses common concerns about traditional data sources and offers a unique perspective on understanding white-collar and corporate criminal behaviour (Rorie et al, 2018).

My PhD research focuses on the deterrence of commercial bribery in China, employing a vignette-based factorial survey to explore the prevention and control of bribery in the private sector. In this method, respondents are invited to complete a survey that includes hypothetical scenarios or vignettes. These vignettes are constructed using multiple factors that may influence bribery intentions (for example, the economic condition of the company, the severity of the bribery act, and corporate norms). The goal is to simulate real-world situations individuals might face when deciding whether to engage in bribery. Researchers can manipulate these factors during survey administration, allowing different respondents to react to slightly varied vignettes. By responding to questions about their perceptions of various interventions and the likelihood of engaging in the behaviour of the role described in the vignette, researchers can integrate individual and organizational-level factors influencing bribery intentions to analyze which interventions, whether applied individually or in combination, are effective in reducing the propensity to bribe.

This chapter aims to explore the application of the factorial survey in the study of white-collar and corporate crime. The first section introduces the basic concepts and methodological advantages of this method. The second section discusses its limitations and practical considerations and suggests strategies to address these challenges. The chapter then reviews how the method has been applied in research on white-collar and corporate crime, including its use in exploring criminal intent, decision-making processes, and in evaluating the effectiveness of crime prevention and control measures. The chapter concludes by analyzing the unique contributions of this method to academic research and policy development.

Description of the factorial survey
What is the factorial survey method?
The factorial survey method was first developed by Peter H. Rossi (1979) to combine the strengths of experimental design and survey research. It aims to improve the internal validity of studies while increasing the generalizability of research findings (Taylor and Zeller, 2007; Aviram, 2012; Auspurg and Hinz, 2015; Piquero et al, 2021). The core of this method is the use of vignettes within the survey. Vignettes are brief, fictional descriptions of social situations or characters, incorporating various dimensions (or variables) relevant to the

research, and are used to simulate real-life contexts (Wallander, 2009; Rorie et al, 2018). Unlike traditional survey methods that directly ask respondents questions, the factorial survey presents respondents with realistic scenarios that simulate real-world situations, prompting them to weigh multiple dimensions before responding (Auspurg and Hinz, 2015). Researchers can infer the underlying factors influencing respondents' intentions, attitudes, decisions, or judgements based on their reactions to the vignettes (Rorie, 2022). For example, Simpson, Gibbs, and colleagues (2013) incorporated several dimensions into their vignette to examine factors influencing managers' involvement in corporate crime. Among these, environmental constraints provided respondents with contextual information about the economic environment of the firm, while ethical culture was identified as a factor shaping managers' perceptions of corporate crime. These perceptions, in turn, could influence their expectations of the benefits or costs associated with violations. Additionally, organizational dimensions such as management level, whether the violation was ordered by a superior, and the internal compliance structure and its operation are also closely linked to crime-related decision-making.

In designing a factorial survey, researchers typically rely on practical knowledge, existing theories, prior studies, or preliminary qualitative research to identify key dimensions and define the levels (specific values that the dimension can take) for each dimension (Taylor, 2005; Rorie et al, 2018). For instance, in the aforementioned study, the dimension 'environmental constraints' included three levels: 'losing ground to foreign competitors', 'economically healthy', and 'economically deteriorating'. Similarly, the dimension 'management level' consisted of two levels: 'a mid-level manager' and 'an upper-level manager'. The dimension concerning superior orders included levels such as 'is asked by a higher-level manager' and 'asks an employee' (Simpson et al, 2013, p 244). These dimensions are then embedded into a series of sentences arranged in a fixed order to construct the vignettes. The levels of each dimension within the sentences are randomly varied across the vignettes, generating multiple distinct vignettes (Taylor, 2005; Taylor and Zeller, 2007; Steiner et al, 2016). For example, vignettes might take forms such as, 'Lee, a mid-level manager at AmCorp, asks an employee to ignore an environmental agency's demand to act on a compliance order' or 'Lee, a low-level manager at AmCorp, is asked by a supervisor to …' (Simpson et al, 2013, p 270). Collectively, these vignettes form what is known as the 'vignette universe', which grows exponentially as more dimensions and levels are increased (Auspurg and Hinz, 2015). For instance, if a vignette includes two dimensions, each with three levels, nine unique vignettes can be generated. Each respondent is randomly assigned one or more vignettes. Therefore, not all respondents receive the same vignette. This design allows researchers to observe differences in respondents' decisions or attitudes across various contexts and to more accurately analyze the independent effects of each dimension (Aviram, 2012; Rorie, 2022).

Like other surveys, factorial surveys include one or more questions at the end of each vignette to capture respondents' attitudes or perceptions related to the vignette (Piquero et al, 2021). These questions take various forms, with Likert scales being the most commonly used (Taylor, 2005). The survey may also include additional questions to collect background information or data on theoretical constructs relevant to the research, such as respondents' demographic characteristics (Piquero et al, 2021).

Why use the factorial survey method?

There are several advantages to using the factorial survey method. Foremost among these is its experimental nature, which allows researchers to manipulate the dimensions (or variables) embedded within the vignettes, thereby enhancing the internal validity of the study, ensuring that observed changes in the dependent variable are caused by the experimental stimuli (Aviram, 2012; Auspurg and Hinz, 2015). In traditional surveys, if two independent variables often appear together and are naturally correlated, it becomes difficult to separate their independent effects (Taylor, 2005). For instance, 'job position' and 'income' are often positively correlated, and those in higher positions tend to earn more. This kind of collinearity makes it difficult to determine whether changes in decision-making are influenced by 'job position' or 'income'. However, in factorial surveys, the random assignment of different levels of dimensions to vignettes, and the random allocation of these vignettes to respondents, ensures that each variable is independent (that is, eliminates natural associations between variables). This design allows researchers to directly test how each variable independently affects respondents' reactions, without interference from confounding factors. As a result, it helps to address the issue of spurious correlations (Taylor and Zeller, 2007; Atzmüller and Steiner, 2010; Auspurg and Hinz, 2015; Nokes and Hodgkinson, 2017). For example, in a vignette, the levels of 'job position' may be randomly combined with those of 'income', producing combinations such as 'a high-level position with low income' or 'a low-level position with high income'. These vignettes are then distributed randomly among respondents. This approach makes it possible to assess the distinct effects of job position and income on decision-making, without being confounded by the natural correlation between these variables. It is worth noting, however, that the random manipulation of dimensions may sometimes lead to vignettes that lack contextual realism. This issue will be further discussed in the limitations section.

Second, factorial surveys combine hypothetical scenarios (vignettes) with survey questions, enabling researchers to manipulate various conditions that may influence decisions, intentions, or judgements. This method provides a way to better understand the complex decision-making processes behind corporate and white-collar crime (Oll et al, 2018). In addition, some scholars argue that individuals are often unable to accurately explain how they make judgements. Factorial surveys allow researchers to study the implicit predictors of judgement through respondents' reactions to vignettes, rather than by relying on direct survey questions (Rorie et al, 2018). For example, when Simpson and Piquero (2002) investigated managerial decision-making in corporate crime, they designed vignettes with eleven dimensions to simulate real-world decision-making situations. These dimensions included, for example, management level, company size, personal benefits of noncompliance (such as, likelihood of promotion and salary bonuses), corporate benefits of noncompliance (such as, cost savings, reputation enhancement), the internal compliance structure (such as, ethics training, audits), personal risks of noncompliance (such as, prosecution, dismissal, acquittal), and risks faced by the company if noncompliance is detected (such as, corporate prosecution, regulatory sanctions, public naming, or immunity from prosecution). By analyzing respondents' reactions, the researchers were able to explore how variations in factors such as crime-related risks and benefits influence decision-making. However, there has been ongoing debate regarding whether behavioural intentions expressed in hypothetical scenarios align with actual behaviours. This issue will be discussed in the next section.

Third, embedding vignette experiments within surveys makes sampling and distribution more flexible and accessible. This helps enhance the external validity of the research and makes it easier to apply findings to broader populations (Atzmüller and Steiner, 2010; Rorie, 2022). Specifically, traditional experiments often face criticism for limited external validity, partly because they rely on unrepresentative samples (for example, convenience samples such as students, which do not reflect the general population), or take place in overly simplified settings. By contrast, factorial surveys address this issue by allowing vignettes and follow-up questions to be distributed in written or online formats. This flexibility enables researchers to reach large, more representative samples, and helps to overcome a key limitation of traditional experimental designs.

The factorial survey method also helps to resolve common issues found in traditional research designs, such as recall bias and problems with temporal order (Piquero et al, 2021). Instead of relying on participants' memories, this method presents respondents with hypothetical scenarios and asks for their immediate reactions. This allows researchers to directly observe how independent variables influence responses in real time (Rorie et al, 2018). Because responses are based on immediate reactions, rather than memories of past behaviours, this method avoids the recall bias often seen in self-report studies. For example, traditional surveys should carefully determine the appropriate recall period to ensure respondents can accurately report past events. Moreover, the factorial survey ensures that the independent variables are presented before the response, maintaining the correct temporal order. This helps to establish a clearer causal relationship between the independent and dependent variables (Taylor and Zeller, 2007; Rorie, 2022).

Moreover, the factorial survey method may help reduce social desirability bias, in which respondents tend to provide socially acceptable answers or present themselves in a positive way (Wallander, 2009). Because factorial surveys can be conducted online and without the presence of researchers, individuals may feel more comfortable responding honestly, particularly when the questions involve sensitive topics (Rorie et al, 2018). In addition, respondents are typically unaware of how the key variables are manipulated within the vignettes. This makes it difficult for them to infer the purpose of the study or adjust their responses accordingly, which increases the likelihood of capturing their genuine attitudes (Piquero et al, 2021). For instance, in a study exploring Austrians' views on income equality between male and female employees, directly asking whether men and women should receive equal pay might have led respondents to express support for equality due to political correctness. Instead, researchers incorporated 'employee gender' as a between-subjects factor in the factorial survey. Some respondents received vignettes describing female employees, while others received ones about male employees (Steiner et al, 2016). This design reduced the likelihood that respondents would adjust their answers to align with perceived social expectations.

Finally, the factorial survey provides a practical way to explore behaviours that are difficult to observe directly or for which conventional data sources are limited (Aviram, 2012; Piquero et al, 2021). In research on white-collar and corporate crime, access to key corporate figures such as executives and senior business managers is often difficult. To address this, some researchers have used student samples, particularly MBA students and participants in executive MBA programmes, when conducting factorial surveys (Simpson and Piquero, 2002; Piquero et al, 2005). Respondents are asked to place themselves in the role described in the vignettes (for example, acting as a manager) and to indicate how likely they would be to engage in specific behaviours under those conditions.

Limitations and practical considerations

Like other methods used to study social phenomena, factorial surveys have certain limitations when it comes to evaluating real-world cognition and behaviour. One key issue is their reliance on hypothetical scenarios to simulate real-life decision-making, which raises concerns about whether the vignettes accurately reflect real-life situations (Eifler, 2010; Exum et al, 2014). The effectiveness of a vignette largely depends on how well it can trigger genuine cognitive processes in respondents. For this reason, ensuring realism in vignette design is essential for maintaining measurement validity (Piquero et al, 2021). In my doctoral research, we aimed to improve the validity of the vignettes by extensively drawing on empirical and theoretical literature to identify relevant dimensions and levels. We also developed the vignette storylines based on more than twenty real-world cases. Experts in corporate and white-collar crime research, who were familiar with the factorial survey method, were invited to review the initial drafts, and we revised the survey based on their feedback. Pilot study was another critical part of the process (Hughes and Huby, 2004; Steiner et al, 2016). We conducted a small-scale pilot study to test the feasibility of the vignette survey. As Aviram (2012) points out, the extent to which a vignette elicits genuine responses from respondents depends on whether they perceive the vignette as realistic. Based on this, we included a question at the end of the survey asking respondents to evaluate the realism of the vignette. This allowed us to exclude responses to vignettes that were perceived as unrealistic during data analysis (Rorie and West, 2022).

Second, a key limitation of factorial surveys is whether self-reported behavioural intentions accurately predict actual behaviour (Eifler, 2010; Oll et al, 2018). Some scholars argue that respondents' reported intentions in hypothetical situations may not reflect how they would act in real-life situations (Eifler, 2010; Oll et al, 2018), challenging both the internal and external validity of this method.

Nevertheless, existing research has shown a strong association between criminal intentions and actual deviant behaviour in real-world settings (Ludwick and Zeller, 2001; Pogarsky, 2004). For example, Pogarsky (2004) combined hypothetical scenarios with laboratory experiments, finding that respondents who cheated during the experiments were more likely to predict that they would engage in misconduct in real-life situations. Researchers should interpret these findings with caution and avoid concluding that respondents will necessarily act in the same way in real-life situations. Intentions expressed in response to hypothetical vignettes are still influenced by the vignette design and respondents' individual characteristics. In practice, people are likely to face more complex factors and pressures. Therefore, the results of factorial surveys are more suited to exploring behavioural tendencies or intentions, rather than providing direct explanations of actual behaviour.

Third, while factorial surveys may help reduce social desirability bias, some scholars remain sceptical about whether the method can fully eliminate it (Auspurg and Hinz, 2015; Auspurg and Jäckle, 2017). For instance, in designs where respondents respond to multiple vignettes, their reaction to the first vignette might influence how they respond to later ones. This can result in autocorrelation between responses, which violates the assumption of uncorrelated error terms required for multivariate linear regression models and potentially affect the reliability and validity of the analysis. Addressing this issue requires careful design choices. For example, randomizing the order of vignette presentation, or employing advanced statistical models such as multilevel models or mixed-effects models, can help mitigate autocorrelation effects (Auspurg and Hinz, 2015). In my doctoral research, to minimize potential bias from vignette or response option order, each respondent was presented only one vignette, which was randomly distributed. We also randomized the order of response options to further reduce order effects.

Fourth, determining the appropriate number of dimensions and levels in vignettes is a practical challenge that requires balancing theoretical depth with feasibility. While including a wide range of dimensions can provide respondents with sufficient contextual information to make decisions, adding too many dimensions or levels causes the number of possible vignettes to grow exponentially, which increases the required sample size (Auspurg and Hinz, 2015). To ensure sufficient statistical power, each level of every dimension should be evaluated by an adequate number of respondents (Piquero et al, 2021). Furthermore, presenting too many dimensions may overwhelm respondents, making it difficult for them to consider each factor carefully. As a result, certain dimensions may be ignored, which could reduce the validity of the study.

To address this issue, Taylor (2005) recommends including five to ten dimensions, although in some cases this number can exceed twenty. Meanwhile, Auspurg and Hinz (2015) suggest limiting the number of dimensions to around seven, with two to three levels per dimension, aiming to use a limited and balanced number of levels whenever possible. They emphasize that additional dimensions should only be introduced if required by the research objectives. On the other hand, if the study focuses on only a few dimensions, the number can be reduced. In such cases, however, each respondent should be assigned only a small number of vignettes (for example, one or no more than five). Otherwise, a lack of variation may make the vignettes feel repetitive, leading to boredom or fatigue effects. Moreover, pilot studies are especially important for selecting appropriate dimensions. By conducting a pilot, researchers can evaluate the applicability of each dimension and level, ensure that key dimensions are included, and remove unnecessary or redundant ones.

Another practical concern in factorial surveys is determining the appropriate sample size. Since the unit of analysis is the vignette, rather than the respondent, researchers must decide how many vignettes to include and how many respondents should evaluate each vignette to ensure the results are reliable and representative (Auspurg and Hinz, 2015). Auspurg and Hinz (2015) recommend that each vignette be evaluated by at least five different respondents. However, this is a practical guideline rather than a statistically grounded requirement. A more precise approach involves conducting a power analysis (Auspurg and Hinz, 2015; Steiner et al, 2016). This technique helps determine the sample size needed to detect a given effect size with a specified level of statistical power (Steiner et al, 2016). Researchers can collect preliminary data during a pilot to estimate effect sizes and variability, which are critical parameters for conducting power analysis and determining the final sample size. While there is no strict rule for the sample size of pilot studies, including 30 to 50 respondents is generally considered sufficient for generating preliminary insights and estimating key parameters (Steiner et al, 2016). That said, the final sample size should always be adjusted based on the complexity of the research design and the resources available.

The application of factorial surveys in the study of corporate and white-collar crime

In the social sciences, the factorial survey method has been widely applied across academic and non-academic fields, including sociology, economics, law, psychology, political science, nursing, and marketing research (Aviram, 2012; Auspurg and Hinz, 2015). As summarized in two reviews, a substantial proportion of factorial survey studies focus on themes related to crime, law, and deviant behaviour (Wallander, 2009; Rorie et al, 2018). However, these reviews also highlight that factorial surveys are still mainly used by a relatively small group of researchers. This is not due to inherent limitations of the method itself, but rather to limited awareness and knowledge sharing, leaving many researchers unaware of its potential value (Wallander, 2009).

In the study of white-collar and corporate crime, the factorial survey has been applied to address two core themes: (1) exploring criminal intentions and decision-making processes, or testing the explanatory power of relevant theories on deviant behaviour, and (2) studying crime prevention and control, particularly the effectiveness of punitive sanctions and non-punitive regulatory measures. This section discusses how the factorial survey method has been used to explore these themes and highlights its unique contributions to the study of white-collar and corporate crime.

Criminal decision-making and intentions

The factorial survey method is widely used to investigate how individuals make decisions to engage in criminal behaviour within specific contexts. Gaining insight into these decision-making processes is essential for understanding issues related to compliance, crime, and justice. This type of research requires a comprehensive consideration of the complex situations in which individuals are situated, as well as reliable ways to measure their decisions in these settings (Piquero et al, 2021). In the field of white-collar and corporate crime, researchers face particular challenges due to significant variations between organizations in terms of size, financial conditions, corporate culture, and compliance histories. These variations make it difficult to measure how decisions are made in complex and dynamic contexts. Moreover, requiring individuals to complete a survey or participate in an interview at every decision point is clearly impractical. The factorial survey method addresses these challenges effectively, particularly when the research focus is on the combination of variables rather than individual respondents (Rorie, 2022). By randomly assigning different levels to various dimensions within the vignettes, this method allows for a flexible integration of individual-level characteristics with meso-level (organizational) and macro-level (community or societal) factors (Oll et al, 2018). These factors include personal self-interest, normative organizational considerations, organizational costs and benefits, authority, and group influences.

In practical applications, respondents are typically asked to read vignettes describing scenarios of noncompliance and then report how likely they would be to act in the same way as the manager depicted in the vignette. The manager in the vignette is always portrayed as engaging in some form of misconduct. Some studies use vignettes to present varying levels of severity for a single type of misconduct. Examples vary from severe acts of pollution (intentionally discharging toxic substances into local waterways) to relatively minor technical violations (failing to act on or comply with an environmental agency's order) (Simpson et al, 2013). Other research explores different types of misconduct within the vignettes. For instance, Paternoster and Simpson (1996) presented respondents with multiple vignettes describing various forms of misconduct, including bribery, manipulation of sales data, price-fixing, and violation of environmental standards.

Researchers manipulate various factors within vignettes that may influence criminal decision-making or intentions, allowing them to estimate how changes in multiple variables affect respondents' decisions or to identify which variables have the most significant impact, even if respondents cannot explicitly articulate the influence of these factors. Existing studies have included a variety of manager-related attributes in vignettes, such as management level, tenure at the firm, authority, and personal benefits of noncompliance (Paternoster and Simpson, 1996; Simpson and Piquero, 2002; Simpson et al, 2013). In addition, company-related attributes have also been incorporated, such as firm size, economic conditions, and internal compliance measures (such as, the presence of ethical guidelines, anonymous reporting hotlines, and random audits) (Paternoster and Simpson, 1996; Simpson and Piquero, 2002; Piquero et al, 2005; Simpson et al, 2013; Rorie, 2015).

After reading the vignette, respondents are typically asked to respond to one or more questions. Studies often use Likert scales to measure respondents' intentions or decisions (Piquero et al, 2021). For instance, Simpson et al (2013) asked respondents to evaluate the likelihood of engaging in similar behaviour as described in the scenario, using a scale ranging from 0 to 10, where 0 = no chance at all and 10 = 100% chance. In addition to assessing behavioural intentions, supplementary questions can be included after the vignette to measure other factors potentially influencing criminal intentions or decisions. For example, Dickel and Graeff (2018) measured the degree of norm internalization (that is, adherence to laws) using additional questions. Respondents rated their agreement with statements such as, 'Corruption is always wrong', 'One has to adhere to generally applicable laws', and 'If norms exist that forbid corruption, then one should adhere to them'. The factor scores from these responses were used as an aggregate indicator of norm internalization. Similarly, Simpson and Piquero (2002) employed this method to measure low self-control by asking respondents about impulsive or unstable behaviours over the past year. These included questions on long-term unemployment, number of divorces, number of sexual partners, frequency of traffic violations, involvement in car accidents, and instances of heavy drinking.

Factorial surveys have made significant contributions to understanding the intentions and decision-making processes associated with white-collar and corporate crime. At the micro-level, studies often draw on self-control theory and rational choice theory. Research has shown that the internalization of moral norms significantly reduces criminal intentions. In other words, individuals with stronger moral beliefs are less likely to intend to commit crimes (Paternoster and Simpson, 1996; Dickel and Graeff, 2018). Additionally, self-control theory has been tested in the context of explaining criminal intentions (Simpson and Piquero, 2002; Piquero et al, 2005; Schoepfer et al, 2014). However, Schoepfer et al (2014) found that while low self-control is associated with traditonal criminal behaviour, it is insufficient to explain corporate crime. In contrast, desire for control, defined as a general tendency to seek control over events in daily life, was found to be a stronger predictor of corporate criminal tendencies.

In contrast to self-control and rational choice theories, which emphasize individual behaviour, organizational theory shifts the focus of analysis to the meso- and macro-levels (Simpson, 2013). At the organizational level, Simpson and Piquero (2002) found that effective compliance programmes and a strong managerial perception of the immorality of illegal activities significantly reduce criminal intentions. In contrast, criminal intentions tend to increase when such behaviours are common within the company, when supervisors direct managers to act illegally, and when corporate reputation is at risk. These findings highlight the critical role of organizational-level factors in explaining white-collar crime. Incorporating organizational characteristics into analytical frameworks not only improves the explanatory power of crime theories, but also provides theoretical support for strengthening organizational-level control measures. For example, improving internal ethics training and refining compliance mechanisms may play a important role in reducing corporate misconduct.

Additionally, research has increasingly focused on the role of emotions in shaping criminal intentions and decision-making. Factors such as shame (Paternoster and Simpson, 1996), the fear of falling hypothesis (Piquero, 2012), and the afraid of arrest hypothesis (Pickett et al, 2018) have been explored. For example, Piquero (2012) examined the impact of the fear of falling on the intention to engage in price manipulation. The fear of falling refers to the strong motivation among white-collar offenders to avoid financial losses, social status decline, or reputational damage to themselves or their families. This fear drives them to commit crimes, not to gain more benefits but to avoid losing their current position or resources. To measure this independent variable, Piquero manipulated the presence of 'fear of falling' conditions within the vignette. Specifically, respondents were randomly assigned to one of two versions of the vignette: one included descriptions reflecting the fear of falling (for example, concerns about a child no longer being able to attend private school and the cessation of annual family vacations to Europe), while the other excluded such descriptions. By comparing respondents' reactions across the two vignettes, the study found that, rather than increasing criminal intentions as hypothesized, the fear of falling actually reduced respondents' criminal intentions. This result suggests that the role of emotions in criminal decision-making may be more complex than traditional theories predict. The focus on emotional factors complements the traditional criminological assumption that individuals always make decisions based on rational choice, offering a more comprehensive perspective for understanding criminal behaviour.

Overall, the factorial survey method provides a robust tool for testing traditional criminological theories and developing new ones. Through this method, researchers can not only validate the applicability of established theories, such as rational choice theory and self-control theory, in the context of white-collar and corporate crime. At the same time, it supports the development of new, field-specific theories, such as the fear of falling hypothesis (Piquero, 2012) and organizational theory (Simpson and Piquero, 2002).

Prevention and control of white-collar and corporate crime

In research on preventing and controlling white-collar and corporate crime, methods such as secondary data analysis (for example, data from official agencies and corporate reports), traditional surveys, and quasi-experiments (for example, pre-test/post-test designs) are commonly used; however, the application of factorial surveys remains relatively limited (Simpson et al, 2014; Rorie et al, 2018). Traditional surveys can help reveal the impact of preventive and control measures on criminal intentions or behaviours. However, they are often limited by spurious correlations. Experimental studies allow precise manipulation of variables to test causal relationships between specific factors and noncompliance. However, in the context of white-collar and corporate crime regulation, experimental designs face practical and ethical challenges. For example, randomly applying stricter regulations to certain entities or regions, as required by experimental designs, may raise fairness concerns, making such approaches less acceptable for widespread use (Rorie et al, 2018). In such cases, factorial surveys provide a useful alternative. By designing hypothetical scenarios that simulate different regulatory measures or their intensities, this method allows researchers to assess the direct effects of interventions on criminal intentions without implementing actual interventions. For example, in the study by Dickel and Graeff (2018), the probability of detection (1%, 5%, and 10%) was manipulated within vignettes to analyze how these changes influenced entrepreneurs' propensity to engage in corruption.

When using factorial surveys to evaluate the effectiveness of interventions, studies often rely on rational choice theory and deterrence theory. These theories assume that rational individuals decide whether to commit crimes based on their perceived risks and benefits: the higher the perceived risk of punishment, the lower the likelihood of criminal intent (Nagin and Pogarsky, 2001; Pogarsky, 2002). In research, researchers typically assess the effectiveness of crime prevention and control measures within the context of personal and organizational factors that may increase or decrease the likelihood of noncompliance. For instance, Simpson et al (2013) incorporated multiple factors into their vignettes, such as the manager's hierarchical level, whether the violation was ordered by a superior, the company's economic condition, the ethical orientation of management, and the organization's internal compliance measures. By controlling for these factors, they investigated the extent to which managers' decisions to violate environmental laws were influenced by command-and-control measures (based on detection and punishment) or self-regulation strategies for prevention and control.

Perceptions of sanction risk are central to deterrence research (Apel, 2022). Existing studies often measure respondents' perceptions of sanctions through questions following the vignette. Specifically, after reading the vignette, respondents are typically asked to report not only their likelihood of engaging in the described misconduct (that is, their criminal intent) but also to evaluate the certainty of sanctions (that is, the probability of detection or being subjected to criminal or civil penalties) and their severity (that is, the impact of legal consequences). For example, Pickett et al (2018) asked respondents to assess the likelihood of being arrested after committing the specific offence described in the vignette on a scale of 1 (very unlikely) to 7 (very likely). Respondents were also asked to rate their fear of being arrested on a scale of 1 (not at all afraid) to 7 (very afraid). These measures allowed the researchers to analyze whether perceptions of sanction threats effectively deterred criminal intent. Furthermore, most deterrence studies ask respondents to consider how various interventions might affect both themselves as individual decision-makers and their organizations. For instance, respondents are often asked to evaluate the likelihood of arrest or prosecution (that is, the certainty of sanctions) and to estimate the degree to which such negative outcomes would pose problems for themselves or their companies (that is, the severity of sanctions) (Simpson and Piquero, 2002; Simpson et al, 2013).

The deterrent effects of formal sanctions remain inconsistent in factorial survey research. The impact of sanction certainty and severity on criminal intent is often moderated by other factors. For instance, Simpson, Garner, and Gibbs (2011) found that formal legal sanctions significantly deter noncompliant behaviour among managers. However, Simpson and Piquero (2002) observed that when sanctions targeted the organization rather than individuals, the certainty of criminal sanctions had little significant effect on managerial decisions. Only the severity of criminal sanctions reduced noncompliance intentions. Notably, when respondents were asked to consider the personal risks associated with sanctions, the deterrent effect of formal legal sanctions became more pronounced. This effect typically emerged only when both organizational-level and individual-level factors were included in the analytical model. Moreover, the deterrent effects of formal sanctions are also moderated by moral beliefs or expectations of outcomes (Simpson et al, 2013).

In addition to formal sanctions, research has also explored the deterrent effects of informal sanctions. For example, respondents are often asked to assess the potential negative consequences of engaging in illegal behaviour, such as the likelihood and severity of losing their job, facing career limitations, or damaging their company's reputation. Results consistently show that informal sanctions have a significant deterrent effect, particularly the impacts of losing respect, employment, or future career opportunities (Piquero et al, 2005; Simpson et al, 2013). Some studies have even found that informal sanctions are more effective in reducing criminal intent than formal sanctions (Elis and Simpson, 1995; Craig Smith et al, 2007).

In addition, some factorial survey studies have examined the deterrent effects of non-punitive regulatory measures. Unlike punitive measures that deter through increased costs of noncompliance, cooperative regulation aims to enhance compliance by fostering information-sharing and promoting a culture of organizational compliance (Rorie, 2015; Rorie et al, 2015). For example, Rorie and West (2022) investigated the impact of corporate ethical codes (documents outlining a company's principles and rules for ethical and acceptable behaviour) on noncompliance intentions by designing fictional ethical guidelines and manipulating their content and presentation in vignette. Their findings revealed that corporate ethical codes can enhance compliance. The study demonstrated that reminding employees of the importance of ethical conduct is effective in reducing noncompliance intentions. These results highlight the potential of non-punitive measures in fostering voluntary compliance.

Overall, the studies discussed here support a comprehensive strategy for effectively preventing and controlling corporate and white-collar crime by combining cooperative regulation with more punitive sanction measures (Simpson, 2002; Simpson et al, 2011, 2013), including formal legal sanctions, informal sanctions, corporate self-regulation, and non-punitive regulatory approaches. However, existing research has rarely examined the combined effects of these prevention and control strategies, particularly in identifying which combinations of strategies are most effective at reducing the risk of noncompliance. Future research could apply the factorial survey method by manipulating multiple strategies and their combinations to address this gap and provide valuable insights into the optimal integration of deterrence measures.

Conclusion

Although factorial surveys have not yet been widely applied in research on white-collar and corporate crime, existing studies show that they can provide valuable insights. Compared to traditional survey methods, factorial surveys allow researchers to manipulate key variables, making it easier to control for confounding factors and directly examine causal relationships. They are also well-suited to large-scale sample studies, offering greater representativeness and external validity than traditional experiments. As a result, factorial surveys are particularly useful in balancing internal and external validity. Nevertheless, scholars should carefully consider whether this method suits their specific research questions. Factorial surveys are particularly effective for exploring perceptions of deviant behaviours and the multiple motivations that drive noncompliance. In contrast, traditional surveys may be better suited for examining how frequently such behaviours occur. For studies that aim to explore the causes of noncompliance in depth, interviews or case studies may be more appropriate.

Existing research has shown that factorial surveys can be effectively used to explore the intentions and decision-making processes behind white-collar and corporate crime, as well as to identify strategies for preventing and controlling such behaviours. The ability of factorial surveys to examine combinations of variables allows for the manipulation of potential consequences, organizational characteristics of potential offenders, and types of noncompliance. This makes it particularly well-suited for analyzing individual judgements and behavioural intentions in relation to multiple influencing factors. Moreover, the factorial survey enables researchers to link these responses to variables operating at the micro-level (individual attitudes and traits), meso-level (organizational characteristics), and macro-level (community or societal factors). This multidimensional design supports the investigation of the various motivations and dynamic trade-offs driving criminal behaviours.

Furthermore, the factorial survey method provides a way to deconstruct complex and ambiguous concepts, allowing researchers to examine how different components influence outcomes and to identify which aspects have the strongest influence (Oll et al, 2018). For example, when studying the impact of 'ethical culture' on compliance, the concept can be broken down into specific dimensions, such as the attitudes of senior management, the existence and enforcement of ethical codes, and supervisors' behavioural expectations. This approach helps identify which aspects of ethical culture have the strongest impact on compliance. Moreover, it is worth noting that most existing factorial survey studies rely on single-country samples. Exploring how individuals from different cultural and national backgrounds respond to the same vignette could provide valuable cross-cultural insights; such insights are especially relevant when investigating corporate behaviour that crosses national boundaries (Rorie et al, 2018).

While factorial surveys have advantages, their limitations should not be overlooked. Respondents' intentions in hypothetical scenarios may not always accurately reflect actual behaviour, and researchers should interpret results with caution, avoiding the assumption that behavioural intentions are equivalent to actual actions. To enhance the realism of factorial surveys, vignettes can be designed based on real cases, theoretical literature, and expert consultations. Pilot studies also play a crucial role by helping identify and resolve potential issues before the main study. Another challenge is the exponential increase in the number of vignettes as more variables are added, which requires a larger number of respondents. However, under budget constraints, researchers often ask respondents to answer multiple vignettes to reduce costs. While this strategy is more cost-effective, it can lead to respondent fatigue, resulting in lower response quality and compromised data reliability. In my pilot study, each respondent was asked to read and answer two vignettes. The results indicated clear signs of fatigue when answering the second vignette, including a decline in response quality. To address this issue, we adjusted the study design for the main study. Based on the pilot findings, we reduced the number of dimensions in the vignettes, keeping only the most essential ones. This reduced the size of the vignette universe and allowed each respondent to complete only one vignette. These modifications improved response quality and the reliability of the study's findings.

References

Apel, R. (2022) 'Sanctions, perceptions, and crime', *Annual Review of Criminology*, 5(1): 205–27.

Atzmüller, C. and Steiner, P.M. (2010) 'Experimental vignette studies in survey research', *Methodology*, 6(3): 128–38.

Auspurg, K. and Hinz, T. (2015) *Factorial Survey Experiments* (7th edn), Sage.

Auspurg, K. and Jäckle, A. (2017) 'First equals most important? Order effects in vignette-based measurement', *Sociological Methods & Research*, 46(3): 490–539.

Aviram, H. (2012) 'What would you do? Conducting web-based factorial vignette surveys', in L. Gideon (ed), *Handbook of Survey Methodology for the Social Sciences*, Springer New York, pp 463–73.

Benson, M.L., Madensen, T.D., and Eck, J.E. (2009) 'White-collar crime from an opportunity perspective', in S.S. Simpson and D. Weisburd (eds), *The Criminology of White-Collar Crime*, Springer New York, pp 175–93.

Brickey, K.F. (2006) 'In Enron's wake: corporate executives on trial', *Journal of Criminal Law and Criminology*, 96(2): 397–434.

Craig Smith, N., Simpson, S.S., and Huang, C.-Y. (2007) 'Why managers fail to do the right thing: an empirical study of unethical and illegal conduct', *Business Ethics Quarterly*, 17(4): 633–67.

Dickel, P. and Graeff, P. (2018) 'Entrepreneurs' propensity for corruption: a vignette-based factorial survey', *Journal of Business Research*, 89: 77–86.

Eifler, S. (2010) 'Validity of a factorial survey approach to the analysis of criminal behavior', *Methodology*, 6(3): 139–46.

Eitle, D.J. (2000) 'Regulatory justice: a re-examination of the influence of class position on the punishment of white-collar crime', *Justice Quarterly*, 17(4): 809–39.

Elis, L.A. and Simpson, S.S. (1995) 'Informal sanction threats and corporate crime: additive versus multiplicative models', *Journal of Research in Crime and Delinquency*, 32(4): 399–424.

Exum, M.L., Bailey, D., and Wright, E.L. (2014) 'False positive and false negative rates in self-reported intentions to offend: a replication and extension', *Journal of Criminal Justice*, 42(1): 1–9.

Hughes, R. and Huby, M. (2004) 'The construction and interpretation of vignettes in social research', *Social Work and Social Sciences Review*, 11(1): 36–51.

Karpoff, J.M., Lee, D.S., and Martin, G.S. (2008) 'The cost to firms of cooking the books', *Journal of Financial and Quantitative Analysis*, 43(3): 581–611.

Ludwick, R. and Zeller, R.A. (2001) 'The factorial survey: an experimental method to replicate real world problems', *Nursing Research*, 50(2): 129–33.

Nagin, D.S. and Pogarsky, G. (2001) 'Integrating celerity, impulsivity, and extralegal sanction threats into a model of general deterrence: theory and evidence', *Criminology*, 39(4): 865–92.

Nokes, K. and Hodgkinson, G.P. (2017) 'Policy-capturing: an ingenious technique for exploring the cognitive bases of work-related decisions', in R.J. Galavan, K.J. Sund, and G.P. Hodgkinson (eds), *Methodological Challenges and Advances in Managerial and Organizational Cognition*, Emerald Publishing, pp 95–121.

Oll, J., Hahn, R., Reimsbach, D., and Kotzian, P. (2018) 'Tackling complexity in business and society research: the methodological and thematic potential of factorial surveys', *Business & Society*, 57(1): 26–59.

Paternoster, R. and Simpson, S. (1996) 'Sanction threats and appeals to morality: testing a rational choice model of corporate crime', *Law & Society Review*, 30(3): 549–83.

Pickett, J.T., Roche, S.P., and Pogarsky, G. (2018) 'Toward a bifurcated theory of emotional deterrence', *Criminology*, 56(1): 27–58.

Piquero, N.L. (2012) 'The only thing we have to fear is fear itself: investigating the relationship between fear of falling and white-collar crime', *Crime & Delinquency*, 58(3): 362–79.

Piquero, N.L., Exum, M.L., and Simpson, S.S. (2005) 'Integrating the desire-for-control and rational choice in a corporate crime context', *Justice Quarterly*, 22(2): 252–80.

Piquero, N.L., Kanvinde, V., and Sanders, W. (2021) 'Factorial surveys and crime vignettes', in B. Van Rooij and D.D. Sokol (eds), *The Cambridge Handbook of Compliance* (1st edn), Cambridge University Press, pp 773–9.

Pogarsky, G. (2002) 'Identifying "deterrable" offenders: Implications for research on deterrence', *Justice Quarterly*, 19(3): 431–52.

Pogarsky, G. (2004) 'Projected offending and contemporaneous rule-violation: implications for heterotypic continuity', *Criminology*, 42(1): 111–36.

Rorie, M. (2015) 'An integrated theory of corporate environmental compliance and overcompliance', *Crime, Law and Social Change*, 64(2–3): 65–101.

Rorie, M. (2022) 'Self-report surveys and factorial survey experiments', in M. Rorie and B. Van Rooij (eds), *Measuring Compliance: Assessing Corporate Crime and Misconduct Prevention* (1st edn), Cambridge University Press, pp 93–107.

Rorie, M. and West, M. (2022) 'Can "focused deterrence" produce more effective ethics codes? An experimental study', *Journal of White Collar and Corporate Crime*, 3(1): 33–45.

Rorie, M., Rinfret, S., and Pautz, M. (2015) 'The thin green line: examining environmental regulation and environmental offending from multiple perspectives', *International Journal of Law, Crime and Justice*, 43(4): 586–608.

Rorie, M., Simpson, S.S. and Boppre, B. (2018) 'Factorial survey research in the study of environmental regulatory processes', in W.H. Van Boom, P. Desmet, and P. Mascini (eds), *Empirical Legal Research in Action: Reflections on Methods and their Applications*, Edward Elgar Publishing, pp 137–72.

Rossi, P.H. (1979) 'Vignette analysis: uncovering the normative structure of complex judgments', in *Qualitative and Quantitative Social Research: Papers in Honor of Paul F. Lazarsfeld*, Simon and Schuster, pp 176–87.

Schoepfer, A., Piquero, N.L., and Langton, L. (2014) 'Low self-control versus the desire-for-control: an empirical test of white-collar crime and conventional crime', *Deviant Behavior*, 35(3): 197–214.

Simpson, S.S. (2002) *Corporate Crime, Law, and Social Control* (Cambridge studies in criminology), Cambridge University Press.

Simpson, S.S. (2013) 'White-collar crime: a review of recent developments and promising directions for future research', *Annual Review of Sociology*, 39(1): 309–31.

Simpson, S.S. and Piquero, N.L. (2002) 'Low self-control, organizational theory, and corporate crime', *Law & Society Review*, 36(3): 509–47.

Simpson, S.S., Garner, J., and Gibbs, C. (2011) 'Assessing punitive and cooperative strategies of corporate crime control for select companies operating in 1995 through 2000 [United States]: archival version', ICPSR – Interuniversity Consortium for Political and Social Research.

Simpson, S.S., Gibbs, C., Rorie, M., Slocum, L.A., Cohen, M.A., and Vandenbergh, M. (2013) 'An empirical assessment of corporate environmental crime-control strategies', *Journal of Criminal Law and Criminology*, 103(1): 231–78.

Simpson, S.S., Rorie, M., Alper, M., Schell-Busey, N., Laufer, W.S., and Smith, N.C. (2014) 'Corporate crime deterrence: a systematic review', *Campbell Systematic Reviews*, 10(1): 1–105.

Steiner, P.M., Atzmüller, C., and Su, D. (2016) 'Designing valid and reliable vignette experiments for survey research: a case study on the fair gender income gap', *Journal of Methods and Measurement in the Social Sciences*, 7(2): 52–94.

Taylor, B.J. (2005) 'Factorial surveys: using vignettes to study professional judgement', *British Journal of Social Work*, 36(7): 1187–207.

Taylor, B.J. and Zeller, R.A. (2007) 'Getting robust and valid data on decision policies: the factorial survey', *The Irish Journal of Psychology*, Routledge, 28(1–2): 27–41.

Van De Bunt, H. (2010) 'Walls of secrecy and silence: the Madoff case and cartels in the construction industry', *Criminology & Public Policy*, 9(3): 435–53.

Wallander, L. (2009) '25 years of factorial surveys in sociology: a review', *Social Science Research*, 38(3): 505–20.

Yeager, P.C. (2016) 'The elusive deterrence of corporate crime', *Criminology & Public Policy*, 15(2): 439–52.

6

Affective Atmosphere and White-Collar Crime: A Case of Transgressive Thrill in the Art Fair

Diāna Bērziņa

Introduction

Warr (2021, p 21), summarizing the work of Michel Serres, notes that we experience the world through 'our embodied perceptions' and we know the world 'through our sensorial experience'. Humans are influenced by a myriad of subconscious stimuli, only a fraction of which filters through to the conscious mind (Thrift, 2000; Walsh, 2002). Yet when it comes to law and analyzing crimes, harms, and justice, there is a separation between senses. For example, forensic investigations are visually oriented (Lam, 2012). Similarly, criminology itself is characterized by the 'ocular-centric way of thinking' (Herrity et al, 2021a, p xxiii). Information is gathered through vision and the researcher is distanced from the object of inquiry, and this distance is related to 'concepts of impartiality and objectivity' (Lam, 2012, p 162). As such there is a disconnect between the way we experience the world, namely via multiple senses, and the way we analyze it criminologically. As Thrift (2000, p 36) notes '[p]robably 95 percent of embodied thought is non-cognitive, yet probably 95 percent of academic thought has concentrated on the cognitive dimension of conscious "I"'.

McClanahan and South (2020) suggest that one way to approach the sensory dimensions of crime is through the concept of 'atmospheres'. I unpack this concept in more detail in the following section but here I want to note that atmospheres can be conceptualized 'as rooms of implicit moods that can be influenced intentionally' (Wolf, 2019, p 210). In other disciplines adjacent to criminology, such as social and cultural geography, law, philosophy, and architecture, research focused on senses and atmospheres has flourished (to name a few, Anderson, 2009; Philippopoulos-Mihalopoulos, 2013; Bille et al, 2015). Yet in criminology, apart from some notable exceptions (for example, Millie, 2019; Young, 2019; McClanahan and South, 2020; Fraser and Matthews, 2021; Herrity et al, 2021b), and more recently with a special issue of *Criminological Encounters* edited by Young, Rogers and McClanahan (2023) dedicated to affective and sensory criminologies, focus on a full sensorial experience has not been well established or embraced in the mainstream. In particular, there has been little sensory research done in the field of white-collar crime.

In white-collar crime research organizational culture has long been looked at 'as a key explanatory and causal variable' (Apel and Paternoster, 2009, p 29). Essentially, organizational culture is 'the shared social knowledge within an organization regarding the rules, norms, and values' (Colquitt et al, 2011, p 557). These norms, while often informal, exert strong influence on individual behaviour as 'they are essentially guidelines for social approval' (Tomlinson and Pozzuto, 2016, p 371) and 'intended to shape individual decisions' (Tomlinson and Pozzuto, 2016, p 369). Yet there is some criticism to the conclusion that 'a particular environment is "criminogenic"' (Apel and Paternoster, 2009, p 21). However, while the notion of organizational culture as it relates to white-collar crime is human-centred and related to the ways one might behave due to wanting to conform to the behaviour and expectations of other humans occupying the same [work]place, as I discuss later, the place itself is not a neutral background. Instead, it is 'active, lively, fragile, powerful and connected in ways that matter' (Franklin, 2017, p 204).

Therefore, in this chapter I discuss how the focus on the sensory and atmospheres has a potential to enrich our understanding of what might influence someone's behaviour and decision-making when it comes to white-collar crime. This chapter is primarily theoretical in nature and seeks to explore what a focus on unobservable structures and sensory modalities can add to our research on organizational culture and contextual factors. I will explore this by focusing on one type of white-collar space, namely sites of commerce related to art such as high-end art fairs. These provide a good example for exploring the importance of a place, atmosphere, and senses, and how those are designed to affect humans and their behaviour and to facilitate certain values. I focus on art fairs such as TEFAF and BRAFA[1] that specifically sell antiques and antiquities and look at them from the sensory/atmospheric perspective. I focus on one sense, namely touch. Through this I look at the ways in which space can be designed to affect people and potentially lead to transgressions or harms. These transgressions do not necessarily have to be illegal or harmful in a particular context, instead they can be seen as a 'safe rebellion' against societal norms and values that are operating outside the borders of the particular space.

By considering senses and atmospheres we can create a more nuanced, 'multi-layered form of theorizing' (Young, 2019, p 777) of organizational culture and norms and values that play out on an active background. This active background and unobservable structures affect us in a way that can be significant and important both theoretically and practically.

Some of the current challenges

On a practical level, white-collar crimes, and, more broadly, crimes of the powerful are difficult to research due in part to issues with access (Mackenzie, 2019; Croall, 2001). For those who operate in white-collar fields there might be a degree of risk involved in taking part in the research and not so much to gain (Mackenzie, 2019). Therefore, in some areas of white-collar crime, a large part of the data comes from a self-selecting group of people who are willing to speak to the researchers or to the media, or who write and publish their own autobiographic stories (Mackenzie and Yates, 2016; Cross, 2018).

On a theoretical level, as mentioned earlier, there is a disconnect between the way we experience the world, namely via multiple senses, and the way we analyze the world criminologically, and there is little attention paid to sensory/atmospheric experiences when it comes to white-collar crime. Prior research in the fields of organizational communication, psychology, and architecture has shown that white-collar spaces are affective (see, for example, Kożusznik et al, 2018). This organizational space is not just a passive backdrop on which human actions play out. Instead as Duff (2010, p 881 emphasis in original) notes '[t]o experience place is to be *affected by place*'. This suggests that it would be worthwhile to include place itself as a meaningful player in the research on white-collar crime, not only on white-collar spaces.

Workplace and affective atmospheres in white-collar crime research

The physical environment affects the way people interact with each other (Shah and Kesan, 2007, pp 351–5). Sailer and Penn (2010, p 12) note that humans participate in multiple networks based on 'spatial and social solidarities that emerge in a complex, simultaneous and multiplex way'. This means that humans are enmeshed in the networks of relationships between other humans and non-humans that constitute a particular space or place, and they exert a degree of influence on each other. In turn, affective atmospheres are inspired by 'the lived sensation, the feel, and emotional resonance of place' (Duff, 2010, p 881). Atmospheres are 'spaces configured in the totality of sensory information' (McClanahan and South, 2020, p 13). Fraser and Matthews (2021, p 4) note that by focusing on affective atmospheres, we can address 'a broad range of material, sensory and affective relations that shape human capacity for action'. In other words, atmospheres can influence people's behaviour. Affect is experienced 'both as a particular feeling state and as a *distinctive variation in one's willingness or capacity to act* in response to that state' (Duff, 2010, p 882, emphasis in original).

While the concept of atmosphere might seem vague, researchers during fieldwork often rely on instinct which is 'often the unconscious ... processing of sensory data ... [and] we [the researchers] can 'sense' a shift in mood or atmosphere' (Herrity et al, 2021a, p xxv). Furthermore, the affect being engineered through material structures is not a vague, theoretical concept only. Miller (2014, p 14) describes the emergent 'biopolitical strategy', which is 'the engineering of affect through urban design'. As Kindynis (2021, p 620) notes, through biopolitical strategies 'certain bodily and emotional dispositions are now being actively designed or "scripted" into (urban) space'.

To bring it back to white-collar crime research, what follows is that if organizational culture and contexts affect the individual's decision-making and behaviour in some way when it comes to white-collar crime, then we also need to consider the place in which the organizational culture comes in contact with people. From what I have already discussed, a place can be conceptualized as an affective and active construction, which is embedded in relations between humans and non-humans. It is created so that it elicits specific bodily and emotional dispositions. By attuning to this, we can understand contexts where white-collar actors operate and better understand relations between people, the material world, and sensory experiences.

Addressing current challenges in white-collar crime research

All of the above said, I propose that perhaps one way to address some of the challenges discussed is by incorporating the concept of atmospheres and the sensory perspective into white-collar crime research. Through this we can approach this crime with a different toolkit, enrich our understanding of what might influence someone's behaviour and decision-making, and supplement more traditional, mainstream criminological approaches.

Additionally, to address the lack of representative diversity we, as researchers, can explore white-collar spaces using our own senses to better understand how the place – the background on which the organizational culture plays out – is experienced by those who work there. We can immerse ourselves in the environment and analyze what circumstances and qualities of a place can perhaps make someone more susceptible to engaging in harmful or illegal behaviour. The researchers can use their own senses and experiences as a tool to understand the less tangible qualities of the settings they are studying. This approach is also necessary in order to not only observe the behaviour of people but also to experience the physical environment ourselves as much as possible to understand 'the "why" of what we observe' (Schein, 1983, p 2). This approach can then be supplemented with interviews.

Methodological note

By attending 'to sensory aspects of social experience' we can traverse boundaries 'between the subjectivity and commonality of experience ... [and] arrive at shared meaning and understanding' (Herrity et al, 2021a, p xxviii). Following this, by focusing on the sensory aspects and atmosphere of a shared place, we can attend to the ways that senses are used to condition us to view certain situations, objects, or encounters in a specific way. Data for this research was gathered during the observational experiential fieldwork carried out as part of the larger European Research Council-funded Trafficking Transformations project.[2] This approach sees the researcher's own experiences as a tool to understand the less tangible qualities of the settings under study. The researcher uses their own senses to experience the space, consider its implications, and then watch how other people appear to navigate the same space. These observations are supplemented in the moment by unstructured and incidental interviews in the form of conversations with people who are also experiencing these spaces.

The approach was inspired by sensory ethnography (Pink, 2009), and research on atmospheres by Young (2019) and Fraser and Matthews (2021). To be able to describe an experience clearly and distinctly it is important to immerse oneself 'in sites of other people's experiences' (Pink et al, 2016, p 21). Additionally, as atmospheres are perceived through the body 'in order to say what they are ... one must expose oneself to them' (Böhme, 2013, p 2). Therefore, I strategically placed myself within art commerce spaces to experience the atmosphere of the place, note sensory elements and observe the actions and reactions of other people present within the particular space.

Staging the high-end art fair

An art fair is 'a booth-style convention show' which brings together various people from the art world, such as dealers, collectors, and curators (Garner, 2020). Art fairs are 'designed to amass a global audience within a single place, and are the epicentres of art business' (Argun, 2022). It is an opportunity for the dealers to display their artworks to a large audience and find new buyers; in the same way, collectors have a chance to view numerous works of art offered by a wide variety of dealers. Large art fairs are essentially 'platforms of sale' (Morgner, 2014, p 38). However, there is some uneasiness that comes with this, with some exhibitors noting that they do not want their galleries to appear like a shop, instead they want 'to represent and mediate the art' (Schultheis, 2017, p 5).

As I have explored in more detail elsewhere (Bērziņa, 2025), despite being places of commerce, art fairs create an atmosphere which masks the sensory experiences that we associate with commerce, while still allowing for commerce to happen as perceptions 'can be manipulated by carefully controlling sensations' (Krishna, 2012, p 14). One way this is achieved is through creating associations with a museum by staging an atmosphere of a museum-like space which then can affect and guide people's behaviour (Böhme, 2013; Bille et al, 2015). It is a particular atmosphere which is 'an enhanced presence of a ... complex idea' (Hauskeller and Rice, 2019, p 150). Art fairs mimic a few chosen familiar attributes (in terms of the physicality of the objects and their setting) of a museum-like space and then 'our brains ... relate incoming sensations to imagery of other events or sensations already in our memory' (Solomon et al, 2010, p 132). Outside of the art fair space, many galleries also reflect 'the distinction between art and commerce' through layouts where the front display area 'is a museum-like space where artwork is exhibited' (Thompson, 2008, p 207). However, the replicated atmosphere is based on a specific idea of a museum experience, which in many instances is now outdated due to museums evolving into 'spaces of learning for people of all ages and backgrounds' (Agbisit, 2021). Yet in the high-end art fairs, it is expressed as a more 'traditional' museum experience. This traditional museum atmosphere can be described as 'temple-like' (Classen, 2017, p 1).

In a traditional museum experience, visitors are meant to show a sensory restraint (Classen, 2007). Cox et al (2016, p 5) note that 'art plays upon our nervous systems but is frequently understood through language, text and reading as the privileged means of analysis and representation'. Instead of touching, we are meant to look at objects from a distance and read the accompanying informative labels. Therefore, historically in a museum space touch has been seen as transgressive and has been linked to concepts of damage, vandalism, and theft (see Candlin, 2008 on history of touch in museums; Classen and Howes, 2006).

Yet within an art fair setting (focusing on antiques and antiquities), touch is encouraged, for example, by dealers who routinely pick the objects up or hand the objects to the buyers for them to look at it more closely. Touching increases the likelihood that the object will be purchased (see Ranaweera, 2021 on the importance of touch for consumers), and touch serves 'as a synecdoche for luxury consumption' (Mathiowetz, 2010). Therefore, art fairs create 'a high-society cultural experience' (Yates and Mackenzie, 2021, p 122), where touch is used as a sales technique and as a way to create a lure and promote desire for the objects offered in art fairs.

Duncan (1995, p 8) has conceptualized the art museums as ritual sites that 'represent beliefs about the order of the world'. Many museums reinforce the specific world order and rules such as that culturally valuable objects should not be touched. Art fairs then, by attempting to mask their commercial nature through a recreation of an atmosphere of a museum-like space, also by extension inherit association with the rules of a particular world order. However, art fairs do not reinforce the rules of a particular world order or social values. On the contrary, they encourage a subtle transgression, in this case expressed through touch, against societal norms and rules inherent in the museum-ritual site space.

Implications for white-collar crime research

Art fairs are white-collar spaces; high-end art fairs attract elite art galleries and elite clientele. Perhaps the best way to describe high-end art fair experience is by looking at the marketing of The Other Art Fair, which aims to provide affordable works of art. The rationale behind its creation was described as 'Art should never be elite. Here, art is for everyone … You belong here'.[3] As such the high-end art fairs are more exclusionary, opulent, and in some ways intimidating for those who are not familiar with this environment. Many types of art crime can be seen as white-collar crimes (Balcells, 2015; Mackenzie, 2019). High-end art fairs are white-collar spaces; therefore, perhaps by analyzing an art fair from a sensory and atmosphere perspective, we can learn some lessons that can be applicable to white-collar spaces and perhaps make some inferences about associated white-collar harms and crimes.

By attempting to avoid the atmosphere of a commerce-space and instead focusing on mimicking features of a museum-space, art fairs have created a by-product: a place which allows for a guided shedding of norms and rules that normally saturate our lives in a museum and outside of it (see Philippopoulos-Mihalopoulos, 2013 on lawscapes). This does not mean that art fairs encourage crime to happen within art fairs themselves. Instead, they recreate specific structures and encourage the emergence of specific atmospheres associated with a specific space, while at the same time controlling for transgressions that normally would not be allowed to occur in the original space. It is a permissible shedding of those norms. It is a transformation of mundane activities such as shopping 'into moments of thrill' (Hudson, 2015, p 293). It is a setting that exerts influence on an unconscious level and can perhaps influence people to believe in an image that on a conscious level they would reject, such as not questioning potential harms that might be bundled with objects with an unclear origin (see Walsh, 2002 on marketing ideas that affect person's unconscious and influence their behaviours and beliefs).

To bring these ideas to white-collar crime, focus on the senses and atmospheres in white-collar crime research would uncover the subtle ways in which people are encouraged to transgress or explore how certain atmospheres can make people more susceptible to not questioning certain behaviours or practices. Huisman (2020, p 141) notes that there is a divide between scholars who argue that the goal-seeking nature of organizations makes them 'inherently criminogenic' while others argue that it is not 'the nature of the goals that is criminogenic, but the pressure to attain them'. While not the focus of this chapter, it is worth considering that while pressure can be put on to employees by other employees and leaders, and can be expressed through the set norms and values (that is, the culture) of the organization, we also need to consider how certain atmospheres can be used to put pressure on people to attain certain goals or create a 'lure'.

Shover and Hochstetler (2010, p 115) have defined lure as 'arrangements or situations that turn heads'. They write that when lure 'is encountered, it serves as a reminder of what is desired', but it is 'not a criminal opportunity, and it does not evoke a uniform response' (Shover and Hochstetler, 2010, p 116). Lure is something that people want; it is a temptation. People can make a choice to follow this temptation or not. However, the seemingly rational economic decision-making is implicated in webs of relations that are more than just about simple cost-benefit analysis (for a similar discussion see Sheller's (2004) research on automobility). As the examples from the art spaces show, environments can be created to promote the lure and desire that can affect at least some people either on a conscious or subconscious level. As Katz (1988, p 5) writes '[o]nly rarely do we actually experience ourselves as subjects directing our conduct'. Hudson (2015, p 293) describes how specific atmospheres can be generated to 'galvanise' human behaviour and transform mundane activities into more exciting moments. Therefore, certain atmospheres can be created around 'objects and ideas' and through that 'focus people's attention on them' (Hauskeller and Rice, 2019, p 149). For example, they can be used to facilitate competitiveness, to emphasize the attainment of particular goals, and to create moments of thrill to attain these goals. In some instances, a 'successful, invisibilisation of the law' (Philippopoulos-Mihalopoulos, 2015, p 107) is achieved, where outside rules seem to be suspended.

Many criminological theories use the insight that 'criminal motives, norms, techniques, and opportunities are influenced by the company one keeps' (Papachristos et al, 2012, p 406). Similarly, when it comes to white-collar crime the focus tends to be on human elements and their interactions, norms, values, and corporate practices. However, the atmospheric qualities of the organization, which can be traced around the sensory, material, and emotive elements of the [work]place, exert a degree of influence on humans as well. While this a felt presence, it is hard to describe and put it into words. As a response to it, people can act in different ways, sometimes in a way that is unexplainable to others or even themselves.

While organizational culture and contextual factors can play an important role in the decision-making process, the place itself and the physical environment can also contribute to this process and affect human behaviour. While these ideas might seem very subtle, and some perhaps might argue that it is people and the company one keeps rather than sensory modalities or material relations affecting people, experiential fieldwork hints at a more complex picture. Just by being in certain settings without other humans directly interacting with us, we can be affected by the place and atmosphere. By attuning to more-than-human affects, we can add another layer to processes that influence the way humans behave.

Rhys-Taylor (2013, p 405) notes that '[w]hat people say about their own lives … will always be important … However, it is at the level of the nondiscursive, or the sensuous, that we get a taste of the processes that are shaping the culture.' Similarly, while insights gathered from the interviews with white-collar actors will always be important, by looking 'seriously [at] the ephemeral and fleeting senses that we encounter in the field but that do not achieve the requisite stability to enter into language, let alone theoretical interpretation' (Cox et al, 2016, p 9), we can better understand the frameworks that guide and reinforce certain beliefs and behaviours. Researching the sensory and atmospheres requires a reflexive approach. This approach requires researchers to look at their own experiences as a tool to understand the 'ephemeral and fleeting senses' (Cox et al, 2016, p 9) at play in the settings under study.

Conclusion

By using as an example high-end art fairs, I briefly highlighted how space can be designed to create an immersive, multisensory experience that is designed to affect people in particular ways, such as encouraging desire and consumption. The sensory and emotional feel of the place inspire affective atmospheres that are supported by utilizing a variety of senses. These atmospheres are designed to affect people on an unconscious level, as other research focusing on traditional consumer spaces (Walsh, 2002; Hudson, 2015) has noted. The place, with its specific atmosphere and sensorial cues, can play a role and affect emotions and actions of the people that are a part of this space.

Organizational culture is argued to play an important role in white-collar crime. However, in white-collar crime research, organizational culture is often conceived of as a collection of values, norms, and beliefs shared by the people of the same organization. Emotional or sensorial components are not often considered as a part of this culture. Furthermore, organizational culture plays out on an active background – that is [work]place. By incorporating the concept of atmospheres, and the sensory perspective into white-collar crime research, we, as researchers, can utilize our own reflexive and critical engagement with a particular setting to understand sensorial, affective, and atmospheric aspects of white-collar spaces. We can attune to the ways the unobservable structures, sensory modalities, and material relations can prompt and deform our perceptions, emotions, and interpretations – and as such affect the actions we take and the decisions we make. As Katz (1988, p 4) writes '[t'he particular seductions and compulsions they [offenders] experience may be unique to crime, but the sense of being seduced and compelled is not. To grasp the magic in the criminal's sensuality, we must acknowledge our own.'

On a more practical level, through accounting for sensorial and atmospheric elements, we can understand better what affects human decision-making processes and behaviour and accordingly look for points of interventions to reduce or prevent illegal or harmful behaviours. Wall (2019, p 148) notes 'a cyclical relation between atmosphere and behaviour', meaning that while atmosphere 'puts pressure' on how to behave, our 'demeanor and behaviour' contribute to the shaping of atmosphere. This is a self-feeding loop: place and atmospheres affect people, but by conforming to them, people re-make and reinforce them. Through being a part of a place with a specific atmosphere some values and behaviours that, outside of this place, might go against social norms and values (such as touching valuable works of art) or bring a range of harms can become normalized. Similarly, place can affect people by creating a discrepancy between the life one leads and 'the idealized self-image' (Walsh, 2002), for example, by trying to fit not only within a specific organizational culture but also within a physical place. Perhaps one possible point of intervention could be limiting the emergence or 'strength' of specific atmospheres through visual cues or sounds. Perhaps this could be achieved through displaying visual signs of potential harms or crimes to make sure that the law does not disappear into the background, and making it impossible to achieve 'successful, invisibilisation of the law' (Philippopoulos-Mihalopoulos, 2015, p 107).

The additions to more traditional approaches and criminological theories of crime might be subtle, but these questions and their implications for white-collar crime research should be at least considered, so that we can better reflect our lived sensorial experiences, and provide a more nuanced, multilayered understanding of human behaviour and decision-making.

Notes

[1] TEFAF – The European Fine Art Fair, an annual art, antiques, and design fair held in Maastricht, the Netherlands; BRAFA – Brussels Art Fair, an annual art and antiques fair held in Brussels, Belgium.

[2] The Trafficking Transformations project has been granted ethical approval by Maastricht University's Ethics Review Committee Inner City Faculties (ERCIC).

[3] The Other Art fair. 'About'. Available from: https://www.theotherartfair.com/about/

Funding acknowledgment
The funding for this research was provided by the European Research Council (ERC) under the European Union's Horizon 2020 research and innovation programme (grant agreement: 804851).

References

Agbisit, J.B. (2021) 'Are traditional museums and galleries on the brink of extinction?', *The Asean*, 19 November. Available from: https://theaseanmagazine.asean.org/article/are-traditional-museums-and-galleries-on-the-brink-of-extinction/

Anderson, B. (2009) 'Affective atmospheres', *Emotion, Space and Society*, 2(2): 77–81.

Apel, R. and Paternoster, R. (2009) 'Understanding "criminogenic" corporate culture: what white-collar crime researchers can learn from studies of the adolescent employment–crime relationship', in S.S. Simpson and D. Weisburd (eds), *The Criminology of White-Collar Crime*, Springer, pp 15–33.

Argun, E. (2022) 'Art Market 101: what is an art fair?', MyArtBroker, 20 October. Available from: https://www.myartbroker.com/collecting/articles/what-is-an-art-fair

Balcells, M. (2015) 'Art crime as white-collar crime', in J. Kila and M. Balcells (eds), *Cultural Property Crime*, Brill, pp 96–110.

Bērziņa, D. (2025) 'Cultivating desire: touch and transgressive thrill in the art fair', *Advances in Archaeological Practice*, 1–14. doi:10.1017/aap.2024.36

Bille, M., Bjerregaard, P., and Sørensen, T.F. (2015) 'Staging atmospheres: materiality, culture, and the texture of the in-between', *Emotion, Space and Society*, 15: 31–8.

Böhme, G. (2013) 'The art of the stage set as a paradigm for an aesthetics of atmospheres', *Ambiances*, 1–9.

Candlin, F. (2008) 'Museums, modernity and the class politics of touching objects', in H. Chatterjee (ed), *Touch in Museums*, Routledge, pp 9–20.

Classen, C. (2007) 'Museum manners: the sensory life of the early museum', *Journal of Social History*, 40(4): 895–914.

Classen, C. (2017) *The Museum of the Senses: Experiencing Art and Collections*, Bloomsbury.

Classen, C. and Howes, D. (2006) 'The museum as sensescape: Western sensibilities and indigenous artifacts', in E. Edwards, C. Gosden, and R.B. Phillips (eds), *Sensible Objects*, Bloomsbury Academic, pp 199–222.

Colquitt, J., LePine, J.A., and Wesson, M.J. (2011) *Organisational Behavior: Improving Performance and Commitment in the Workplace* (2nd edn), McGraw-Hill Irwin.

Cox, R., Irving, A., and Wright, C. (2016) 'Introduction', in R. Cox, A. Irving, and C. Wright (eds), *Beyond Text? Critical Practices and Sensory Anthropology*, Manchester University Press, pp 1–19.

Croall, H. (2001) *Understanding White Collar Crime*, Open University Press.

Cross, C. (2018) 'Victims' motivations for reporting to the "fraud justice network"', *Police Practice and Research*, 19(6): 550–64.

Duff, C. (2010) 'On the role of affect and practice in the production of place', *Environment and Planning D: Society and Space*, 28(5): 881–95.

Duncan, C. (1995) *Civilizing Rituals: Inside Public Art Museums*, Routledge.

Franklin, A. (2017) 'The more-than-human city', *The Sociological Review*, 65(2): 202–17.

Fraser, A. and Matthews, D. (2021) 'Towards a criminology of atmospheres: law, affect and the codes of the street', *Criminology and Criminal Justice*, 21(4): 1–17.

Garner, A. (2020) 'What is an art fair? How to run a successful booth', *Tribeca Printworks*, 22 April. Available from: https://www.tribecaprintworks.com/what-is-an-art-fair/

Hauskeller, M. and Rice, T. (2019) 'A jungly feeling: the atmospheric design of zoos', in T. Griffero and M. Tedeschini (eds), *Atmosphere and Aesthethics: A Plural Perspective*, Palgrave Macmillan, pp 147–58.

Herrity, K., Schmidt, B.E., and Warr, J. (2021a), 'Introduction: welcome to the sensorium', in K. Herrity, B.E. Schmidt, and J. Warr (eds), *Sensory Penalities: Exploring the Senses in Spaces of Punishment and Social Control*, Emerald Publishing, pp xxi–xxxiv.

Herrity, K., Schmidt, B.E., and Warr, J. (eds) (2021b) *Sensory Penalities: Exploring the Senses in Spaces of Punishment and Social Control*, Emerald Publishing.

Hudson, C. (2015) 'ION Orchard: atmosphere and consumption in Singapore', *Visual Communication*, 14(3): 289–308.

Huisman, W. (2020) 'Blurred lines: collusions between legitimate and illegitimate organizations', in M.L. Rorie (ed), *The Handbook of White-Collar Crime*, Hoboken: Wiley-Blackwell, pp 139–58.

Katz, J. (1988) *Seductions of Crime*, Basic Books.

Kindynis, T. (2021) 'Persuasion architectures: consumer spaces, affective engineering and (criminal) harm', *Theoretical Criminology*, 25(4): 619–38.

Kożusznik, M.W., Peiró, J.M., Soriano, A., and Navarro Escudero, M. (2018) '"Out of sight, out of mind?": The role of physical stressors, cognitive appraisal, and positive emotions in employees' health', *Environment and Behavior*, 50(1): 86–115.

Krishna, A. (2012) 'An integrative review of sensory marketing: engaging the senses to affect perception, judgment and behavior', *Journal of Consumer Psychology*, 22(3): 332–51.

Lam, A. (2012) 'Chewing in the name of justice: the taste of law in action', *Law Text Culture*, 16(1): 155–82.

Mackenzie, S. (2019) 'White-collar crime, organised crime and the challenges of doing research on art crime', in S. Hufnagel and D. Chappell (eds), *The Palgrave Handbook on Art Crime*, Routledge, pp 839–53.

Mackenzie, S. and Yates, D. (2016) 'Collectors on illicit collecting: higher loyalties and other techniques of neutralization in the unlawful collecting of rare and precious orchids and antiquities', *Theoretical Criminology*, 20(3): 340–57.

Mathiowetz, D. (2010) 'Feeling luxury: invidious political pleasures and the sense of touch', *Theory and Event*, 13(4): 1–31.

McClanahan, B. and South, N. (2020) '"All knowledge begins with the senses": towards a sensory criminology', *The British Journal of Criminology*, 60(1): 3–23.

Miller, J.C. (2014) 'Malls without stores (MwS): the affectual spaces of a Buenos Aires shopping mall', *Transactions of the Institute of British Geographers*, 39(1): 14–25.

Millie, A. (2019). 'Crimes of the senses: yarn bombing and aesthetic criminology', *The British Journal of Criminology*, 59(6): 1269–87.

Morgner, C. (2014) 'The art fair as network', *The Journal of Arts Management, Law, and Society*, 44(1): 33–46.

Papachristos, A.V., Meares, T.L., and Fagan, J. (2012) 'Why do criminals obey the law? The influence of legitimacy and social networks on active gun offenders', *Journal of Criminal Law and Criminology*, 102(2): 397–440.

Philippopoulos-Mihalopoulos, A. (2013) 'Atmospheres of law: senses, affects, lawscapes', *Emotion, Space and Society*, 7: 35–44.

Philippopoulos-Mihalopoulos, A. (2015). *Spatial Justice: Body, Lawscape, Atmosphere*: Routledge.

Pink, S. (2009) *Doing Sensory Ethnography*, Sage.

Pink, S., Horst, H., Postill, J., Hjorth, L., Lewis, T., and Tacchi, J. (2016) *Digital Ethnography: Principles and Practice*, Sage.

Ranaweera, A.T. (2021) 'When consumers touch: a conceptual model of consumer haptic perception', *Spanish Journal of Marketing – ESIC*, 26(1): 23–43.

Rhys-Taylor, A. (2013) 'The essences of multiculture: a sensory exploration of an inner-city street market', *Identities*, 20(4): 393–406.

Sailer, K. and Penn, A. (2010) *Towards an Architectural Theory of Space and Organisations: Cognitive, Affective and Conative Relations in Workplaces*, 2nd Workshop on Architecture and Social Architecture, Brussels, Belgium. Available from: https://discovery.ucl.ac.uk/id/eprint/1342930/

Schein, E.H. (1983) *Organizational Culture: A Dynamic Model*, Massachusetts Institute of Technology.

Schultheis, F. (2017) 'On the price of priceless goods: sociological observations on and around Art Basel', *Journal for Art Market Studies*, 1(1): 1–15.

Shah, R.C. and Kesan, J.P. (2007) 'How architecture regulates', *Journal of Architectural and Planning Research*, 24(4): 350–9.

Sheller, M. (2004) 'Automotive emotions: feeling the car', *Theory, Culture & Society*, 21(4–5): 221–42.

Shover, N. and Grabosky, P. (2010) 'White-collar crime and the Great Recession', *Criminology & Public Policy*, 9(3): 429–33.

Solomon, M.R., Bamossy, G., Askegaard, S., and Hogg, M.K. (2010) *Consumer Behaviour: A European Perspective* (4th edn), Pearson Education.

Thompson, D. (2008) *The $12 Million Stuffed Shark: The Curious Economics of Contemporary Art and Auction Houses*, Aurum.

Thrift, N. (2000) 'Still life in nearly present time: the object of nature', *Body and Society*, 6(3–4): 34–57.

Tomlinson, E.C. and Pozzuto, A. (2016) 'Criminal decision making in organizational contexts', in S. Van Slyke, M.L. Benson, and F.T. Cullen (eds), *The Oxford Handbook of White-Collar Crime*, Oxford University Press, pp 367–81.

Wall, I.R. (2019) 'Policing atmospheres: crowds, protest and "atmotechnics"', *Theory, Culture and Society*, 36(4): 143–62.

Walsh, B. (2002) 'Media literacy for the unconscious mind', *Journal of New Media & Culture*, 1(1). Available from: https://www.ibiblio.org/nmediac/winter2002/mind.html

Warr, J. (2021) 'Fire! Fire! The prison cell and the thick sensuality of trappedness', in K. Herrity, B.E. Schmidt, and J. Warr (eds), *Sensory Penalities: Exploring the Senses in Spaces of Punishment and Social Control*, Emerald Publishing, pp 19–33.

Wolf, B. (2019) 'Atmospheres of learning, atmospheric competence', in T. Griffero and M. Tedeschini (eds), *Atmosphere and Aesthethics: A Plural Perspective*, Palgrave Macmillan, pp 209–22.

Yates, D. and Mackenzie, S. (2021) 'Crime, material and meaning in art world Desirespaces', in N. Oosterman and D. Yates (eds), *Crime and Art: Sociological and Criminological Perspectives of Crimes in the Art World*, Springer Nature Switzerland, pp 119–34.

Young, A. (2019) 'Japanese atmospheres of criminal justice', *The British Journal of Criminology*, 59(4): 765–79.

Young, A., Rogers, J., and McClanahan, B. (2023) Special Isssue, *Criminological Encounters: Affective and Sensory Criminologies*, 6(1).

7

Beyond Mafia: Considerations on Criminal Infiltration in the Legal Economy

Giovanni Nicolazzo

Introduction

The infiltration of organized crime into legitimate businesses is a theme consistently discussed in academia. This phenomenon is characterized by the channelling of resources and exertion of control by organized crime syndicates into legal enterprises, a concept well supported by the literature (Savona et al, 2016; von Lampe et al, 2016). Savona et al (2016) map out this process: the existence of criminal organizations, actions carried out on their behalf, techniques used to infiltrate businesses, and finally, the active participation of criminals in business decision-making. This definition, while providing a conceptual framework, presents operational challenges due to the elusive nature of defining a criminal organization (Ruggiero, 1996; Levi and Maguire, 2004; Edwards and Levi, 2008).

The definition of 'criminal infiltration in the legal economy' has been applied across various contexts and sectors (Ferwerda and Unger, 2016; Palomo et al, 2016; Skinnari et al, 2016; Slak et al, 2016; May and Bhardwa, 2018).[1] Nonetheless, much of the literature has focused primarily on mafia-type organizations, mainly due to the Italian institutional landscape being suited for this area of research (Savona et al, 2016), initiating a series of studies focusing specifically on mafia-type infiltration in the legal economy. As the discipline became compartmentalized, scholars questioned whether the research focus should shift beyond the specific typology of criminal groups, proposing that the study of criminal infiltration should not be limited to the Italian mafia or similar structured criminal groups.

Structured criminal organizations, such as mafia-type groups, infiltrate the legal economy to invest revenues from illicit actions, among other reasons. Nevertheless, criminal activities are not monopolized by large, structured mafia groups. A wide array of actors, from individual freelance criminals to the mafia, coexist in illegal markets, and there is no reason why they should not coexist because of the criminal infiltration in the legal economy. As pointed out by Savona (2015), the international literature constantly rejects the hypothesis that large structured mafias operate as monopolies or oligopolies (Reuter and Haaga, 1989; Dorn et al, 2005). These findings are further supported by studies conducted on situations in Italy, which have only identified monopolistic behaviours in small areas, such as small villages or specific neighbourhoods in larger cities (Becchi, 1996; Paoli, 2002; Paoli and Reuter, 2008).

Understanding criminal infiltration of the legitimate economy requires overcoming the compartmentalization experienced in the literature and broadening its scope to include a range of structures, from large organizations to loosely connected networks (Ruggiero, 1996). This chapter explores the possibility of broadening the study of criminal infiltration in the legal economy, considering whether an integrated approach is advisable due to overlapping motivations, strategies, and tendencies among different criminal actors, or at least due to the validity of standard theoretical models.

Literature review

Since the 1970s, economists have focused on crime, with early studies by Schelling (1967),[2] Becker (1968),[3] and Reuter (1986)[4] exploring the economic interpretation of criminal activities and their intersection with the legal economy. These studies did not significantly address the profile of the actors involved, aside from recognizing their criminal nature.[5] In current studies on the topic, actor-centred approaches have become predominant, emphasizing understanding the influence of specific actors, typically structured organized crime groups, on the legal economy.

Building on the entrepreneurial paradigm of organized crime, Savona et al (2016) defined 'organized crime infiltration' into the legal economy as the channelling of resources and the exercise of control by organized crime syndicates into legal businesses. Their definition implies the existence of criminal organizations, actions carried out on their behalf, techniques used to infiltrate the business, and the active participation of criminals in business decision-making. Studies adopting this definition, while adhering rhetorically to a common conceptual framework, faced the dilemma of identifying who exactly infiltrates the legitimate economy and defining what an organized crime is (von Lampe et al, 2016). This created an illusion of coherence which highlights points of difference but did not engage in a discussion of them (von Lampe et al, 2016). In fact, the illegality of the actions under study was defined independently of the nature of the actors involved. At the same time, illegal practices among business executives have existed as long as those within criminal syndicates (Simpson, 2002). Nonetheless, the discipline experienced a compartmentalization into different branches in relation to the nature of the actors.

The definition provided by Savona et al (2016) was initially oriented towards the infiltration actions of mafia-type crime syndicates, aligning with Fantò (1999). In *L'impresa a partecipazione mafiosa (The Mafia-infiltrated Enterprise)*, Fantò (1999) identified the mafia enterprise as an economic unit partly fuelled by capital from criminal activities, aiming to produce and exchange licit services and goods, operating in official markets either legally or illegally. Similarly, Dalla Chiesa (2012) considered the mafia enterprise as formally legal but directly emanating from criminal organizations operating in a particular sector of agriculture, industry, or services, up to the most sophisticated financial services.

Scholars started doubting whether the focus on organized crime was justified and whether the focus should shift from organized crime groups to actual offences or their outcomes (Wall et al, 2016).[6] Some suggested that the viability of business should be studied, instead of merely focusing on the profile of criminals (Ruggiero, 1996; von Lampe et al, 2016).

Ruggiero (1996) pointed out that the division in studying economic crimes and crimes by criminal syndicates goes back to Sutherland (1983)'s concept of white-collar crime. Sutherland observed that economists, though well acquainted with business methods, rarely considered them in terms of crime. Conversely, sociologists, though often focused on criminal behaviour, seldom viewed crime as an element within business operations (Geis, 2016). Sutherland aimed to bridge this gap by integrating economic and sociological perspectives, presenting a comparison of crime in the upper or white-collar crime class, composed of respectable – or at least respected – business and professional men, and crime in the lower class, composed of those with low socioeconomic status. This approach led to the development of literature on white-collar crime and gave rise to the subcategory of corporate crime, which is defined as the 'conduct of a corporation, or employees acting on behalf of the corporation, which is proscribed and punishable by law' (Braithwaite, 2013).

Notably, this definition closely resembles that one criminal infiltration in the legal economy, which is different primarily in the nature of the actors involved – corporate entities and white-collar individuals in the former, and criminal syndicates in the latter. This division, leading to scattered knowledge in criminology, contradicts Sutherland (1983)'s initial goal of enhancing understanding of criminology by including crimes by non-traditional criminals, known as white-collar criminals, without aiming to split knowledge (Ruggiero, 1996). The profit-oriented nature of economic systems makes companies vulnerable to economic crime. Criminal action in the legal economy can be viewed as practices within the economic system that operate under a normative code prioritizing wealth accumulation – often at the expense of collective well-being. This criminogenic normative code, as articulated by Ruggiero (2013), facilitates the removal of moral constraints in the pursuit of wealth, inherently creating conditions conducive to economic crime.

Non-organized criminals may exploit legal economy for illicit purposes primarily for personal gain, rather than for the strategic objectives of criminal organizations (Gottschalk, 2023). Nonetheless, to analyze the plausible effect of different types of criminal presence in the legal economy, it is essential to adopt a conceptual framework that accounts for the motivations, opportunities, and willingness of individuals to engage in economic crime. This should be done without isolating the discipline into separate, non-communicating areas.

The problem of calling it 'infiltration'

This area of study is traditionally referred to as 'criminal infiltration in the legal economy'. The term 'infiltration' is widely used in the study of mafia-type groups and generally refers to cases where something initially absent is introduced and spreads in a new context. It is often used in discussing the translocation of mafia-type groups from their traditional origins in southern Italy to new territories, such as in central and northern Italy (Buonanno and Pazzona, 2014; Alessandri, 2016).[7]

The term 'infiltration', in conjunction with the terminology of 'penetration', appeared primarily in the US in the first study on criminal infiltration in the legal economy, where the central theoretical perspective used to decipher the phenomenon was still that of the alien theory. According to this theory, an external body penetrates and pollutes what was previously pure, creating the idea of an external threat (Cressey, 2017). This perception persists today. When the literature talks about infiltration, it describes or conceptualizes a phenomenon that comes from outside: the movement of mafia-type criminal groups from their traditional place to new places or the takeover of existing companies by criminal organizations. This is where the term 'infiltration' causes most of the problems.

The term 'infiltration' causes problems in three ways. First, it fails to consider whether the economic environment itself generates a threat to the criminal enterprise. Sometimes, the economic environment itself creates the conditions that stimulate the commission of economic crimes without needing an external underworld threat. Nonetheless, the conceptualization of infiltration still suggests an external threat generated outside the economic system. This perspective justifies a focus on criminal organizations that have their first source of income and specialization in illegal enterprises, such as drug trafficking, loan sharking, and gambling, aiming to pollute the legitimate system with this dirty money. This focus on such organized groups overlooks the fact that criminal organizations often commit and obtain resources from economic crimes that find their beginnings and their ends in the enterprise's environment.

Second, a strict conceptualization of the term 'infiltration' fails to consider the most common way for criminal groups or individuals to gain control of a business is to set it up in the first place rather than infiltrating an existing one. Studies using the term 'infiltration' may differ in what is being studied. A minority adopt a purist approach, considering only those cases where criminal groups take control of an existing company and thus infiltrate it. The vast majority, however, analyze all companies under the control of the criminals, including those set up directly by them. It is generally explained that it is not the company being infiltrated, but rather the legal, economic system as a whole, which ends up being also infiltrated in the case of a company incorporated by criminals since the beginning.

A third reason for departing from the use of the concept of 'criminal infiltration of the legal economy' is that it has been conceptualized as the action of a criminal organization. This definition generally implies that the tasks are planned collectively, the proceeds are shared, and further activities are attempted collectively (Ruggiero, 1996). However, this conceptualization has been inappropriate because the units of analysis have also included actions that, even if carried out by members of a criminal organization, were carried out independently, and proceeds were not necessarily shared.

For these reasons, this chapter replaces the terminology of 'criminal infiltration in the legal economy' with 'criminal participation' or 'criminal component'. These terms refer to all cases where company control is linked to criminals (or persons allegedly responsible for crimes). This shift in terminology aims to provide a more accurate and inclusive understanding of the phenomenon, encompassing both organized groups and individual actors operating within the economic system.

The need for a new case

Beyond the problem of terminology, it is a fact that research on organized crime infiltration in the legal economy has flourished in the context of mafia-type criminal groups. However, in those studies, the theoretical reasoning has not adopted theoretical models beyond the lens of the mafia-type paradigm, as it has not taken a comparative approach with other types of criminal groups to justify a standard theoretical interpretation of the different or similar features of those phenomena. Indeed, currently, the factors driving differences in the criminal component in relation to different types of criminal groups are not well understood, and a similar question has not yet been asked: is it advisable to adopt an integrated approach to the criminological study of infiltration into the legal economy due to overlapping motivations, strategies, and tendencies among different criminal actors – or at least due to the validity of standard theoretical models?

Considerations towards an integrated approach

Throughout the literature on criminal participation in the legal economy, it has been customary to analyze economic crime separately in relation to the profile of the actors. As Ruggiero (1996) reports, this separation, embryonically present in Sutherland (1983), has gradually crystallized, in many cases giving rise to two respective and distinct criminological disciplines: that of the analysis of criminal entrepreneurship by white-collar actors and that of the analysis of criminal participation by organized crime. In later years, the latter strand has further compartmentalized the analysis of criminal participation by mafia-type groups and the analysis of other types of criminal syndicates.

Ruggiero (1996) repeatedly suggested paying attention to the characteristics underlying the criminal component in the legal economy beyond limiting the study to the profile of the perpetrators. According to him, the hypothesis of a potential contagious effect in relation to the dynamic adopted by actors of a different nature to infiltrate the legal economy would allude to the fact that the techniques used in the commission of crimes should be more central than the social characteristics of those who use them (Ruggiero, 1996). This statement does not suggest that there are no differences with respect to the various forms of criminal participation. The features of criminal components may be influenced by the nature of actors, mainly when they are differently targeted by law enforcement, creating operational characteristics distinct from companies which are not under criminal control (Reuter, 1983). Nonetheless, moving beyond compartmentalization aims to encourage the development of holistic concepts that can be tailored to specific elements, lifting the necessity to examine similar phenomena through distinct analytical approaches as currently happens. Lifting such compartmentalization, indeed, may help identify patterns in other criminal actors that may be seen sooner and then applied to further criminal actors. By comparison, it is possible to better highlight the specificity of some criminal actors and in so doing further improve the reasoning and the understanding of the overall phenomena.

For instance, in the mid-1990s, the intense emotion aroused in public opinion by the mafia massacres led Italian economists to undertake systematic research on the mafia-type criminal economy; various explanations and interpretations were given for mafia-type entrepreneurial crime, some of them divergent, but all agreed that the mafia phenomenon was so specific in some features that it was not to be confounded or collapse with other types of criminal phenomena (Paoli, 1998; Champeyrache, 2017). This specificity even led to criticism of the application of models of entrepreneurial analysis to the mafia criminal phenomenon for overestimating the modernity of mafia groupings, neglecting both the historical time and place in which they were formed and the limitations imposed on their evolutionary path by their condition of opposition to state laws (Paoli, 1998).

These considerations seem to reject the call for a standard and integrated analysis of criminal entrepreneurship. But only apparently. Indeed, an integrated analysis would not avoid taking the profile of the actors into consideration, but would consider this in comparison with other actors, looking for theoretical references that may be more valid in general. Champeyrache (2017) advocated for considering the peculiarities of mafia-type infiltration, given that mafia operators are subject to severe constraints on several fronts which may affect the characteristics of their involvement in the legal economy, such as the difficulty of securing the commitment of their underworld partners in transactions, or the constant risk of being discovered by law enforcement authorities, which puts them very much under the radar. Nevertheless, these considerations – which call for not overlooking the specific environment and constraints in which mafia actors operate – are well established in the discipline of organised crime and do not apply exclusively to the mafia context. Some studies have suggested the hyper-simplicity of techniques employed by mafia-type actors in the realm of economic crime in relation to non-mafia actors. For instance, Nazzari and Riccardi (2024) analyzed 2,818 Italian offenders involved in money laundering. They showed a difference between mafia and non-mafia launderers, where the former were associated with the use of fewer jurisdictions and higher use of false invoicing, as well as of figureheads.

In contrast, for non-mafia criminals (predominantly tax offenders), a higher prevalence of misuse of the banking system was observed (Riccardi and Reuter, 2024). Nonetheless, these considerations – that call for the specificity of studying within the mafia-type declination mirror concept and theoretical formulation – are well established in the discipline of organized crime and do not refer exclusively to the mafia context. They are already addressed in the work of Reuter (1983) and, more broadly, assimilable to the famous paradigm of a trade-off between security and efficiency in criminal networks (Morselli et al, 2007). In fact, mafia individuals are under relevant law enforcement targeting, and this restricts the range of formal entrepreneurship they can declare; this is in line with what Reuter (1983) formulated in relation to the criminal enterprise paradigm. This justifies, for instance, the need for the mafia entrepreneurs to recruit frontmen. One notable manifestation of this practice is the disproportionately high level of female ownership observed in companies associated with mafia-type organizations (Savona et al, 2016). While increased female entrepreneurship is generally a positive development in a society, in this context, it often reflects a tactical response to law enforcement pressure. Research has shown that the rate of female ownership in such organizations significantly exceeds the average in the legitimate economy, suggesting that women are being used as nominal owners to shield the true controllers of these businesses. The security-efficiency trade-off is not the only example of a way in which the specificity of criminal components of the legal economy can be dealt with in a comparative analysis that expands the different types of profiles of criminal actors. The necessity and opportunity paradigms are suited for analysis of this kind. Among the most important antecedents to criminal participation in the legal economy and the techniques through which it is carried out, there are necessities felt by the offenders and the opportunities they face.

In that regard, criminal behaviour, independent of the type of criminal organization of which the criminal is part, acts as an essential explanation for the need for sophistication. This translates into identifying the characteristics of the criminal background of the subject, explaining what techniques he or she had to employ to achieve their ends, and thus to which techniques he or she is inclined: Levi and Soudijn (2020), in considering the factors determining the choice of money-laundering methods of organized crime actors, suggest that the form in which the revenues are generated – the amounts, the frequency, and regularity – influence the money-laundering decisions.

Apart from necessities, the opportunities clearly shaped the techniques used to put economic crime in place (Riccardi and Reuter, 2024). The rationality of offenders is never absolute (Cornish and Clarke, 1986), and it is constrained by both personal and environmental limits (Simon, 1955). Personal constraints, and the way these interact with the environment or evolve over the offender's life course, are at the centre of a wide variety of criminological perspectives, from age-graded theory (Sampson and Laub, 1995) to social learning (Akers, 1973), general strain or social disorganization theories, and others. As suggested by social embeddedness theory (Kleemans and van De Bunt, 1999), criminals can benefit from the social and cultural proximity of their peers to mitigate the risk implicit in criminal domains. When laundering money, offenders can rely on compatriots or extended family members (Malm and Bichler, 2013) by involving them as cash smugglers (Soudijn and Reuter, 2016) or as beneficiaries in informal financial transfer methods employed by their ethnic communities. Similarly, high-level corrupt politicians could benefit from the network of entrepreneurs and government officials in which they are embedded to facilitate the laundering of corruption money. Many forms of white-collar crimes are often depicted as highly technical offences (Gilmour, 2016; Tiwari et al, 2023), where the skills of offenders, their awareness and knowledge of accounting and financial techniques, are crucial in determining the likelihood of engaging in those offences, and the specific techniques employed.

Conclusion

An aggregate analysis of the criminal component of the legal economy is possible and feasible. Encouraging such aggregate analysis would help us better understand how the unique characteristics of different criminal actors interact with and shape the nature of criminal participation in the legal economy. An integrated approach allows us to consider the full complexity of these interactions, acknowledging the logic behind the actors' choices and the various constraints they face.

Traditionally, studies in this field have been compartmentalized, focusing narrowly on specific types of criminal activities or groups of offenders. This compartmentalization limits our ability to identify the specific features of criminal involvement and prevents us from applying general models of economic crime that have been developed in broader economic crime research. So far, the study of criminal participation in legitimate enterprises has not held a significant place within criminology and has often been examined predominantly from an economic perspective. Removing the compartmentalization and developing a comparative perspective may increase the criminological relevance of this area of study.

The goal of such an approach should be to demonstrate that it is both possible and beneficial to analyze criminal involvement in the legal economy on an aggregate level, rather than in isolated segments, by emphasizing that without compartmentalization the researcher can better identify the unique characteristics and patterns of criminal involvement across different contexts. Future research should aim to create integrated models that capture the complexities of criminal participation in the legal economy, combining insights from criminology, economics, sociology, and other relevant disciplines. Conducting comparative analyses across different jurisdictions and types of criminal actors can reveal how various legal, social, and economic environments influence criminal behaviours and strategies. A deeper understanding of the aggregate features of criminal involvement can inform the development of more effective policies and law enforcement practices aimed at preventing and combating criminal infiltration of legitimate businesses. At the same time, it may encourage collaboration between scholars from different fields which could lead to innovative approaches and methodologies, enhancing the overall quality and impact of research in this area.

In conclusion, moving beyond compartmentalized studies and embracing an integrated, comparative approach holds significant promise for advancing our understanding of criminal participation in the legal economy. This shift not only enriches academic discourse but also has practical implications for developing strategies to address and mitigate the impact of criminal activities within legitimate economic systems.

Notes

[1] For instance, in *Organised Crime in European Business* (Savona, Riccardi, and Berlusconi 2016), the definition of criminal infiltration in the legal economy has been widely applied across diverse contexts and sectors. Examples range from transportation companies facilitating transit crimes in the Netherlands (Ferwerda and Unger 2016), to bars and nightclubs connected to the sex market in Slovenia (Slak et al 2016), and welfare fraud schemes in Sweden (Skinnari, Korsell, and Ronnblom 2016). This demonstrates the adaptability of organized crime in exploiting sector-specific vulnerabilities and national contexts to integrate illicit activities into legitimate enterprises.

[2] Referring to the lack of interest in economic theory in the phenomena of criminal enterprise, Schelling pointed to the need for a more careful study capable of providing the analytical elements to understand the incentive structure and limits of organized crime, to assess the various types of social costs of criminal activity, and consequently to design appropriate repressive responses (Patalano, 2020 on Schelling, 1967). According to Schelling, an essential characteristic of a criminal organization is its exclusivity, that is, its monopoly. What counts, according to Schelling, is not the ability to provide illegal services but to suppress competing services and protect them from corruption. Schelling provided one of the first economic characterizations of criminal activity, leading to the abandonment of the ethnic characterization (Patalano, 2020, on Schelling, 1967).

[3] In the late 1960s, Becker initiated what became known as the economic model of crime, explaining criminal choice as the solution to an individual's decision to maximize his or her welfare (Becker, 1968). Becker's approach was later criticized due to the fact that it reduced criminal action to a game of possible gains and losses, ignoring plans of greater complexity that were later dealt with in other studies, such as Ehrlich (1973). See an overview in Marselli and Vannini (1999) or Masciandaro (1999).

[4] Reuter (1986) proposed a definition of organized crime as consisting of organizations characterized by longevity, hierarchy, and involvement in a variety of criminal activities, which, through violence or the credible threat thereof, have gained monopoly control of some critical illegal markets. Reuter added two other elements to the monopoly that characterizes criminal organizations: the systematic use of violence to obtain economic benefits, and the corruption of public authorities necessary to maintain and extend the privileges acquired.

[5] On the contrary, any ethical connotation was removed by defining a conceptual paradigm of organized crime based on the triad of monopoly-violence-corruption. The approach was then deepened by subsequent scholars who expanded the range of elements to include, for example, hierarchical structure and organization, continuity in the pursuit of criminal activity, the use or threat of violence, solidarity and links between members, illegal entrepreneurial activity, corrupt activity, and non-secondary penetration of legitimate markets. Over the years, various definitions of organized crime have been established: the German academic Klaus von Lampe identifies at least 180 (von Lampe et al, 2016).

[6] Wall, Chistyakova, and Bonino (2016, p 112) wrote: 'Are the right questions about organised crime being asked? Are investigators still tending to focus on the organised

crime groups rather than exploring the actual offence or its outcome? In other words, should an "enterprise approach" be taken that looks at the viability of the business rather than looking for criminals?'

7   For example, Buonanno and Pazzona (2014) use the term infiltration several times in their paper on the 'migrating mafia' to describe the expansion of the sphere of influence of Italian southern mafia organizations into the traditionally immune northern regions. It has also been used by Ravenda et al (2020), for example, to describe the process by which mafia-type organizations have taken part in public procurement, referring to it as 'infiltration in public procurement', or it is easily used to refer to the case where municipal councils are dissolved for mafia-related reasons, because the mafia exerts influence on the dynamics of the municipal council itself. In this case, the expression 'infiltration in municipal council' is generally used (Occhiuzzi, 2019). The word infiltration has a strong connotation and is used in a mafia context.

References

Akers, R.L. (1973) *Deviant Behavior: A Social Learning Approach*, Wadsworth Publishing Co.

Alessandri, A. (2016) 'L'espansione della criminalità organizzata nell'attività di impresa al Nord', *Rivista di Studi e Ricerche sulla Criminalità Organizzata*, 2: 3–62.

Becchi, A. (1996) 'Italy: "Mafia-dominated drug market"?', in N. Dorn, J. Jepsen, and E. Savona (eds), *European Drug Policies and Enforcement*, Palgrave Macmillan, pp 119–30.

Becker, G.S. (1968) 'Crime and Punishment: An Economic Approach', *Journal of Political Economy*, 76(2): 169–217.

Braithwaite, J. (2013) *Corporate Crime in the Pharmaceutical Industry*, Routledge.

Buonanno, P. and Pazzona, M. (2014) 'Migrating mafias', *Regional Science and Urban Economics*, 44: 75–81.

Champeyrache, C. (2017) 'La non neutralità dell'identità del proprietario: elementi di teorie dell'impresa legale-mafiosa', in *La mafia come impresa. Analisi del sistema economico criminale e delle politiche di contrasto*, FrancoAngeli.

Cornish, D.B. and Clarke, R.V.G. (1986) *The Reasoning Criminal: Rational Choice Perspectives on Offending*, Springer Verlag.

Cressey, D. (2017) *Theft of the Nation: The Structure and Operations of Organized Crime in America*, Routledge.

Dalla Chiesa, N. (2012) *L' impresa mafiosa: tra capitalismo violento e controllo sociale*, Cavallotti University Press.

Dorn, N., Levi, M., and King, L. (2005) 'Literature review on upper level drug trafficking', London: Home Office.

Edwards, A. and Levi, M. (2008) 'Preface: The organization of serious crimes: developments in research and theory', *Criminology & Criminal Justice*, 8(4): 359–61.

Fantò, E. (1999) *L'impresa a partecipazione mafiosa: economia legale ed economia criminale* (Strumenti/scenari, 5), Bari: Dedalo.

Ferwerda, J. and Unger, B. (2016) 'Organised crime infiltration in the Netherlands', in E.U. Savona, M. Riccardi, and G. Berlusconi (eds), *Organised Crime in European Businesses*, Routledge, Taylor & Francis Group, pp 35–50.

Geis, G. (2016) *White-Collar and Corporate Crime*, Oxford University Press.

Gilmour, N. (2016) 'Understanding the practices behind money laundering: a rational choice interpretation', *International Journal of Law, Crime and Justice*, 44: 1–13.

Gottschalk, P. (2023) 'The national authority in Norway is no serious economic crime office anymore? An empirical study of press releases', *Journal of Economic Criminology*, 2: 100021.

Kleemans, E.R. and van De Bunt, H.G. (1999) 'The social embeddedness of organized crime', *Transnational Organized Crime*, 5: 19–36.

Levi, M. and Maguire, M. (2004) 'Reducing and preventing organised crime: An evidence-based critique', *Crime, Law and Social Change*, 41(5): 397–469.

Levi, M. and Soudijn, M. (2020) 'Understanding the laundering of organized crime money', *Crime and Justice*, 49(1): 579–631.

Malm, A. and Bichler, G. (2013) 'Using friends for money: the positional importance of money-launderers in organized crime', *Trends in Organized Crime*, 16(4): 365–81.

Marselli, R. and Vannini, M. (2020) *Economia della criminalità: delitto e castigo come scelta razionale*, Economia e istituzioni.

Masciandaro, D. (1999) *Mercati e illegalità: economia e rischio criminalità in Italia*, Ricerche di base, Università commerciale Luigi Bocconi.

May, T. and Bhardwa, B. (2018) *Organised Crime Groups Involved in Fraud*, Palgrave Macmillan.

Morselli, C., Giguère, C., and Petit, K. (2007) 'The efficiency/security trade-off in criminal networks', *Social Networks*, 29(1): 143–53.

Nazzari, M. and Riccardi, M. (2024) 'Cleaning mafia cash: an empirical analysis of the money laundering behaviour of 2800 Italian criminals', *European Journal of Criminology*, 21(4): 583–608.

Occhiuzzi, F. (2019) 'The dissolution of municipal councils due to organized crime infiltration', *European Journal of Interdisciplinary Studies*, 5(2): 16–29.

Palomo, J., Marquez, J., and Laguma, P. (2016) 'From drug trafficking to wholesale trade business', in E.U. Savona, M. Riccardi, and G. Berlusconi (eds), *Organised Crime in European Businesses*, Routledge, Taylor & Francis Group, pp 65–85.

Paoli, L. (1998) 'Il contratto di status nelle associazioni mafiose', *Quaderni di Sociologia*, 18: 73–97.

Paoli, L. (2002) 'The paradoxes of organized crime', *Crime, Law and Social Change*, 37(1): 51–97.

Paoli, L. and Reuter, P. (2008) 'Drug trafficking and ethnic minorities in Western Europe', *European Journal of Criminology*, 5(1): 13–37.

Patalano, R. (2020) *Capitalismo criminale: Analisi economica del crimine organizzato*, Giappichelli Editore.

Ravenda, D., Argilés-Bosch, J.M., and Valencia-Silva, M.M. (2020) 'Detection model of legally registered mafia firms in Italy', *European Journal of Political Economy*, 64: 101923.

Reuter, P. (1983) *Disorganized Crime: The Economics of the Visible Hand*, MIT Press.

Reuter, P. (1986) *Disorganized Crime: The Economics of the Visible Hand* (3rd edn), MIT Press.

Reuter, P. and Haaga, J. (1989) 'The organization of high-level drug markets: an exploratory study', Rand Corporation. Available from: https://www.rand.org/pubs/notes/N2830.html

Riccardi, M. and Reuter, P. (2024) 'The varieties of money laundering and the determinants of offender choices', *European Journal on Criminal Policy and Research*, 30: 333–58.

Ruggiero, V. (1996) *Economie sporche. L'impresa criminale in Europa*, Bollati Boringhieri.

Ruggiero, V. (2013) *I crimini dell'economia: una lettura criminologica del pensiero economico*, Feltrinelli (Campi del sapere).

Sampson, R.J. and Laub, J.H. (1995) *Crime in the Making: Pathways and Turning Points Through Life*, Harvard University Press.

Savona, E.U. (2015) 'The businesses of Italian mafias', *European Journal on Criminal Policy and Research*, 21(2): 217–36.

Savona, E.U., Riccardi, M., and Berlusconi, G. (eds) (2016) *Organised Crime in European Businesses*, Routledge, Taylor & Francis Group.

Schelling, T.C. (1967) *Arms and Influence* (10th edn), Yale University Press.

Simon, H.A. (1955) 'A behavioral model of rational choice', *The Quarterly Journal of Economics*, 69(1): 99.

Simpson, S.S. (2002) *Corporate Crime, Law, and Social Control*, Cambridge University Press.

Skinnari, J., Korsell, L., and Ronnblom, H. (2016) 'Welfare fraud and criminal infiltration in Sweden', in E.U. Savona, M. Riccardi, and G. Berlusconi (eds), *Organised Crime in European Businesses*, Routledge, Taylor & Francis Group, pp 87–102.

Slak, B., Modic, M., Eman, K., and Ažman, B. (2016) 'The sex market, bars, and nightclubs: criminal infiltration in Slovenia', in E.U. Savona, M. Riccardi, and G. Berlusconi (eds), *Organised Crime in European Businesses*, Routledge, Taylor & Francis Group, pp 51–64.

Soudijn, M. and Reuter, P. (2016) 'Cash and carry: the high cost of currency smuggling in the drug trade', *Crime, Law and Social Change*, 66(3): 271–90.

Sutherland, E.H. (1983) *White Collar Crime*, Greenwood Press.

Tiwari, M., Ferrill, J., Gepp, A., and Kum, K. (2023) 'Factors influencing the choice of technique to launder funds: the APPT framework', *Journal of Economic Criminology*, 1: 100006.

von Lampe, K., Savona E.U., Riccardi M., and Berlusconi G. (eds) (2016) 'Organised crime in European businesses', *Crime, Law and Social Change*, 67: 223–8.

Wall, D., Chistyakova, Y., and Bonino, S. (2016) 'Organised crime infiltration in the UK', in E.U. Savona, M. Riccardi, and G. Berlusconi (eds), *Organised Crime in European Businesses*, Routledge, Taylor & Francis Group, pp 102–17.

8

A Novel Typology of Frauds in Sports: Scripts, Perpetrators, and Bearers of the Associated Harm

Sofie Gotelaere and Letizia Paoli

Introduction

Over the past decades, numerous scandals have revealed various fraudulent activities in the sports sector. These scandals have frequently made the headlines across traditional and social media, and elicited strong emotional reactions from millions of sports fans and the general public (see, for example, Strauss et al, 2024). While often not explicitly presented as such, these frauds constitute very prominent cases of white-collar crime. In fact, they are often exemplars of the well-honed conceptual categories used in the white-collar crime literature (see, for example, Friedrichs, 2009), as they range from corporate to occupational crime and deviance, and involve 'legitimate' sportspeople and sports organizations, both as perpetrators and victims.

Some of the fraudulent activities occurring in sports are specific to the sports sector, such as doping and match-fixing. These are usually committed by athletes, though rarely in isolation. Doping frequently involves the complicity of teams and, in some cases, the encouragement or instigation by national sport federations and/or state authorities. Similarly, athletes participating in match-fixing are often manipulated and bribed by illegal entrepreneurs eager to make money in the gambling industry. Notable examples include the multiple doping cases that have 'rocked' cycling since the Festina scandal in 1998 (see, for example, Paoli et al, 2022), the state-sponsored doping of dozens of Russian athletes participating in Olympic competition (see, for example, Rodchenkov, 2020), and the repeated uncovering of match-fixing schemes across various sports, like football and tennis (see, for example, Hill, 2010a; Sieff, 2023).

Other fraudulent activities in sports are generic, resembling frauds that also occur in other economic sectors. These range from tax and subsidy fraud to embezzlement and are perpetrated by individuals – whether athletes or other stakeholders – and organizations, most often sports clubs. Although these non-sports-specific frauds usually attract less attention than their sports-specific counterparts, several high-profile scandals have disclosed the former, too. For instance, the 2015 FIFA corruption scandal exposed bribery, tax evasion, and wire fraud involving multiple executives of football's global governing body – one of the world's wealthiest sports organizations (Conn, 2017). That same year, the release of the 'Football Leaks' reports shed light on numerous instances of fraud involving major European clubs, players, and agents, including tax fraud and violations of financial fair play regulations (Buschmann and Wulzinger, 2018). In Belgium, the criminal investigation 'Clean Hands', which became public in 2018, revealed that various types of fraud also repeatedly occurred in Belgian professional football, ranging from match-fixing to tax evasion and money laundering (Gotelaere and Paoli, 2024).

Probably due to the numerous manifestations of frauds in sports (and other economic sectors), no comprehensive effort has yet been made to develop a typology, or even a conceptualization, of sports-related fraud that encompasses both the sports-specific and the generic variants. Public, policy, and even academic attention has rather tended to focus on individual types of sports-specific fraud at a time. Conversely, generic frauds in sports have long been overlooked in academia and in the public and policy debate, supposedly due to the perception that they pose a less pressing threat to sports integrity (Nelen, 2022).

The lack of an overarching conceptualization and the neglect of sports-related generic frauds have hindered both a realistic assessment of the extent and seriousness of the fraud problem in sports and the development of adequate and effective countermeasures. Instead, they have favoured the adoption of piecemeal responses to the specific types of sports-specific fraud that are prioritized at any given time. Furthermore, the opportunity to connect the analysis of sports-related fraud with the broader literature on white-collar and corporate crime has also largely been missed.

To address this gap, we propose in this chapter a typology of frauds in sports, which focuses on generic frauds, although it also encompasses sports-specific frauds. Inspired by Layder's (1998) adaptive theory, we have identified the six types of generic frauds on the basis of extensive fieldwork in Belgium and in close dialogue with the relevant criminological and sports science literature. Drawing from the literature and policy documents, we also outline the five main types of sports-specific fraud that are primarily defined by international sports regulations (though these are discussed only briefly, because they are, as mentioned, already better known).

It is our claim that our typology enhances the understanding of sports-related fraud in several ways. It (1) carefully delineates each of the eleven identified types of fraud; (2) singles out the types of laws, rules, and procedures that are used to tackle them, thus specifying whether they constitute 'real' criminal offences or rather white-collar crimes in the broader sense as proposed by Sutherland (1949); (3) reconstructs the core scripts of these frauds, identifying the envisaged advantages and the perpetrators most frequently involved; and (4) identifies the primary and other/possible bearers of harm, and indicates the types of harm suffered, based on Greenfield and Paoli's (2013; 2022) harm assessment framework.

By examining sports fraud through this structured approach, the chapter raises awareness of the multiple types of fraud occurring in sports, including those that are often overlooked, and provides a much-needed evidence-based conceptual framework to address some of the sector's most serious malfeasances.

The remainder of this chapter is structured as follows. First, we briefly review the literature on fraud in sports and discuss previous typologies. In the second section, we define the key concepts central to this study. Next, we outline the research design of the underlying study. We then present our typology of frauds in sports, illustrating the types of generic and sports-specific fraud, along with their bearers of harm. In the final section, we draw the main conclusions, recall the limitations of the study, and suggest potential directions for future research.

Literature review
Academic accounts of fraud in sports

Fraud is a multifaceted phenomenon that takes place in virtually all sectors and societies (Punch, 1996). Albanese (2005) has even claimed that fraud constitutes the characteristic crime of the twenty-first century. While many frauds lack the obvious, direct, and measurable harms associated with crimes such as burglary and assault (Croall, 2001), frauds collectively generate serious economic and social harms, affecting individuals, private and public entities, and even the whole society. VAT-frauds alone, for example, have been reported to generate more revenues throughout the 2010s than all other organized crime activities, including illegal drug trafficking (Hulme et al, 2021).

In recent decades, awareness has grown that the sports sector, too, is vulnerable to different types of fraud (Button et al, 2008; Brooks et al, 2013). As with many other crimes, it is difficult to reach conclusive estimates about the extent of fraud in sports. Andreff (2019b), for example, estimates that approximately 90 per cent of sports corruption remains unknown. Because of this significant dark number, and the fact that many victims are not even aware of having been victimized, not much is known about the different manifestations of fraud in sports, nor about the individuals, entities, or communities impacted by these frauds.

Over the past few decades, academic interest in fraud in sports has increased. Since the 1990s, most research has focused on doping, and since the 2010s, match-fixing has become a 'hot topic' too (Groombridge, 2016). Much less academic attention has been given to generic fraud in sports, such as social security or tax fraud. Moreover, such research, if it takes place at all, is usually narrowed down to men's (professional) football (for example, Manoli et al, 2016; Nelen, 2022), or presented in a journalistic and even anecdotal manner, referring mainly to highly mediatized scandals involving prominent players or clubs. Some notable exceptions we are aware of are the recent studies by Andreff (2019a; 2019b; 2019c), who examined different types of fraud in various sports, and by Kihl et al (2021) and Wicker et al (2023) who investigated occupational fraud in community sports.

A further weakness of the literature on sports-related fraud is its conceptual imprecision. First, different types of sports-related fraud are frequently presented as corruption (see, for example, Masters, 2015; Chappelet, 2016). Second, various definitions of corruption and fraud are used (see, for example, Maennig, 2005, p 189; Gorse and Chadwick, 2011, p 8), an ambiguity that Brooks et al (2013, p 17) had already criticized in 2013. Third, different offences, such as money laundering, corruption, and fraud, are often lumped together without consistent delineation, a conceptual weakness that Lord (2023, p 219) has also pointed out.

Typologies of frauds in sports

Much like the research, institutional and academic typologies of unethical and illicit behaviour in sports tend to focus primarily on frauds that are unique to the sports sector (see, for example, Council of Europe, 2020). A few typologies also include generic frauds in sports, but often only superficially. In the widely cited classification developed by Maennig (2005) and later refined by Chappelet (2016) and Manoli (2018), for example, a distinction is made between 'competition' (or 'on field') and 'management' (or 'off field') corruption. The latter category, in particular, includes some corrupt and fraudulent activities that can also be found in other economic sectors. Neither this nor others, though, consistently define what is (and, perhaps equally important, what is not) meant by 'fraud' in sports or delineate different types of generic fraud in sports.

Research on fraud in general (that is unrelated to sports) does not offer much solace either. Such research, in fact, covers many forms of fraudulent conduct, ranging from insider trading to credit card fraud, so it cannot be applied to the sports sector one-to-one. However, Levi and Burrows (2008, p 302) have interestingly developed a 'victims-centric' typology of fraud, distinguishing between 'victims from the sector', ranging from individuals to financial and non-financial services entities, and 'victims from the public sector', including both central and local government entities. This typology echoes the distinction often made in the Dutch-speaking literature between 'horizontal fraud' (among citizens and private-sector entities) and 'vertical fraud' (involving public money and harming the public sector and hence society as a whole; see, for example, De Bie and Verhage, 2010).

Levi and Burrows (2008, p 304) also distinguish between primary and secondary victims. While the first are those immediately harmed by the fraudulent act, the second category includes 'those who ultimately pay for the economic components of fraud losses', ranging from insurance entities to taxpayers. Levi and Burrows (2008) note, though, that the two categories of victims might coincide in some instances.

For the development of our typology, we have taken inspiration from the latter victim-centric approach as well as from Greenfield and Paoli's (2013; 2022) taxonomy of harms and the latter's bearers of harm, which is one of the tools of their harm assessment framework.

Conceptualization of the key concepts

In this section we define the key concepts of 'fraud in sports' and its 'bearers of harm' and justify the choices made.

Fraud in sports

Despite the numerous manifestations of fraud and the different perpetrators and victims involved, the core of fraud is clear: namely, deception in an attempt to secure some type of benefit. Reflecting such a core, we have adopted the definition of fraud proposed by Transparency International (Transparency International, nd). This defines fraud as 'the offense of intentionally deceiving someone in order to gain an unfair or illegal advantage (financial, political or otherwise)'. We note that in sports such advantages are not only financial or political, as shown by cases of state doping in Soviet and post-Soviet countries (Yesalis and Bahrke, 2002). They often also concern the sports competition itself. In other words, the unfair or illegal advantages sought through fraud can also be sportive.

While the scope of fraud in sports is broad, it remains confined to intentional deceptive behaviour, making it narrower than concepts such as 'sports dysfunctions'. Sports dysfunctions include violations of explicit or implicit rules, such as gender discrimination or weak governance within sports clubs and governing bodies (Andreff, 2018), which do not necessarily involve intentional deceit. Conversely, we stress that 'offence' in the context of sports needs to be understood broadly and to encompass not only criminal law offences but also violations of civil, administrative, or disciplinary rules, as is routinely done in the white-collar crime literature (see Sutherland, 1949; Huisman et al, 2015).

Bearers of harm

Rather than 'victims', we more broadly speak of 'bearers of harms', following Greenfield and Paoli (2022). They define harm as 'a setback to a rightful stakeholder's legitimate interests' (p 1) and distinguish four 'classes' of bearers of harms, namely: individuals; private-sector entities; public sector entities; and the social and physical environment. Applying these categories to the sports context, we note that the individuals first affected are likely to be sportspeople and, among them, primarily the athletes, that is, sportspeople who engage in competitions at some level (see Paoli and Donati, 2014, p xxv). This first category of bearers, however, can also encompass referees and employees of sports clubs or sports governing bodies in addition to members of the general public. The category of private-sector entities specifically includes sports clubs, sports governing bodies, sponsors and other third-party entities in addition to unrelated businesses and NGOs. Following Greenfield and Paoli (2022, p 266), we define the social environment 'as consisting of the interactive regions (that is, relationships) between and among individuals and institutions and their associated cultural practices, including but not limited to communities'. Greenfield and Paoli use this category for harms that cannot be easily attributed to the specific bearers. In the sport sector, the social environment primarily refers to fan communities of a specific club and the organized sports world in addition to society as a whole.[1]

Unlike Levi and Burrows (2008), Greenfield and Paoli (2022) do not restrict their focus to financial harm. According to their framework, bearers in each class experience harm as damages to one or more 'interest dimensions', consisting of functional integrity, material support, reputation, and privacy and autonomy. They note that not all interest dimensions relate to all classes of bearers and that harm to functional integrity may occur differently by class. In fact, functional integrity refers to physical, psychological, and intellectual integrity for individuals, to operational integrity for private and public sector entities, and to physical, operational, and aesthetic integrity for the environment. The interest dimensions represent, in their view, categories of capabilities that create paths to attaining: a certain quality of life or standard of living for individuals (Von Hirsch and Jareborg, 1991, citing Sen, 1987); a mission for institutions; or sustainability for the environment.

Drawing on Greenfield and Paoli's (2013; 2022) harm assessment framework, the typology identifies not only the perpetrators of each type of fraud, but also the possible bearers of harm. Although an empirical assessment of the fraud-related harms is beyond the scope of this chapter and would require much better data than is currently available, this partial analysis singles out both the primary and other possible bearers of harm, thus showing who stands to lose the most from each type of fraud.

Research design

Inspired by Layder's (1998) adaptive theory, we developed the typology in an iterative dialogue between theoretical frameworks, Belgian sports-related laws and regulations, and our empirical data. The data were collected with a mixed-method research design. We identified and analyzed a total of 37 proceedings (that is, 10 criminal, 24 administrative, and 3 disciplinary proceedings) concerning generic fraud in sports, to see which laws and regulations had been violated and to understand how the frauds had been committed. To further investigate these issues and to gain insight into the harms associated with the frauds, we also conducted 33 expert interviews. Specifically, we interviewed 21 experts, including police officers, prosecutors, and representatives of several public inspectorates, as well as 12 representatives of sports ruling bodies and clubs.

By triangulating data from these different sources, we have attempted to reach a fuller overview of sports-related fraud in Belgium than either approach could do by itself. In particular, we have delineated the types of generic sports frauds and, for each type, we also indicate whether it is defined and addressed by 'criminal', 'administrative' and/or 'disciplinary' rules and procedures.

For each category of fraud, we have reconstructed their 'script' or 'scripts' (Cornish, 1994), as some of them, and especially tax fraud, have many variants. While we report more extensively on these scripts elsewhere (see Gotelaere and Paoli, 2024), we have provided brief summaries of such scripts here. On this basis, we establish whether the unfair advantage sought through each fraud type is sportive or financial or a combination of both, and we identify the perpetrators involved. For each fraud type, we also single out the primary and other possible bearers of harms, considering not only direct financial harms but also harms to the other interest dimensions discussed earlier (see Greenfield and Paoli, 2022).

In the second part of the typology, drawing on the literature and on public and sports regulation, we also delineate the main types of sports-specific frauds. Here, too, we consider the defining rules and procedures, the core scripts, the advantages aimed at, the perpetrators, and the bearers of harm.

We present an overview of all fraud types in Table 8.1, categorized into six types of generic fraud and five types of sports-specific frauds. The former category includes tax fraud, subsidy fraud, social fraud, licence fraud, occupational fraud, and outsiders' fraud. The latter includes sports-specific

Table 8.1: Typology of frauds in sports

Types of fraud in sports	Definitions and procedures			Characteristics (core scripts)	Main envisaged advantage		Main perpetrators	Bearers of harm	
	Criminal	Administrative	Disciplinary		Sportive	Financial		Primary	Other/possible
Generic fraud									
Tax fraud	x	x		Not (correctly) declaring income or assets (for example, via false tax status, forged contracts/ invoices, hidden payments, offshore companies, over– and undervaluation of transfer values)		x	Clubs, athletes, trainers, sponsors, sports agents, intermediaries (for example, lawyers, tax advisors)	Public bodies, citizens[a]	Other clubs, leagues, sports sector,[b] sponsors,[b] fan communities, athletes and other sportspeople
Subsidy fraud	x	x		False or misleading application, breach of subsidy requirements, misappropriation (for example, via false declarations, forged documents)		x	Clubs, athletes	Public bodies, citizens[a]	Other clubs, leagues, sports sector,[b] sponsors,[b] fan communities, athletes and other sportspeople
Social fraud	x	x		Not (correctly) reporting activities (for example, via		x	Clubs, athletes, trainers	Public bodies, citizens,[a]	Other clubs, leagues, sports sector,[b]

Table 8.1: Typology of frauds in sports (continued)

Types of fraud in sports	Definitions and procedures			Characteristics (core scripts)	Main envisaged advantage		Main perpetrators	Bearers of harm	
	Criminal	Administrative	Disciplinary		Sportive	Financial		Primary	Other/possible
				forged contracts, hidden payments, no (correct) residence or work permit, breach of permit requirements (for example, via false declarations, forged documents)				offending athletes, offending trainers	sponsors,[b] fan communities, athletes and other sportspeople
Licence fraud	x	x	x	No licence, false or misleading licence application, breach of licence requirements (for example, via false declarations, forged documents)	x	x	Clubs, sports agents	Other clubs, other agents	Leagues, sports sector,[b] sponsors,[b] fan communities, athletes and other sportspeople
Occupational fraud	x			Misappropriation of funds (monetary or in kind), embezzlement		x	Members or employees (for example, accountants, board members) of the clubs	Affected clubs	Athletes and other sportspeople

(continued)

Table 8.1: Typology of frauds in sports (continued)

Types of fraud in sports	Definitions and procedures			Characteristics (core scripts)	Main envisaged advantage		Main perpetrators	Bearers of harm	
	Criminal	Administrative	Disciplinary		Sportive	Financial		Primary	Other/possible
Outsiders' fraud	x			Identity theft, phishing, other scams		x	Third parties (individuals and entities)	Affected clubs	Athletes and other sportspeople
Sports-specific fraud									
Sports-specific financial fraud		x		Fraudulent breaching of sports-specific financial regulations		x	Clubs' management (including owners), sports agents, intermediaries (for example, lawyer, tax advisor), third parties (individuals or entities)	Other clubs, other athletes	Leagues, sports sector,[b] sponsors,[b] fan communities
Doping	x		x	The use of a substance or technique to fraudulently improve athletic performance	x		Athletes, trainers, clubs, sports governing bodies, third parties (for	Other clubs, other athletes	(Offending) athletes and other sportspeople (doping),

Table 8.1: Typology of frauds in sports (continued)

Types of fraud in sports	Definitions and procedures			Characteristics (core scripts)	Main envisaged advantage		Main perpetrators	Bearers of harm	
	Criminal	Administrative	Disciplinary		Sportive	Financial		Primary	Other/possible
Match-fixing	x		x	Fraudulent interference in the natural course of a sporting event or competition	x	x	example, physicians, illegal gambling networks)		leagues, sports sector,[b] sponsors,[b] fan communities
Personal information fraud			x	Use of false information (personal data, physical or intellectual capabilities) relating to an athlete	x				
Playing surface and equipment fraud			x	Fraudulent modifications relating to playing surface, sporting venue, equipment, technology, software	x				

Note: [a] In their capacity as taxpayers and recipients of public services; [b] Negatively affecting their reputation.

financial fraud, doping, match-fixing, personal information fraud, and playing surface and equipment fraud. Given the evolving nature of fraud. and considering that not all real-world cases fit neatly and unequivocally within one of these types, the categories are not definitive, but they do provide a useful starting point for further analysis.

Generic frauds in sports

In this section, we present the first part of our typology, which singles out six types of generic fraud: tax, subsidy, social, licence, occupational, and outsiders' fraud.

The first four types of generic fraud involve violations of specific laws and regulations committed with fraudulent intent. Unlike some jurisdictions (for example, England and Wales, where fraud has been codified under the Fraud Act 2006[2]; Brooks et al, 2013), Belgian criminal law does not contain a single offence encompassing all types of fraud. Instead, behaviours considered fraudulent are addressed through a variety of laws and regulations, such as specialized social security and taxation legislation.

The laws and regulations affected usually belong to the sphere of administrative law, although criminal sanctions are sometimes imposed for particularly serious offences. In addition to the police and the public prosecutor's office, several public bodies are involved in the detection and prosecution of these types of fraud, such as specialized inspectorates and non-criminal courts. In the case of licence fraud, some requirements are also issued by private entities, *in casu* sports governing bodies, and prosecuted by national and international disciplinary bodies, like the Belgian and International Courts of Arbitration for Sport. Unlike the first four fraud types, occupational and outsiders' fraud are usually defined by the criminal code in Belgium and other civil law countries and prosecuted by the public prosecutor's office.

Financial advantages are the primary drivers of most generic frauds, although they might be complemented by sportive advantages in some cases of social and licence fraud. The main perpetrators are sports clubs (including their members and employees), athletes, trainers, or sports agents. In some cases – especially the more serious fraud types – the perpetrators are assisted by intermediaries. Only in the case of outsiders' frauds, are the main perpetrators, by definition, third parties.

Types

As for 'tax fraud', our data indicates that several athletes and sports clubs have omitted to declare their activities to the competent tax authorities, made under-the-table payments, or set up specific (cross-border) tax evasion schemes. Instances of serious tax fraud have involved cases of residence tax fraud and tax fraud involving image rights; they have been reported especially in elite cycling and football. In the latter sport, the criminal investigation 'Clean Hands' has also revealed concealed payments to evade taxes on salaries, on players' transfer fees, and on football agents' fees. To do so, specific constructions such as transfer bungs, kickbacks, and fictitious scouting contracts were used. Notably, in these more serious cases of fraud, our data suggests that the perpetrators are frequently aided by intermediaries, including lawyers and tax advisors.

'Subsidy fraud' is premised on the large subsidies received by the sports sector in Belgium and most other countries (for some data, see Gotelaere and Paoli, 2024). In sports, subsidy fraud occurs when clubs use false declarations or documents to obtain subsidies (for example, by lying about the number of members); when information is withheld in violation of a specific obligation, resulting in undue subsidies (for example, failure to comply with the obligation to engage youth players); or when subsidies are deliberately used for purposes other than those for which they were intended (for example, to pay professional players instead of investing in infrastructure). Though no proceedings documented this type of fraud in Belgium, several interviewees reported that some sports clubs and athletes had engaged in different forms of subsidy fraud, indicating that they are the main perpetrators.

'Social fraud' encompasses violations of social security or labour laws. As for social security laws, our data indicates that, to evade social security contributions, activities in the sports sector have repeatedly not been declared to the competent authorities (so-called 'undeclared work')[3] and that employees of sports clubs (usually trainers or coaches) have fraudulently pretended to be self-employed (so-called 'fictitious self-employment'). In violation of labour laws, Belgian sports clubs have employed foreign athletes or trainers without a (valid) residence permit and/or work permit. In those cases, sports clubs have falsely claimed, among other things, that the athletes were only in Belgium for a try-out or employed them on the basis of a tourist visa. The conditions for obtaining such permits are also frequently violated, particularly via fraudulent schemes designed to avoid paying the guaranteed minimum annual salary. Our data show that, alongside sports clubs, athletes and trainers are the main perpetrators of social frauds.

With regard to 'licence fraud', licences regulate admission to certain professions (such as sports agent) or certain events (such as sports leagues). With regard to the former, sports agents in Belgium are only allowed to offer their services to athletes, clubs, or teams if they are registered with the regional Belgian authorities. However, some agents fraudulently circumvent this obligation or deliberately fail to register. Regarding the latter, interviewees reported that some Belgian sports clubs have attempted to obtain a licence by submitting false information or forged documents to fraudulently demonstrate that all financial and legal conditions relating to the licence have been met. As these examples show, licence fraud in Belgium involves mainly sports agents and clubs.

'Occupational fraud' involves fraudulent activities committed against sports entities by 'insiders' of these entities, such as board members or accountants. In the non-profit sector, the term 'occupation' also includes volunteer positions and roles on an association board (Greenlee et al, 2007; Kihl et al, 2021). We identified two criminal proceedings detailing occupational fraud. Both concerned embezzlement by accountants in amateur sports clubs. During an interview, the representative of a Belgian amateur sports club revealed that his club had also been a victim of occupational fraud at the hands of a board member.

We identified two criminal proceedings in Belgium regarding 'outsiders' fraud', where sports clubs fell victim to fraud by third parties. The first was a phishing case, while the second case involved several scams that could be classified as 'identity theft', in which the club's name was misused to sell fictitious sponsorship packages. Furthermore, several interviewees reported incidents where individuals with suspected ties to organized and/or white-collar crime had attempted to invest large sums of money in or even to purchase sports clubs. These so-called 'benefactors' often do this to enhance their image and/or influence in local communities or to launder illegally obtained money. The main perpetrators of outsiders' fraud are thus third parties, who according to our Belgian data, usually had no connection to the sports sector prior to the fraud.

Bearers of harm

The sports sector and its fans generally do not lose sleep over generic fraud in sports, which stands in stark contrast to the collective indignation that usually follows the exposure of sports-specific fraud, such as doping (Nelen, 2022). However, as evident from our typology, generic fraud in sports also has wide-ranging direct and indirect effects on individuals, entities, and society as a whole.

The first three types – tax, subsidy, and social frauds – can be classified as 'vertical' frauds, that is, perpetrators primarily defraud public bodies, which are the immediate bearers of a direct financial harm. Ultimately, however, such bodies will pass this cost on to the taxpayers; in other words, as Greenfield and Paoli (2022, p 165) note in reference to similar harms, 'the government is the near-ultimate bearer of the harm, but not the ultimate bearer'. Yet, these harms are hardly perceived, because they are 'accumulative' (see Greenfield and Paoli, 2022, p 101, citing Feinberg, 1984, pp 225–7), that is, they arise only if the act that triggers the harm is combined with other similar acts.

In addition to public bodies and citizens, there are also other possible bearers, who have to be identified on a case-by-case basis and sometimes coincide with the perpetrators. Especially in the case of social fraud, the same person who benefits in the short term might also suffer in the long term or in case of illness. Athletes and trainers receiving payments without declaring them or (fully) paying social security contributions have an extra untaxed income, but lose protection in the event of an accident or illness and see their pension base reduced in the long-term. Likewise, foreign athletes who are enrolled with a sports club without the required work permit are able to pursue their sportive ambitions in the short term, but they are also unable to obtain all the (financial) benefits of an official contract and have no or only partial access to social security. In some cases, foreign athletes' illegal (work) status may even prevent them from leaving the club, or – in extreme cases – the country. Hence, the harms suffered might involve not only their material support but also their autonomy.

Other sports clubs might also suffer harms to their material interests and possibly to their reputation and functional integrity, because the fraud committed primarily to gain an unfair or illegal financial advantage is also likely to result in a sportive advantage. Research indicates a positive correlation between financial resources and sportive performance (Szymanski and Smith, 1997; Dobson and Goddard, 2001). As such, illicit financial gains from tax, social, or subsidy frauds create an uneven playing field, enabling fraudulent clubs to hire better players or coaches than their law-abiding competitors. The distorting effect on the sports competition can be even more serious than that of match-fixing. The latter, in fact, is usually limited to single matches, whereas the impact of systemic fraud is longer-lasting and accumulates over time. Honest clubs are less likely to achieve a good position within a league when competing against fraudulent players or teams, which reduces their chances of winning prizes or attracting sponsorship.

In addition to these predominantly material harms, reputational harms are also likely to accrue from these various types of fraud, affecting both the implicated leagues and the sports sector more generally. Although the reputational harms may initially appear less serious than the material harms, their severity might increase over time as multiple cases of frauds are revealed, and the harms hence become accumulative. These cumulative harms can erode public trust, potentially disrupting the functional integrity of fan communities. Fans, feeling betrayed by their favourite athletes and clubs, may grow disenchanted and disengaged, thereby undermining the social fabric that sustains the popularity of sports.

Sponsors of the affected clubs (or even leagues), in their turn, might also experience both reputational and material harms. Through the process of image transfer (Hughes and Shank, 2005), consumers may attribute negative traits associated with fraudulent athletes or teams to their sponsors. Such associations can compel sponsors to seek alternative advertising opportunities, resulting in reduced sponsorship revenues and adding to the material harms to the sports sector (Chadwick et al, 2018).

An accumulation of fraud in sports also threatens the integrity and credibility of sports, which might in the long term reduce its overall attractiveness and profitability. As trust erodes, the perceived risks of investing in sports may escalate to levels deemed unacceptable for financial institutions, a scenario that has already been observed in the football sector in Belgium and other European countries (Steenwijk, 2021).

Especially in the case of subsidy fraud, but possibly also in the case of tax and social fraud, harms might also accrue to the functional integrity and reputation of young athletes and other sportspeople, and to the material interests and reputation of trainers who belong to clubs that do not receive the funding to which they are entitled by law and hence cannot unlock their sporting potential. This is the case, for example, when subsidies are misused to pay professional athletes instead of being invested in youth development.

Licence frauds primarily affect the peers of the clubs or agents committing such frauds, that are likely to be harmed in their material interests. The club committing such fraud might also endanger its own material support and functional integrity, as they may lose their licence or face a penalty (see, for example, Richford and James, 2024). Hence, this affects the sporting ambitions, reputation, and functional integrity of its members, no matter whether these are athletes, other sportspeople, managers, or volunteers. Licence fraud might also compromise the material interests of the offending club's sponsors, and possibly even the material interests, reputation, and functional integrity of its league. More indirectly, accumulative reputational harm might also accrue to the whole sports sector. As for the earlier types of generic fraud, fan communities might also suffer harm to their functional integrity, if the cases of licence fraud in a given sport multiply and an accumulative harm ensues.

The last two types of generic fraud – occupational and outsiders' fraud – are even more horizontal than licence fraud. Their primary victims are the clubs or leagues, which are hurt in their material interests. Especially in the case of occupational fraud, there might also be an emotional or psychological impact on the clubs' or leagues' managers, especially if trust has been violated. More indirectly, the sporting ambitions and functional integrity and, in some cases, the material interests of the athletes and other sportspeople of the affected clubs and leagues might also be jeopardized.

Sports-specific frauds

In this section, we present the second part of our typology, which singles out five types of sports-specific fraud: sports-specific financial fraud, doping, match-fixing, personal information fraud, and playing surfaces and equipment fraud.

Unlike generic frauds in sports, sports-specific frauds constitute mainly disciplinary infractions, as they violate rules and regulations issued by sports governing bodies. Some of them, though, can also be investigated by the police and prosecuted by public prosecutors. For instance, criminal proceedings are possible for doping trafficking and for administering of doping. In some countries, including Italy, even athletes who use doping substances can face criminal charges (see, for example, Italy in Paoli and Donati, 2014). Match-fixing can be dealt with via a disciplinary procedure, but, via the provisions of 'passive and active private bribery', such conduct can also give rise to criminal prosecution in Belgium and other countries (Vandercruysse and Baert, 2022).

The main perpetrators of sports-specific financial fraud are individuals or private entities that are part of the sports sector, but are relatively peripheral to sports events, such as clubs' managers (including their owners) or sports agents, with the occasional assistance of intermediaries. Their decisions to commit fraud are primarily driven by financial advantages. In contrast, the latter four types of sports-specific fraud are rather perpetrated by individuals who are directly involved in a sports event, such as athletes, trainers, or (more rarely) clubs, in some cases assisted by third parties. Such perpetrators focus predominantly on the outcome of a sports event and are thus primarily driven by sportive advantages (although they may also be motivated by financial gain, particularly in the case of betting-related match-fixing). Referring to Maennig's (2005) classification, the first frauds are primarily conducted off-field, whereas the latter are on-field.

Types

'Sports-specific financial fraud' refers to practices that, while legal under common business laws, are prohibited by the governing bodies of specific sports. These sports-specific rules and regulations have predominantly emerged in sports with large financial transactions, most notably professional football. A first example of sports-specific financial fraud involves violations of budgetary constraints, like financial fair play rules. Such rules have been introduced in various sports leagues, from football to Formula 1, to promote financial stability and fair competition among clubs (Morrow, 2013). Despite their objectives, they have been violated on several occasions (see, for example, Dimitropoulos et al, 2016). A recent example is the case of the Italian football club Juventus, which was found guilty of violating UEFA's financial fair play rules between 2012 and 2019. Because of that, the club was banned from participating in UEFA competitions for one year and fined €20 million (of which €10 million is conditional) in 2023 (Horncastle, 2023).

A second type of sports-specific financial fraud involves so-called third-party ownership (TPO),[4] a practice in which a third party – distinct from the two clubs involved in a player's transfer – is granted the right to pocket part of the player's future transfer fee (Andreff, 2019a). This arrangement is typically used by clubs in dire financial situations, as it allows the third party to make a speculative investment in a player. TPO raises a number of controversial economic and governance issues (see, for example, Brocard, 2015; Andreff, 2019a). To address these issues, the Fédération Internationale de Football Association (FIFA) banned TPO. The ban aimed to eliminate outside influence on clubs and players' careers, ensuring that clubs retain full control over their playing staff and that transfer decisions are based on sporting considerations rather than the financial interests of third parties. Despite FIFA's ban, TPO practices have persisted, as evidenced, for example, by the financing contracts published via Football Leaks (Buschmann and Wulzinger, 2018). An example from Belgium is the FC Seraing/Doyen case, where the football club FC Seraing was found to have violated the TPO rule when the investment entity Doyen added €300,000 to the club's budget in exchange for 30 per cent of the economic rights of certain players. The club was subsequently fined more than €150,000 and given a transfer ban (Neeraj, 2016). These examples demonstrate that the main perpetrators of sports-specific financial fraud are clubs' management, often with the assistance of intermediaries, such as lawyers, or other third parties.

The next category is 'doping', which, according to the World Anti-Doping Agency (WADA), refers to the occurrence of one or more of the eleven anti-doping rule violations set forth in its 2021 World Anti-Doping Code (WADC). Among them, the two main ones are the 'use or attempted use by an athlete of a prohibited substance or a prohibited method'[5] and 'trafficking or attempted trafficking in any prohibited substance or prohibited method by an athlete or other person'.[6]

While numerous scandals have demonstrated systematic state-sponsored doping among the Olympic teams of several states (Yesalis and Bahrke, 2002; Yang and Leung, 2008), the largest doping case in Belgium goes back to twenty years ago. In 2003, a criminal investigation uncovered a network of doping practices involving several athletes, physicians, and suppliers. As a result, several professional cyclists – including Johan Museeuw, a specialist in classic races – were banned for using Erythropoietin (better known as 'EPO') and other performance-enhancing drugs (Christiansen, 2005). They were later also fined in a criminal proceeding and given suspended sentences (Maeckelbergh, 2008). Whereas athletes are the most immediate perpetrators of doping offences, other people might commit doping offences as well, including trainers, physicians, and the suppliers of other substances prohibited by WADA through its prohibited list.

The following three sports-specific fraud types are singled out by the Council of Europe's 2020 Macolin Convention.[7] The first and most important category relates to 'match-fixing', which is defined by the Council of Europe (2020) as a direct interference in the natural course of a sporting event or competition. This refers to the manipulation of sports competitions, or elements thereof, in order to gain an unfair sporting advantage or corrupt financial benefit (for example, when an athlete deliberately loses a sporting event or competition). Match-fixing is generally categorized into two major types: betting-related match-fixing and sporting-related match-fixing (see, for example, Spapens and Olfers, 2015). The manipulation may target either the overall outcome of the match or specific events within the match (also referred to as 'spot-fixing'; Serby, 2015). The recent Belgian criminal investigation 'Maestro' revealed widespread betting-related match-fixing in semi-professional tennis, with at least 375 matches fixed between 2014 and 2018. The organizer of the match-fixing was sentenced to five years in prison, and more than €9.5 million in gambling winnings were confiscated (Sieff, 2023). As this and other known match-fixing cases show, athletes or trainers are 'necessary' perpetrators of match-fixing, but they are sometimes supported, or even enticed and coordinated, by external figures, who are often linked to illegal betting networks (Hill, 2010b; UNODC, 2024) or, like the lead perpetrator in the Maestro case, involved in betting themselves.

The next type of sports-specific fraud defined by the Macolin Convention (2020) is 'personal information fraud', that is, the modification of an athlete's identity or personal data, physical characteristics, or capabilities (mental or physical). A common example is the manipulation of age, which may be done to facilitate competing against younger opponents or to secure more favourable contracts. The latter practice arises largely from the perception that older athletes are closer to the end of their careers, making clubs less inclined to offer them lucrative contracts (Tosam, 2015). A notable example of age-related fraud is the case of Chancel Mbemba Mangulu, a Congolese football player, who faced scrutiny over inconsistencies in his reported birth dates while playing for the Belgian football club Anderlecht (Sinnott and Molina, 2013). An even more egregious case of personal information fraud occurred at the Sydney 2000 Paralympic Games, where it was revealed that the majority of the Spanish basketball team, which had won the gold medal, were not disabled. Following the revelation, the team was officially disqualified and ordered to return the gold medals, and the then president of the Spanish Sports Federation for People with Intellectual Disabilities was fined €5,400. The scandal had far-reaching consequences, leading to a complete ban on athletes with intellectual disabilities from participating in the 2004 and 2008 Paralympics, effectively ending the careers of thousands of athletes worldwide (Tremlett, 2004). As these examples show, perpetrators are not limited to the athletes themselves, but may also include their trainers or representatives of clubs or even sports governing bodies.

The last category of sports-specific fraud introduced by the Macolin Convention (2020) is 'playing surface and equipment fraud'. This type consists of modifications that are noncompliant with laws or sport rules relating to playing surfaces, playing equipment, or sporting venues (Council of Europe, 2020). Concretely, it might involve tampering with the playing surface or sports equipment (for example, balls or rackets) during a competition or the use of unauthorized or banned equipment. Examples include allegations of so-called 'mechanical doping' in cycling, where riders use small hidden motors to gain an advantage. The most notable case of mechanical doping was that of Femke Van den Driessche, a Belgian cyclist, during the 2016 UCI cyclo-cross world championships. A hidden motor was found in her bike, for which she was banned from the sport for six years (Smith, 2022). For this type of fraud, too, perpetrators might include – in addition to the athletes themselves – their trainers, managers, or even their clubs and sports governing bodies.

Bearers of harm

Sports-specific regulations have been created primarily to protect the fairness of competitions, even if other motivations might be added, such as the protection of athletes' health, as seen in the case of anti-doping efforts. Even in that case, though, the protection of competition fairness overrules other aims. As noted by Fincoeur (2016, p 115), WADA's motto is 'Play true', not 'Play healthy'. Consistent with such aims, it is not surprising that the primary bearers of harms resulting from sports-specific frauds are other clubs or athletes. Victimized clubs and athletes might be hurt not only in their sportive ambitions but also in their material interests and functional integrity, if they are prevented from winning or achieving outstanding results by cheating competitors.

Subordinately, sports governing bodies, the broader sports sector, and sponsors are susceptible to reputational harm in the event of a scandal. As Carpenter (2012) emphasizes, even honest actors within the sector may suffer reputational harm when fraud is suspected. Such harms can also extend to their material interests, as diminished trust in the integrity of sports may lead sponsors and media outlets to reduce their sponsorship and broadcasting agreements (Gorse and Chadwick, 2010). In a similar way, scandals can weaken fan communities' engagement, resulting in decreased interest, attendance, and overall support for sports (Amenta and Di Betta, 2021; Hardyns et al, 2022).

The losses associated with these scandals are not just reputational or economic. According to Harvey and McNamee (2019), threats to the integrity of sports can also weaken deeply rooted sociocultural ties, as sports hold a unique position in culture and society with lifelong and generational attachments often made to clubs and sports.

Research further highlights the psychological impact on athletes, who may become the target of negative public reactions due to allegations or confirmed cases of fraud in sports (Robinson and Parry, 2018). Such public scrutiny may also compromise their privacy and autonomy.

In the case of doping, there might also be harms to the physical and psychological integrity of the doping athletes. This was certainly the case in the past. Between the late 1960s and early 1990s, many elite athletes in multiple countries were given high doses of anabolic steroids and other performance-enhancing substances in state-run schemes or with the tacit complicity of national sport authorities (Franke and Berendonk, 1997; Paoli and Donati, 2014; Paoli et al, 2022). Whether and to what extent such harm to athletes' physical integrity still accrue ought to be determined for each doping substance and method on WADA's prohibited list. The spread of new doping substances, such as EPO, and of the practice of micro-dosing supports the tentative hypothesis that such physical harm, for many doping athletes, has in the meanwhile decreased (see, for example, López, 2011; Marijon et al, 2013; Birzniece, 2015).

Conclusion

In this chapter, we have proposed a novel typology of frauds in sports. In our view, this typology is innovative vis-à-vis the literature in a number of ways. It makes a distinction between sports-specific fraud and non-sports-specific or generic fraud in sports and focuses on the latter, a subset of frauds that have received much less academic and policy attention than sports-specific frauds. Drawing on an extensive data collection in Belgium, an analysis of Belgian and international laws and regulations, and a thorough literature review, the typology singles out six types of generic fraud in sports (tax, subsidy, social, licence, occupational and outsiders' fraud) and five types of sports-specific fraud (sports-specific financial fraud, doping, match-fixing, personal information fraud, and playing surface and equipment fraud).

For each fraud type, we identify the main perpetrators, showing that some types only involve individual perpetrators, whereas others often entail some cooperation between individuals and sports organizations, closely resembling patterns seen in corporate crime. However, except for major cases of generic fraud, both the existence and the strength of such cooperation have to be investigated on a case-by-case basis.

The typology further specifies whether each type of fraud is defined and addressed by 'criminal', 'administrative', or 'disciplinary' rules and procedures, or by varying combinations of these rules and procedures. Additionally, it provides the core scripts of the eleven identified fraud types, and details the main advantage sought by perpetrators – be it sportive, financial, or a combination of both. Moreover, the typology identifies the primary and other possible bearers of the harms resulting from each fraud type and, on the basis of Greenfield and Paoli's (2022) harm assessment framework, it singles out the interest dimensions of each category of bearers that are potentially affected.

Through such analysis, our study indicates that frauds in sports affect multiple stakeholders and extend far beyond a mere financial impact. Specifically, it indicates that sports-related generic frauds, despite their relative neglect in the policy, public, and academic discourses, potentially generate harms to the multiple interest dimensions of several stakeholders, including individuals (as taxpayers, athletes, and other sportspeople), private sector entities (*in primis* sports clubs and leagues), public bodies, and fan communities. The range of affected interest dimensions and bearers appears broader for generic frauds compared to sports-specific frauds.

Notably, the typology and its underlying empirical analyses (Gotelaere and Paoli, 2024) show that the generic frauds committed by some sports clubs could also result in a sportive disadvantage for the other competing clubs, thereby affecting the fairness of competitions. In other words, much like sport-specific frauds, generic frauds might also constitute a form of competition fixing. While the different types of sports-related frauds might differ in how and how much they harm sports functioning, needless to say, all of them are contrary to any kind of fair play concept.

To this end, we call for increased attention for the different types of fraud in the sports sector, especially the generic ones. Such attention should drive, in our view, the adoption of more proactive and systematic measures to prevent and control all sports-related frauds by both sports organizations and state regulators.

A limitation of our typology is that its generic fraud types reflect Belgian laws, regulations, and enforcement practices. As detailed in Gotelaere and Paoli (2024), this regulatory landscape might create opportunities for some specific fraud variants that are absent elsewhere. Yet, given the harmonization of national laws and regulations promoted by both EU and international sports governing bodies, we are confident that the main categories of our typology can also be useful in other regulatory contexts, especially in civil law countries. It will be the task of future analyses to test this assumption empirically.

Next, it was beyond the scope of the present chapter to explore the accompanying or enabling activities associated with the different fraud types, as Greenfield and Paoli (2022) have done in the script analyses of several crimes. Many frauds are likely to be linked to money laundering, and some, such as subsidy fraud, may involve the corruption of government officials or representatives of sports governing bodies. The labour variant of social fraud might enable the exploitation of young foreign athletes, which might in some conditions even amount to human trafficking. Future empirical studies are needed to ascertain which other criminal activities accompany or are enabled by the various fraud types identified in our typology.

Future studies building on this typology should also aim to assess and compare, within specific contexts, the incidence and severity of the harms to the interest dimensions and their bearers that our analysis suggests are associated with different fraud types. As Greenfield and Paoli (2022) argue, such empirical harm assessments are a necessary pre-condition for a real evidence-based policy, because they help identify the most harmful types of sports fraud and hence those that should be prioritized for intervention.

Notes

1. We do not discuss the physical environment as we have no proof of harms resulting from sports-related fraud to such bearer.
2. Fraud Act 2006, c. 35. Available from: http://www.legislation.gov.uk/ukpga/2006/35.
3. Undeclared work is a form of both social and tax fraud, as neither social contributions nor taxes are paid.
4. In response to FIFA's prohibition of TPO, investment funds have developed a workaround known as third-party investments (TPI). Under TPI arrangements, clubs take on loans from investment funds to purchase players on the transfer market. When the player is sold, the proceeds are used to repay the debt. While TPI does not directly violate FIFA's ban on TPO, as the investment fund holds a financial claim rather than an ownership stake in the player's value, the distinction is largely technical (Andreff, 2019a).
5. Article 2.2 of the WADC 2021.
6. Article 2.7 of the WADC 2021.
7. The Macolin Convention, officially known as the Council of Europe Convention on the Manipulation of Sports Competitions, is an international treaty aimed at combating the manipulation of sports organizations.

References

Albanese, J. (2005) 'Fraud: the characteristic crime of the twenty-first century', *Trends in Organized Crime*, 8(4): 6–14.

Amenta, C. and Di Betta, P. (2021) 'The impact of corruption on sport demand', *International Journal of Sports Marketing and Sponsorship*, 22(2): 369–84.

Andreff, W. (2018) 'Different types of manipulation in sport', in M. Breuer and D. Forrest (eds), *The Palgrave Handbook of the Economics of Manipulation in Sport*, Palgrave Macmillan, pp 13–35.

Andreff, W. (2019a) *An Economic Roadmap to the Dark Side of Sport. Volume I: Sport Manipulation*, Palgrave Macmillan.

Andreff, W. (2019b) *An Economic Roadmap to the Dark Side of Sport. Volume II: Corruption in Sport*, Palgrave Macmillan.

Andreff, W. (2019c) *An Economic Roadmap to the Dark Side of Sport. Volume III: Economic Crime in Sport*, Palgrave Macmillan.

Birzniece, V. (2015) 'Doping in sport: effects, harm and misconceptions', *International Medicine Journal,* 45(3): 239–48.

Brocard, J.F. (2015) 'Transferts de joueurs et "Third Party Ownership"', *Reflets et Perspectives de la vie économique,* 54(3): 57–69.

Brooks, G., Aleem, A., and Button, M. (2013) *Fraud, Corruption and Sport,* Palgrave Macmillan.

Buschmann, R. and Wulzinger, M. (2018) *Football Leaks: Uncovering the Dirty Deals Behind the Beautiful Game,* Faber and Faber.

Button, M., Johnston, L., and Frimpong, K. (2008) 'The fraud review and the policing of fraud: laying the foundations for a centralized fraud police or counter fraud executive?', *Policing,* 2(2): 241–50.

Carpenter, K. (2012) 'Match-fixing: the biggest threat to sport in the 21st century?', *International Sports Law Review,* 2(1): 13–24.

Chadwick, S., Roberts, S., and Cowley, R. (2018) 'The impact of sports corruption on organisational stakeholders', in L. Kihl (ed), *Corruption in Sport: Causes, Consequences, and Reform,* Routledge, pp 110–25.

Chappelet, J.L. (2016) 'Autonomy and governance: necessary bedfellows in the fight against corruption in sport', in G. Sweeney (ed), *Global Corruption Report: Sport,* London: Routledge, pp 16–28.

Christiansen, A.V. (2005) 'The legacy of Festina: patterns of drug use in European cycling since 1998', *Sport in History,* 25(3): 497–514.

Conn, D. (2017) *The Fall of the House of FIFA: The Multimillion-dollar Corruption at the Heart of Global Soccer,* Hachette Book Group.

Cornish, D.B. (1994) 'The procedural analysis of offending and its relevance for situational prevention', in R. Clarke (ed), *Crime Prevention Studies 3.1,* Criminal Justice Press, pp 151–96.

Council of Europe (2020) 'Macolin Convention on the manipulation of sports competitions: typology of sports manipulations', Group of Copenhagen.

Croall, H. (2001) *Understanding White Collar Crime,* Open University Press.

De Bie, B. and Verhage, A. (2010) 'Fraudebestrijding in België anno 2010: Quo vadis?', *Orde van de Dag,* 51: 7–16.

Dimitropoulos, P.E., Leventis, S., and Dedoulis, E. (2016) 'Managing the European football industry: UEFA's regulatory intervention and the impact on accounting quality', *European Sport Management Quarterly,* 16(4): 459–86.

Dobson, S. and Goddard, J. (2001) *The Economics of Football,* Cambridge University Press.

Feinberg, J. (1984) *Harm to Others,* Oxford University Press.

Fincoeur, B. (2016) 'Le marché du dopage dans le cyclisme sur route belge et français: Analyse de la demande, de l'offre et de l'impact de la lutte antidopage', Thèse de doctorat en criminologie.

Franke, W. and Berendonk, B. (1997) 'Hormonal doping and androgenization of athletes: a secret program of the German Democratic Republic government', *Clinical Chemistry,* 43(7): 1262–79.

Friedrichs, D.O. (2009) *Trusted Criminals: White Collar Crime in Contemporary Society* (4th edn), Cengage Learning.

Gorse, S. and Chadwick, S. (2010) 'Conceptualising corruption in sport: implications for sponsorship programmes', *The European Business Review*, [Online] volume July/August. Available from: http://www.europeanbusinessreview.com/?p=1973

Gorse, S. and Chadwick, S. (2011) 'The prevalence of corruption in international sport: a statistical analysis', report prepared for the Remote Gambling Association, the European Gaming and Betting Association and the European Sports Security Association.

Gotelaere, S. and Paoli, L. (2024) 'Een verkennend onderzoek naar fraude in sport', *Panopticon*, 45(3): 266–85.

Greenfield, V. and Paoli, L. (2013) 'A framework to assess the harms of crimes', *The British Journal of Criminology*, 53(5): 864–85.

Greenfield, V. and Paoli, L. (2022) *Assessing the Harms of Crime: A New Framework for Criminal Policy*, Oxford University Press.

Greenlee, J., Fischer, M., Gordon, T., and Keating, E. (2007) 'An investigation of fraud in non-profit organisations: occurrences and deterrents', *Nonprofit and Voluntary Sector Quarterly*, 36: 676–94.

Groombridge, N. (2016) *Sports Criminology: A Critical Criminology of Sport and Games*, Policy Press.

Hardyns, W., Vanwersch, L., and Constandt, B. (2022) 'Should football care about its fans' trust? A study into the consequences of a large-scale fraud scandal on sports fans' integrity perception', *Managing Sport and Leisure*, 30(2): 172–87.

Harvey, A. and McNamee, M. (2019) 'Sport integrity: ethics, policy and practice. An introduction', *Journal of Global Sport Management*, 4(1): 1–7.

Hill, D. (2010a) *The Fix: Soccer and Organized Crime*, McClelland & Stewart.

Hill, D. (2010b) 'A critical mass of corruption: why some football leagues have more match-fixing than others', *International Journal of Sports Marketing and Sponsorship*, 11(3): 38–52.

Horncastle, J. (2023) 'Juventus handed one-year ban from European competitions and fined by EUFA for FFP breach', *New York Times*, [Online] 28 July. Available from: https://www.nytimes.com/athletic/4678937/2023/07/28/juventus-ban-europe-conference/

Hughes, S. and Shank, M. (2005) 'Defining scandal in sports: media and corporate sponsor perspectives', *Sport Marketing Quarterly*, 14(4): 207–16.

Huisman, W., van Erp, J., Vande Walle, G., and Beckers, J. (2015) 'Criminology and white-collar crime in Europe', in W. Huisman, J. van Erp and G. Vande Walle (eds), *The Routledge Handbook of White-Collar and Corporate Crime in Europe*, Routledge, pp 1–22.

Hulme, S., Disley, E., and Blondes, E.L. (2021) *Mapping the Risk of Serious and Organised Crime Infiltrating Legitimate Businesses: Final Report*, Publications Office of the European Union.

Kihl, L.A., Misener, K., Cuskelly, G., and Wicker, P. (2021) 'Tip of the iceberg? An international investigation of fraud in community sport', *Sport Management Review*, 24(1): 24–45.

Layder, D. (1998) *Sociological Practice: Linking Theory and Social Research*, Sage.

Levi, M. and Burrows, J. (2008) 'Measuring the impact of fraud in the UK: a conceptual and empirical journey', *The British Journal of Criminology*, 48(3): 293–318.

López, B. (2011) 'The invention of a 'drug of mass destruction': deconstructing the EPO myth', *Sport in History*, 31(1): 84–109.

Lord, N. (2023) Book review: Nelen, H. (2022) 'Ostrageous: how greed and crime erode professional football and we all look the other way', *Crime, Law and Social Change*, 79(2): 217–22.

Maeckelbergh, B. (2008) 'Ex-wielrenners veroordeeld', *De Standaard*, 17 December.

Maennig, W. (2005) 'Corruption in international sports and sport management: forms, tendencies, extent and countermeasures', *European Sport Management Quarterly*, 5(2): 187–225.

Manoli, A.E. (2018) 'Mapping of corruption in sport in the EU', Report to the European Commission.

Manoli, A.E., Antonopoulos, G., and Levi, M. (2016) 'Football clubs and financial crimes in Greece', *Journal of Financial Crime*, 23(3): 559–73.

Marijon, E., Tafflet, M., Antero-Jacquemin, J., El Helou, N., Berthelot, G., Celermajer, D.S. et al (2013) 'Mortality of French participants in the Tour de France (1947–2012)', *European Heart Journal*, 34(40): 3145–50.

Masters, A. (2015) 'Corruption in sport: from the playing field to the field of policy', *Policy and Society*, 34(2): 111–23.

Morrow, S. (2013) 'Football club financial reporting: time for a new model?', *Sport, Business and Management: An International Journal*, 3(4): 297–311.

Neeraj, T. (2016) 'The future of third party ownership and influence in football following the FC Seraing Case', *Lawyerissue*, [blog] 15 March. Available from: https://lawyerissue.com/the-future-of-third-party-ownership-and-influence-in-football-following-the-fc-seraing-case/

Nelen, H. (2022) *Ostrageous: How Greed and Crime Erode Professional Football and We All Look the Other Way*, Eleven.

Paoli, L. and Donati, A. (2014) *The Sports Doping Market: Understanding Supply and Demand, and the Challenges of their Control*, Springer.

Paoli, L., Hoppeler, H., Mahler, H., Simon, P., Sörgel, F., and Treutlein, G. (2022) *Doping für Deutschland: »Die Evaluierungskommission Freiburger Sportmedizin«: Geschichte, Ergebnisse und sportpolitische Forderungen*, Transcript.

Punch, M. (1996) *Dirty Business: Exploring Corporate Misconduct: Analysis and Cases*, Sage.

Richford, S. and James, K. (2024) 'The Rangers FC liquidation and lessons learned in football finance', *International Journal of Engineering Technologies and Management Research*, 11(6): 145–22.

Robinson, S. and Parry, J. (2018) 'The impact of corruption on individual athletes, teams, and organisations', in L. Kihl (ed), *Corruption in Sport: Causes, Consequences, and Reform*, Routledge, pp 91–109.

Rodchenkov, G. (2020) *The Rodchenkov Affair: How I Brought Down Russia's Secret Doping Empire*, WH Allen.

Sen, A. (1987) 'The standard of living: Lecture I, concepts and critiques' and 'The standard of living: Lecture II, lives and capabilities', in G. Hawthorn (ed), *The Standard of Living: The Tanner Lectures, Clare Hall, Cambridge, 1985*, Cambridge University Press, pp 1–38.

Serby, T. (2015) 'The Council of Europe Convention on Manipulation of Sports Competitions: the best bet for the global fight against match-fixing?', *The International Sports Law Journal*, 15: 835–100.

Sieff, K. (2023) 'Game, set, fix', *Washington Post*, [Online] 7 September. Available from: https://www.washingtonpost.com/world/interactive/2023/tennis-match-fixing-gambling-investigation-belgium?itid=lk_inline_enhanced-template

Sinnott, J. and Molina, R. (2013) 'Football's age fraud: FIFA probes player with 'four birthdays', *CNN*, [Online] 4 February. Available from: https://edition.cnn.com/2013/02/01/sport/football/age-african-football-mbemba/

Smith, C. (2022) 'Doping in cycling: past, present and future trends', in G.B. Norcliffe, U. Brogan, P. Cox, B. Gao, T. Hadland, S. Hanlon et al (eds), *The Routledge Companion to Cycling*, Routledge, pp 345–54.

Spapens, T. and Olfers, M. (2015) 'Match-fixing: the current discussion in Europe and the case of the Netherlands', *European Journal of Crime, Criminal Law and Criminal Justice*, 23(4): 333–58.

Steenwijk, P.J.W. (2021) 'Kwade zaken in het voetbal', *Ondernemersrecht*, 61: 3535–64.

Strauss, B., Beunemann, S., Behlau, C., Tietjens, M., and Tamminen, K. (eds) (2024) *Psychology of Crises in Sport: Causes, Consequences and Solutions*, Springer Nature Switzerland.

Sutherland, E.H. (1949) *White Collar Crime*, Dryden Press.

Szymanski, S. and Smith, R. (1997) 'The English football industry: profit, performance and industrial structure', *International Review of Applied Economics*, 11(1): 135–53.

Tosam, J.M. (2015) 'The ethical and social implications of age-cheating in Africa', *International Journal of Philosophy*, 3(1): 1–11.

Transparency International (nd) 'Fraud', [Online] Available from: https://www.transparency.org/En/Corruptionary/Fraud

Tremlett, G. (2004) 'The cheats', *The Guardian*, [Online] 16 September. Available from: https://www.theguardian.com/sport/2004/sep/16/gilestremlett.features

UNODC (2024) 'Casinos, money laundering, underground banking, and transnational organized crime in East and Southeast Asia: a hidden and accelerating threat', January, United Nations Office on Drugs and Crime Southeast Asia and the Pacific (UNODC).

Vandercruysse, L. and Baert, M. (2022) 'Private omkoping en matchfixing: Geen perfecte match', *Nullum Crimen*, 17(5): 343–58.

Von Hirsch, A. and Jareborg, N. (1991) 'Gauging criminal harm: a living-standard analysis', *Oxford Journal of Legal Studies*, 11(1): 1–38.

WADA (2021) '2021 World Anti-Doping Code', [Online] Available from: https://www.wada-ama.org/sites/default/files/resources/files/2021_wada_code.pdf

Wicker, P., Misener, K., Kihl, L., and Cuskelly, G. (2023) 'Vulnerability to fraud in community sport organizations: a multicountry study on the role of organizational capacity', *Journal of Sport Management*, 37(2): 88–101.

Yang, D.L. and Leung, A. (2008) 'The politics of sports anti-doping in China: crisis, governance and international compliance', *China: An International Journal*, 6(1): 121–48.

Yesalis, C.E. and Bahrke, M. (2002) 'History of doping in sport', *International Sports Studies*, 24(1): 42–76.

9

White-Collar Crime in Kenyan Agri-Food Markets: Violations of Agri-Food Safety Laws in the Agri-Food Chain

Emmanuel K. Bunei

Introduction

The Kenyan agricultural sector contributes approximately 34 per cent to Kenya's GDP annually and accounts for 65 per cent of total exports and more than 75 per cent of rural employment (Kenya National Bureau of Statistics [KNBS], 2020). In terms of agricultural market participation, small-scale farmers account for 63 per cent of marketed farm produce in Kenya (Republic of Kenya, 2019a). In fact, small-scale farmers account for over 80 per cent of milk production, 70 per cent of maize farming, 70 per cent of beef production, 65 per cent of coffee production, and 50 per cent of tea farming (KNBS, 2019). Efforts (for example, development of agri-food safety policies such as the National Food Safety Policy 2021 (Republic of Kenya, 2021b) and the National Livestock Policy 2019 (Republic of Kenya, 2019b) have been made to ensure that Kenyans have access to safe and quality food as specified by Article 43 of the Constitution of Kenya (Republic of Kenya, 2010, p 31). However, creating a culture of compliance with agri-food safety regulations has remained a significant challenge within the Kenyan agricultural sector (Kutto et al, 2011; Odwar et al, 2014). Importantly, compliance with critical food safety regulations, especially in the marketing of contaminated farm produce, still exists (Republic of Kenya, 2019a).

Some of the hazards and harmful substances that have the potential to cause food poisoning or contamination on farms include antibiotics, drugs, and pesticides (Republic of Kenya, 2017; Gitaka et al, 2020). Critical to the use of these vital farm inputs is compliance with label requirements and general safety requirements before consumption or sale. This chapter is limited to fraudulent activity in the sale of contaminated farm produce (an example of white-collar crime) by farmers and other actors in the agri-food chain. Therefore, for the purposes of this chapter, contaminated farm produce includes food items that are not fit for human consumption because food safety requirements have not been followed. Examples of sale of contaminated farm produce include the sale of sick, dead, or drugged livestock or poultry; the sale of milk from drugged stock; the sale of crop produce before the expiration of the withdrawal period of pesticide; and the sale of livestock or poultry fed inappropriate farm produce.

While there are various studies that have recognized the problem of safety in agricultural products in Kenya (for example, Kiama et al, 2016; Senerwa et al, 2016), unfortunately, they do not fully address the problem of the sale of contaminated farm produce. Furthermore, most of these studies on agri-food safety compliance have to date focused on the presence and prevalence of harmful substances in farm produce (Kutto et al, 2011); rarely have they empirically explored and provided understanding of the factors that shape law-breaking decision-making in the marketing of farm products in Kenya by farmers and other actors in the agri-food chain. Also, attention to agri-food safety regulations has primarily focused on the export market, especially high-value horticultural products, and compliance with international regulations and standards. With respect to the domestic market, a few studies have examined compliance with agri-food safety regulations concerning farm produce for local markets (Muriithi et al, 2011; Harcourt-Brown et al, 2018). Lastly, studies that have comprehensively investigated the issue from a multidisciplinary perspective – and combined theories from the disciplines of economics, criminology, law, psychology, political science, and sociology – are sparse.

Consequently, this chapter aims to contribute to the analysis and understanding of rule violations by farmers and other actors such as transport drivers, supermarkets, and food vendors in agricultural marketing (production and sale of farm produce). It presents a picture of the significant issues faced by farmers and other actors from emerging economies on issues of markets and marketing farm produce through a criminal entrepreneurship perspective. Criminal entrepreneurship is a business activity in which an individual or group of people deliberately place an illegal commodity or service to legal market or exploit an illegal market opportunity (for example, high demand for goods not meeting legal standards) (Gottschalk 2010). The chapter utilizes Beckert and Wehinger's (2012) ideas to understand how actors in the agri-food market, especially farmers, make their decisions in terms of price valuations, managing stiff competion, and cooperating with other players in the agri-food chain. In this chapter, the concern is how farmers and other actors in the agri-food market maintain the stability and continuity of their businesses, albeit in an illegal way.

This chapter draws upon focus group discussions with farmers and in-depth interviews with experts and key stakeholders in the agri-food chain. This includes government officers (such as agricultural extension officers, livestock production officers, veterinary officers, public health officers, and so on), farmers' organization leaders, food traders, and community leaders (for example, the local chief, an assistant chief, a village elder, and ward[1] administrator) in the Uasin Gishu County of Kenya. The chapter has five major sections. The first section of the chapter provides the context of the study by defining the problem and its purpose. In the second, I discuss markets, marketing, and crime. The third section provides a discussion of the current study. The fourth section discusses the results of the study. The final section offers discussion, recommendations, and concluding thoughts.

Markets, marketing, and crime

Criminologists have long been examining criminality in markets (Spencer et al, 2018; Lord et al, 2019; Rizzuti, 2022). Market is a 'place or platform where buyers and sellers meet to facilitate exchange or transact goods and services' (Republic of Kenya, 2021a, p xi). Practically, there are at least three actors or players: one actor selling or buying, and at least two actors who want to sell or buy the same commodity or service. The actors in the market have the same but conflicting and competing interests in the price and value (that is quality and quantity) of goods and services (Beckert and Wehinger, 2012). This creates competition, which threatens the profit and value expectations of all the actors in the market. This may cause some actors to engage in unethical or illegal behaviours to buy or sell their services or goods (Beckert and Wehinger, 2012).

Governments have a mandate to protect consumers, workers, and producers, as well promoting fair competition among businesspeople by introducing interventions and laws (for example, subsidies and import tariffs, food safety laws, labour laws, and anti-trust laws) (Beckert and Dewey, 2017). Similarly, actors in the market may introduce regulations or organize themselves to protect their interests, such as a guaranteed price or quality (for example, cooperatives, contract farming). While some interventions are meant for the common good, they sometimes constitute barriers to entry into the market, especially if they are not well thought out. For example, strict standard requirements on goods mean that those who cannot meet the requirements have to find another place to purchase or sell goods or services. Yet in some circumstances, some interventions or regulations may be backed by individuals who have an interest in the market. Thus, these competing interests may sometimes produce unintended consequences, such as sale of illegitimate produce or services. This creates what Beckert and Wehinger (2012) term as an 'illegal market'.

A market becomes illegal when the good or service itself is not permitted by law or the rules are violated in the way the service or goods are exchanged (Beckert and Dewey, 2017). For crime to occur in the marketing process, three conditions must exist: (1) product (illegal or legal), (2) willing sellers, and (3) willing buyers. Both the willing buyer and seller are ready to compromise product price and requirements in terms of quantity, quality, process, and those involved. On the supply side, crime occurs when producers or sellers want to offer goods and services that do not meet quality standards of market specifications at the same price or compromise quantity at a lower price, or sometimes both quality and quantity are compromised and offered to the market. On the demand side, crime occurs when purchasers or consumers want cheaper or compromised goods or services than legally sourced ones. Further, sometimes the product or service is legal but offered in an illegal place or through an illegal process (Beckert and Wehinger, 2012). As such, there are different categories of markets that emerge depending on the kind of goods or services being marketed and how it is done. There are those that are legal (both the goods or services and marketing are done according to law), illegal (either or both the product and marketing do not follow law), or 'ethically' dubious, where the legal goods or services are marketed with questionable tactics. Legitimate and illegitimate markets are often mediated by the legitimacy of goods or services and transactions made (Beckert and Wehinger, 2012; Dewatripont and Tirole, 2019). For instance, illegitimate markets involve legitimate business owners who can source illegal farm produce, or illegitimate businesses can source legitimate goods, and vice versa. Thereby, there are interdependencies between licit and illicit economic behaviours in the illegal markets.

In this chapter, the focus is on the infringement of government regulations on food safety by farmers and other actors in the food chain through the sale of illegal farm produce. Illegal farm produce refers to contaminated farm produce, and rule violations revolve around the selling and buying of contaminated farm produce. Finally, the concern in this chapter is with illegal farm produce being placed in legal or illegal farm markets. Rule violation in the food market by the deliberate sale of farm produce that does not meet food safety standards or regulatory specifications is a form of food fraud (Lord et al, 2017). Food fraud is a criminal entrepreneurial activity that involves the exploitation of gaps in business transactions or enforcement for monetary gain (Lord et al, 2017). According to Lord et al (2017), associated criminal entrepreneurial behaviours in the exchange of illicit food products disguised as licit products within a legal market entail behaviours, relations, and acts (commissions or omissions), such as non-disclosure of characteristics of farm produce or mislabelling of food items, which is the focus of this chapter.

Research also shows that some illegal practices in food business, such as meat fraud, are highly organized, involving more than one motivated entrepreneurial actor who sees opportunities in both legitimate and illegitimate farm produce markets (Manning et al, 2016; McElwee et al, 2017). There is evidence in Kenya that the sale of contaminated meat, and the stealing of coffee cherries and avocados may be highly organized (Bunei et al, 2021). The key actors (that is, food traders, farm managers, farm workers, and law enforcers) in the food market may respond 'rationally' by cutting corners or acting illegally so as to survive in a competitive or challenging business environment. According to Smith et al (2017), farmers are at the lower end of organized crime groups (OCGs) who conspire to pass illicit food into the food market for profit. Smith et al (2017) define rogue actors as individuals who breach regulations by deliberately selling or supporting the sale of rule violations in the market for financial gain. It is important to note that some actors are not organized criminals but opportunists who take advantage of existing gaps in markets and enforcement whenever they arise.

While there are a few studies (for example, Muriithi et al, 2011; Hoffmann et al, 2013) that have examined sale of contaminated farm produce in Kenya, unfortunately, most of them have focused on the export market and less on domestic markets. This study addresses this gap by bringing forth knowledge from the context of an emerging economy, such as Kenya. In Kenya, the agri-food market is composed of both formal and informal markets. However, a large portion of farm produce is sold informally. Informal markets include livestock agents, grain traders, neighbours, butchers, and local hotels. Formal markets are mostly government or private grain millers, milk processors, schools, and hospitals. Most small-scale farmers engage in on-the-spot market transactions, involving selling to local markets that are poorly regulated (Hoffmann et al, 2013; Woolverton and Neven, 2014). This context provides a unique opportunity to understand the phenomenon of white-collar crime. In the next section, I provide the methodology for this study.

Current study

The current study was conducted in Uasin Gishu County, Kenya, regarding law-breaking in agricultural marketing in Kenya. The study utilized criminological, sociological, and economic frameworks to understand rule-breaking in agricultural markets in Kenya. Data collection for this study involved a focus group discussion with 54 farmers (six groups), and in-depth interviews with 29 experts and key stakeholders in the agri-food chain that were conducted in Uasin Gishu County, Kenya, between September and December 2019. Participants in in-depth interviews were individuals working in the agri-food chain whose knowledge was important for understanding the behaviour of farmers and other actors

Table 9.1: Profile of key informants

Participant	Area of expertise
#01	Large-scale farmer
#02	Veterinary officer, regular newspaper columnist, and food safety expert
#03	Public health
#04	Representative of farmers' group
#05–#12	Extension service
#13	Business community – milk
#14	Business community – maize/livestock agent/middlemen
#15	Business community – butcher owner
#16	Policing
#17–#19	Business community/livestock agents/middlemen
#20	Governance and farmer
#21	Farmer groups/farmer activist
#22–#25	Community administration
#26	Farmer, farm activist, farm governance, reader in farming and farm policy
#27	Slaughterhouse operator
#28	Business community – maize
#29	Business community/livestock agents/middlemen

in the food chain when participating in the marketing of contaminated food. The key informants (KI) included farmers, government officers (for example, extension officers, veterinary and public health officers), private agronomists, community administrators, leaders of farmers' organizations, food traders, and newspaper columnists on food safety (see Table 9.1 for summary of profile of Key Informants). Additional information was obtained from official government and industry statistical reports, journal articles, industry newsletters, newspaper articles, and World Bank and UN agency reports. Transcripts and notes from reviews of government documents, relevant literature, focus group discussions (FGDs), and in-depth interviews were analyzed thematically, utilizing codes derived from literature reviewed and reoccurring observations.

Results

Presences of stringent formal markets and informal markets

Study participants observed that small-scale farmers view agri-food safety regulations as a barrier to accessing formal markets. The strict requirements of the formal markets (for example, commercial and government food processors, public hospitals, supermarkets, public schools, boards, and other government institutions) mean extra costs, as farmers are required to implement operational changes to guarantee the safety and quality of farm produce. One participant said: 'Some regulations are not fair, practical, and not appropriate for some of us who produce small quantities' (FGD#3). Some participants mentioned that some food regulations exclude small-scale farmers from participating in mainstream formal markets, such as supermarkets and government institutions: 'Because you cannot sell [maize not having required moisture content] to formal buyers, it is better we sell to informal traders who do not demand a lot of things like (moisture level). Also, informal buyers sometimes do not use weight to buy maize' (FGD#5).

Further, some focus group participants reported that they would rather sell to informal markets that do not have stringent requirements. In addition to tight restrictions and regulations by formal buyers, farmers believed that the bureaucratic nature of payment by the formal markets creates unnecessary delays and possibly increases financial pressure on farmers, especially small-scale farmers. One participant said: 'Even if the processors refuse your milk, there are a lot of small hotels who require milk. You just come and ask if they want milk, and they will buy' (FGD#6). Informal markets are arenas where the exchange of goods and services is unregulated or not strictly enforced, easy to enter, farm produce is sold in small quantities, usually below standard requirements, labour intensive (the tendency to utilize human labour in their operations, which can be prone to human errors), and operations are small-scale (Roesel and Grace, 2014). The buyers in the informal market are usually of low means and marginalized in society. In Kenya, informal markets include local open farm produce markets, greengrocers, peri-urban roadside markets, and traders (for example, livestock agents, grain traders) who purchase farm produce from farmers and resell it to retailers or wholesalers, hotels, and restaurants. Factors that contribute to farmers, especially small-scale farmers, preferring informal markets include immediate payment and the avoidance of the stringent safety and quality requirements of the formal markets that are regulated. Rogue farm produce traders have found informal markets to be lucrative places to sell their contaminated farm produce because of the existence of ready buyers and because they are mostly poorly regulated.

The impact of farm size

In this study, some participants believed that most farmers in Kenya are smallholders, and therefore, their incomes are insufficient to support avoidable investments in the farm. Thus, study participants observed that complying with regulations may mean additional costs (fixed, variable, or transactional) and, therefore, a higher selling price. One focus group participant reported the following: 'This smallness of operations greatly impedes their daily decisions including compliance with the law. When it comes to the priority of spending [gain], complying comes among the last things to consider' (KI#6). Another focus group participant discussed how capital costs such as changes to farm structures or equipment to ensure food safety can disproportionately affect small-scale farmers:

> Not all people can ensure food safety. For example, the issue of milk; you need to spend a lot of money such as constructing milking shade, buying aluminium containers, and having cold storage. To ensure all these, it requires money, and yet you may be a farmer who is struggling. (FGD#2)

As represented by the above comments, the size of farm operations has a strong influence on how farmers participate in the market in terms of the price of farm produce and the urgency of payment. In this study, the term small-scale farmer is defined as farmers who farm less than two hectares and use their own labour full-time, or in some cases part time, and for whom agricultural production is their primary source of food supply and income. This has implications for the competitiveness of farm produce in the market. Consequently, some farmers may opt to sell contaminated farm produce to raise money or avoid costs or losses.

Lack of farmers' organizations

Farmers' organizations refer to groups of producers who have come together to influence their bargaining power and protect their reputation in the market. This includes cooperatives and farmer common interest groups, aggregators, and associations. Some participants in the study observed that a lack of an effective farmers' organization has led to law-breaking in agricultural marketing, as it is difficult to police many small-scale farmers, who are a highly fragmented group. One participant remarked: 'We need to organize farmers, especially small-scale farmers, into groups so that they self-regulate. This is good because the government monitors cooperatives and cooperatives monitor their members. If one person [farmer] does the wrong thing [violate] ... all of us suffer. So, you are forced to be disciplined because you do not want to ruin the image of your cooperative' (FGD#3). Another agreed: 'I am a small-scale farmer. I cannot sell one litre to a milk processor. So, I opt to sell to milk traders who collect milk from farmers like me who are not able to produce five litres' (FGD#2).

These quotes show that market participation in cooperatives not only increases guardianship measures, but also fosters the normative role of acting appropriately. Another important aspect of farmers' organizations is the capacity to instil self-discipline, a practice referred to as 'self-regulation'. Thus, organizing farmers into cooperatives increases compliance, as the fear of ruining the reputation of the group drives farmers to comply with the law.

Presence of rogue traders

Business intermediaries or traders (for example, open farm produce markets, greengrocers, peri-urban roadside markets, hotels and restaurants, livestock agents, and grain traders) play a crucial role in linking farmers with buyers of farm products. However, business intermediaries may face unfavourable business conditions which may tempt them to violate laws or take advantage of emerging business opportunity to recover cost or generate profit, albeit illegally. One participant remarked the following in relation to business intermediaries who became rogue by engaging in illegal trading of contaminated farm produce:

> There is a business that has come. Meat brokers have found a black [illegal] market in towns and slums [informal settlements] because *okoa* [meat from livestock that is sick, under medication, or drought stricken] is cheap. A broker buys *okoa* at KES 3000 and he can easily sell at KES 10,000. It has become a business. There is a network facilitating illegal trade starting from farmers through brokers to consumers. The beneficiaries are brokers. (#FGD4)

One key informant remarked: 'Although it is a crime to add milk water, it does not mostly occur on farm premises. It mostly occurs after milk has exited the farm gate' (KI#6).

As observed, unscrupulous or rogue traders in the food chain act as supporters of law-breaking in agricultural marketing by providing financially constrained farmers with the opportunity to dispose of their contaminated farm produce. Unscrupulous traders act as buyers of illegal farm produce and sell it in informal and poorly regulated formal markets, sometimes with the aid of rogue law enforcers. This suggests that farmers may become victims of organized crime in agri-food business, either deliberately or innocently.

Farm produce of high demand and value

Farm produce that is in high demand and of high value is a lucrative business venture for some rogue traders. Thus, if such farm produce becomes illegitimate (for example, contaminated meat), it can be very lucrative to rogue business traders, who can source it cheaply and sell it like legal goods. One key informant remarked the following about farm produce of high value: 'There is need for price premiums on food produced by following the law. If a farmer can receive good money from the sale of goods [farm produce] when they have followed the law, they will not be motivated to sell contaminated farm produce' (KI#12). A focus group participant agreed: '*Okoa* is lucrative. You can easily make a good profit' (KI#23).

As indicated by these quotes, farm produce that is illegal because it is not meeting safety standards can be attractive to both financially constrained farmers and rogue traders: both benefit by selling illegal produce to the market. In this study, these products were meat, milk, maize, and vegetables. For example, meat and milk are in high demand in informal markets. Rogue traders find these farm products easily disposable and very profitable.

Presence of rogue law enforcers

Law enforcers in the market are supposed to ensure that any exchange of goods or services is legal and/or that the exchange of a product or service is done within the law. For food markets, law enforcers are present from farms to the platforms where the final consumer buys the farm produce. This includes food inspectors, market inspectors, public health officers, veterinary officers, and many others. Participants, especially farmers and key informants, discussed how some rogue law enforcers support or encourage the sale of illegal farm produce, especially high-value, high-demand farm produce such as meat (livestock) and milk. This is not surprising, as some law enforcers may spot an opportunity to make money by allowing rogue farmers or other food traders to sell or buy illegal farm produce or violate food safety laws while buying or selling legal farm produce. One focus group participant said: 'there is the possibility that you [farmer] can opt not to comply and fail to be caught by police, or even if you are caught, you can escape – courtesy of corruption!' (FGD#4). Further, participants identified transportation routes and food processors as points where most rule violations occur in the food chain. Specifically, it was noted that bribery or corruption tends to occur among inspectors at the roadblocks and among those in the food processors (for example, abattoirs, aggregation centres). A meat trader stated: 'I blame corruption. It is not possible for sick livestock to pass so many regulatory bodies on the way to town' (KI#19). Overall, a lack of reliable safety and quality checks by law enforcers, presence of rogue (corruptible) law enforcers, and the absence of traceability systems create opportunities for rule violations in farm produce markets.

As shown in Figure 9.1, the presence of strict formal markets coupled with the existence of informal markets tends to generate push and pull factors to offend in the farm markets. Thus, it is not surprising that factors like the inability of small farms to place their products in formal markets (such as big meat processors) displace them to informal markets, where they can at least find somewhere to sell their farm produce. Informal markets may be difficult

Figure 9.1: The interrelationship between key study observations

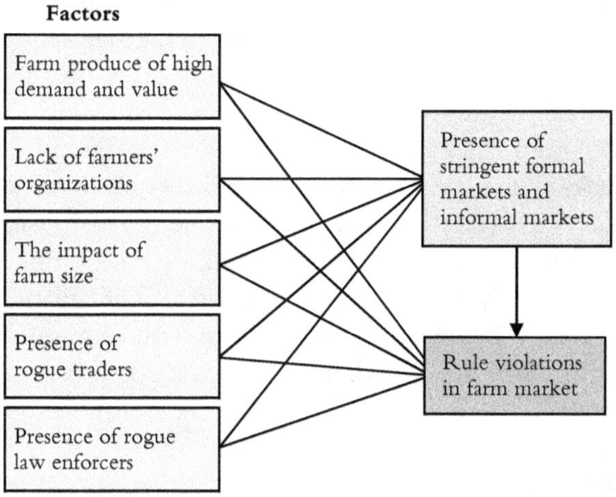

Factors

- Farm produce of high demand and value
- Lack of farmers' organizations
- The impact of farm size
- Presence of rogue traders
- Presence of rogue law enforcers

→ Presence of stringent formal markets and informal markets
→ Rule violations in farm market

to regulate and therefore lack guardianship, which provides opportunities for rogue traders to source contaminated farm produce. Consequently, designing effective and acceptable agri-food safety compliance strategies requires an understanding of these local dynamics in Kenya.

Conclusion

The current study has sought to identify – through the lenses of criminology, economics, and market sociology – the key factors or conditions that make farmers or other actors participate in the violations of agri-food safety regulations by marketing or selling contaminated farm produce. The study framed noncompliance as an economically driven behaviour that is mediated by social, political, and legal factors. Overall, noncompliance with food safety regulations by farmers and other actors in the food chain through the deliberate sale of contaminated farm produce was largely determined by two factors: motivation and opportunities in the legal (enforcement gaps) and illegal (economic) markets. These actors' motivation for rule violations in the markets and opportunities for law-breaking are determined by the structural, institutional, and sociocultural structures present in society.

Regarding motivation, the overarching driver for the sale of contaminated food is monetary gain in terms of avoiding costs or losses, especially in relation to small-scale farmers. This finding is consistent with the findings of previous regulatory studies (Muriithi et al, 2011; Siddiki et al, 2012). Small-scale farmers, like other actors in the market, when faced with constraints that emanate from complying with regulations in the production and distribution of farm produce, have to avoid costs to make a profit.

Small-scale farmers viewed agri-food safety as a constraint that prevents them from participating in the sale of farm produce; this is consistent with the findings in other regions of Kenya (Mwambi et al, 2020) as well as in developed societies (Winter and May, 2001; Hendrickson and James, 2005; Chen et al, 2021). This suggests that designing effective and acceptable agri-food safety compliance strategies requires an understanding of the size of farm operations, the local needs of the farmer, and local dynamics. For example, some small-scale farmers face the dilemma of losing income or going hungry because they cannot sell the milk from their one cow for three days in order to comply with the agri-food safety regulations regarding the withholding period. Therefore, as complying with food safety regulations has differential implications for their lives, some farmers breach agri-food safety regulations for socioeconomic reasons. The implications are that the government needs to make compliance with agri-food safety regulations financially attractive by supporting farmers to modernize their operations.

Second, in relation to the existence of opportunities in the legal and illegal markets, the results show that farmers and other food traders tend to exploit opportunities or enforcement gaps that arise from their normal business. As Lord et al (2019) observe, there is a need to understand those inherent factors, conditions, or drivers that provide opportunity for offending in farm produce (food) markets. Some of the opportunities are licit, while others are quasi-legal or outright illegal. In this study, rogue food traders (illegal) and informal settlements (quasi-legal) provided economic opportunity for unscrupulous farmers to sell their illegitimate farm produce. For example, strict formal regulations in the formal markets motivate some farmers and other actors to sell their illegitimate farm produce in informal markets, where there are minimal barriers in terms of safety and quality checking. This finding about strict formal markets, the existence of illegal markets or strained formal markets, and the noncompliance behaviour of farmers mirrors what other scholars have found on the impact of unstable markets on individual decisions (Beckert and Wehinger, 2012; Lord et al, 2017).

The existence of informal settlements, mostly in urban centres, has provided rogue traders as well as unscrupulous farmers with the opportunity to sell their contaminated food as there is minimal guardianship. This finding is similar to the findings of Hoffmann and Moser (2017) in Kenya in relation to rejected contaminated maize that is redirected to lower-value markets (that is, informal markets in this study). This implies that sometimes good intentions (laws) may lead to unintended consequences. Furthermore, contaminated farm produce that is in high demand and easily sold is more likely to be targeted by rogue farm produce traders. Specifically, milk, meat, maize, and vegetables were in high demand because of the increasing population in urban centres, especially in informal settlements; this is similar to findings by van Ruth and de Pagter-de Witte (2020), who found that pork and olives were more likely to be targeted for fraudulent practices than eggs and bananas, partly because of their attractiveness in terms of value and demand. Farm produce that is not in high demand might not be targeted by rogue traders because it is not a major staple in Kenya, such as wheat, rice, and millet; it is, therefore, not attractive to source contaminated farm produce from these groups.

Another important finding relates to enforcement gaps in legal markets. This includes a lack of reliable safety and quality checks for farm produce, a lack of farm produce traceability systems, and a lack of education for farmers, traders, and consumers. This problem is compounded by the presence of corrupt law enforcers who are ready to benefit from allowing the sale of contaminated farm produce. This provides an opportunity for the sale of illegal farm produce on legal markets. This observation mirrors what Cheng (2012) found in China: illegal practices in the food chain occur 'in the context of "cheap capitalism", characterized by low prices, inferior quality of products, and degraded social morality and business ethics'. This shows that food fraud practices are affected by a number of factors situated in economic, social, cultural, and political contexts, echoing the observation by Lord et al (2017) that food fraud is socially organized around commercial opportunities.

In conclusion, by addressing the agri-food safety compliance problems identified in this study, the likelihood of securing livelihoods, promoting economic development, and, more importantly, public health is enhanced. Importantly, if the sale of illegal farm produce is not checked, it can bring serious social consequences and harm to society (for example, consumers, farm workers, farmers, and food traders). For example, the increased proliferation of the sale of illegal farm produce can affect the economic relationship between rural and urban areas. Further, as alluded to in the introduction, the sale of illegal farm produce would undermine the livelihoods of 70 per cent of small-scale farmers in Kenya who depend on growing and supplying farm produce to earn income. Thus, there is a need for concerted efforts to protect and support farmers experiencing difficulties in producing food. There is also a need to support consumers in informal settlements to access affordable food. In relation to rogue traders, the government needs to expand monitoring and detection strategies and introduce punitive strategies, such as harsh fines and the threat of loss of licence for traders or public shaming via mainstream media (for example, newspapers) and/or social media (for example, Facebook, X). The public could be encouraged to report rogue traders or enforcers anonymously via secure online links. These strategies not only address the motivation to sell illegal farm produce but also reduce the opportunities for disposing of such products. Innovative non-deterrence tactics like affordable insurance could significantly lessen farmers' or food traders' struggles for economic survival. Also, the government needs to increase guardianship measures, especially traceability measures, food safety checks, and the activities of rogue traders.

This chapter concludes by suggesting that there is a need for an increased interdisciplinary approach (a conflux of criminology, sociology, economics, public health, law, political science, and social psychology) to the study of white-collar crimes in the agri-food sector, so as to provide critical points of view that enrich understanding of law-breaking in the sale of contaminated farm produce.

Note

[1] Ward is the lowest electoral unit within a sub-county that is delimited for purposes of representation in the county governments of Kenya in accordance with Article 89 of the Constitution. It is usually represented by a person elected as a member of the County Assembly for five years. There are 1,450 wards across Kenya and 30 in Uasin Gishu County (Republic of Kenya, 2010).

References

Beckert, J. and Dewey, M. (2017) 'Introduction: the social organization of illegal markets', in J. Beckert and M. Dewey (eds), *The Architecture of Illegal Markets: Towards an Economic Sociology of Illegality in the Economy*, Oxford University Press, pp 1–34.

Beckert, J. and Wehinger, F. (2012) 'In the shadow: illegal markets and economic sociology', *Socio-Economic Review*, 11(1): 55–30.

Bunei, E., Barclay, E., and Kotey, B. (2021) 'Routine activity theory and farm produce sale in Kenya: an analysis of non-compliance with agri-food safety laws', *Crime Prevention and Community Safety*, 23: 400–15.

Chen, H., Ellett, J. K., Phillips, R., and Feng, Y. (2021) 'Small-scale produce growers' barriers and motivators to value-added business: food safety and beyond', *Food Control*, 130: 108192.

Cheng, H. (2012) 'Cheap capitalism: a sociological study of food crime in China', *The British Journal of Criminology*, 52(2): 254–73.

Dewatripont, M. and Tirole, J. (2019) *Incentives and Ethics: How Markets and Organizations Shape Our Moral Behavior*, Working Paper.

Gitaka, J., Kamita, M., Mureithi, D., Ndegwa, D., Masika, M., Omuse, G., et al (2020) 'Combating antibiotic resistance using guidelines and enhanced stewardship in Kenya: a protocol for an implementation science approach', *BMJ Open*, 10(3): e030823.

Gottschalk, P. (2010) 'Criminal entrepreneurial behaviour', *Journal for International Business and Entrepreneurship Development*, 5(1): 635–76.

Harcourt-Brown, L., Alonso, S., Lindahl, J.F., Varnell, H., Hoffman, V., and Grace, D. (2018) *Regulatory Compliance in the Kenyan Dairy Sector: Awareness and Compliance Among Farmers and Vendors*, International Food Policy Research Institute. Available from: http://ebrary.ifpri.org/cdm/ref/collection/p15738coll2/id/133046

Hendrickson, M.K. and James, H.S. (2005) 'The ethics of constrained choice: how the industrialization of agriculture impacts farming and farmer behavior', *Journal of Agricultural and Environmental Ethics*, 18(3): 269–91.

Hoffmann, V. and Moser, C. (2017) 'You get what you pay for: the link between price and food safety in Kenya', *Agricultural Economics*, 48(4): 449–58.

Hoffmann, V., Mutiga, S., Harvey, J., Nelson, R., and Milgroom, M. (2013) Asymmetric Information and Food Safety: Maize in Kenya, Agricultural and Applied Economics Association (AAEA) 2013 Annual Meeting (4–6 August), Agricultural and Applied Economics Association.

Kenya National Bureau of Statistics [KNBS] (2020) *Economic Survey 2020*. Kenya National Bureau of Statistics. Available from: https://www.knbs.or.ke/?wpdmpro=economic-survey-2020

Kenya National Bureau of Statistics [KNBS] (2019) *2019 Kenya Population and Census*, Kenya National Bureau of Statistics. Available from: https://www.knbs.or.ke/download/2019-kenya-population-and-housing-census-volume-iv-distribution-of-population-by-socio-economic-characteristics/

Kiama, T.N., Lindahl, J.F., Sirma, A.J., Senerwa, D.M., Waithanji, E.M., Ochungo, P.A. et al (2016) 'Kenya dairy farmer perception of moulds and mycotoxins and implications for exposure to aflatoxins: a gendered analysis', *African Journal of Food, Agriculture, Nutrition and Development*, 16(3): 11106–25.

Kutto, E.K., Ngigi, M.W., Karanja, N., Kangethe, E., Bebora, L., Lagerkvist, C.J. et al (2011) 'Bacterial contamination of kale (brassica oleracea acephala) along the supply chain in Nairobi and its environment', *East African Medical Journal*, 88(2): 46–53.

Lord, N.J., Campbell, L.J., and Van Wingerde, K. (2019) 'Other people's dirty money: professional intermediaries, market dynamics and the finances of white-collar, corporate and organized crimes', *The British Journal of Criminology*, 59(5): 1217–36.

Lord, N., Flores Elizondo, C.J., and Spencer, J. (2017) 'The dynamics of food fraud: the interactions between criminal opportunity and market (dys)functionality in legitimate business', *Criminology & Criminal Justice*, 17(5): 605–23.

Manning, L., Smith, R., and Soon, J.M. (2016) 'Developing an organizational typology of criminals in the meat supply chain', *Food Policy*, 59: 44–54.

McElwee, G., Smith, R., and Lever, J. (2017) 'Illegal activity in the UK halal (sheep) supply chain: towards greater understanding', *Food Policy*, 69: 166–75.

Muriithi, B.W., Mburu, J., and Ngigi, M. (2011) 'Constraints and determinants of compliance with EurepGap standards: a case of smallholder french bean exporters in Kirinyaga district, Kenya', *Agribusiness*, 27(2): 193–204.

Mwambi, M., Bijman, J., Mshenga, P., and Oosting, S. (2020) 'Adoption of food safety measures: the role of bargaining and processing producer organizations', *NJAS – Wageningen Journal of Life Sciences*, 92 (December): 100337.

Odwar, J.A., Kikuvi, G., Kariuki, J.N., and Kariuki, S. (2014) 'A cross-sectional study on the microbiological quality and safety of raw chicken meats sold in Nairobi, Kenya', *BMC Research Notes*, 7: 627.

Republic of Kenya (2010) *The Constitution of Kenya*. Government Printer.

Republic of Kenya (2017) *National Policy on Prevention and Containment of Antimicrobial Resistance*. Ministry of Agriculture, Livestock, Fisheries and Irrigation. Available from: https://www.health.go.ke/wp-content/uploads/2017/04/Kenya-AMR-Containment-Policy-_Final_April.pdf

Republic of Kenya (2019a) *Agricultural Sector Transformation and Growth Strategy: 2019–2029*. Ministry of Agriculture and Livestock Development. Available from: https://www.agck.or.ke/Downloads/ASTGS-Full-Version-1.pdf

Republic of Kenya (2019b) *TheNational Livestock policy*. Ministry of Agriculture and Livestock Development. Available from: https://kilimo.go.ke/wp-content/uploads/2024/08/Livestock-Policy-Sessional-Paper-Number-3-of-2020-2.pdf

Republic of Kenya (2021a) *National Agricultural Marketing Strategy 2021–2030*. Ministry of Agriculture and Livestock Development. Available from: https://kilimo.go.ke/wp-content/uploads/2021/11/Draft-National-Agricultural-Marketing-Strategy-2021.11.04-edited.pdf

Republic of Kenya (2021b) *The Draft National Food Safety Policy*. Ministry of Agriculture and Livestock Development. Available from: https://kilimo.go.ke/wp-content/uploads/2022/02/Draft-Food-Safety-Policy-2021.pdf

Rizzuti, A. (2022) 'Organized crime in the agri-food industry', in Z. Yuliya and K. Thachuk (eds), *The Private Sector and Organized Crime*, Routledge, pp 163–79.

Roesel, K., and Grace, D. (eds) (2014) *Food Safety and Informal Markets: Animal Products in Sub-Saharan Africa*, Routledge.

Senerwa, D.M., Sirma, A.J., Mtimet, N., Kang'ethe, E.K., Grace, D., and Lindahl, J.F. (2016) 'Prevalence of aflatoxin in feeds and cow milk from five counties in Kenya', *African Journal of Food, Agriculture, Nutrition and Development*, 16(3): 11004–21.

Siddiki, S., Basurto, X., and Weible, C.M. (2012) 'Using the institutional grammar tool to understand regulatory compliance: the case of Colorado aquaculture', *Regulation and Governance*, 6(2): 167–88.

Smith, R., Manning, L., and McElwee, G. (2017) 'Critiquing the interdisciplinary literature on food fraud', *International Journal of Rural Criminology*, 3(2): 250–70.

Spencer, J., Lord, N., Benson, K., and Bellotti, E. (2018) '"C" is for commercial collaboration: enterprise and structure in the "middle market" of counterfeit alcohol distribution', *Crime, Law and Social Change*, 70: 543–60.

van Ruth, S.M. and de Pagter-de Witte, L. (2020) 'Integrity of organic foods and their suppliers: fraud vulnerability across chains', *Foods*, 9(2): 188.

Winter, S.C. and May, P.J. (2001) 'Motivation for compliance with environmental regulations', *Journal of Policy Analysis and Management*, 20(4): 675–98.

Woolverton, A. and Neven, D. (2014) *Understanding Smallholder Farmer Attitudes to Commercialization: The Case of Maize in Kenya*. Available from: http://www.fao.org/3/a-i3717e.pdf

Index

References to endnotes show both the page number and the note number (231n3).

A

abductive reasoning 67
ABN AMRO 41
accountability 52
adaptive theory 126, 131
administrative law 17, 136
adolescent crime 10
affective atmospheres 3, 97–110
age and crime 10
age-graded theory 118
agri-food sector 153–69
alien theory 114
amoral calculators 16–17
analytical dualism 62
Andreff, W. 127, 128, 129
anti-cartel enforcement 49
anti-money laundering (AML) 3, 41–57, 58–77
Apel, R. 98
Archer, M.S. 62
arrest, fear of 89, 91
art fairs 97–110
Auspurg, K. 79, 80, 81, 84, 85, 86
automated transaction monitoring systems 60, 62
Aviram, H. 79, 81, 83, 84, 86
awareness raising 50
Ayres, I. 43, 54

B

'bad apples' 15, 72
banking systems 41, 58–77, 117
Beach, D. 31, 32
'bearers of harm' 130–1, 132–5, 138–40, 144–5
Beckert, J. 154, 155, 156, 164
Belgium 126, 131, 132–45
beliefs, collective 61
beliefs, underlying 25, 27–8, 62, 103
Benson, M.L. 26
Betlem, R. 48
Bhaskar, R. 60–1, 62, 64

biopolitical strategy 100
Bovens, M.A.P. 52
BP 26
BRAFA (Brussels Art Fair) 98
Braithwaite, J. 43, 50, 52, 53, 54
bribery 78–96, 125, 141
Bunei, E. 157
Burrows, J. 128–9, 130

C

Cameron, K.S. 27
career impacts 91
Carpenter, K. 144
cartels 43–4, 49
case study methods 28, 31, 33, 78
causal explanations 10
causal process tracing method 31–2, 33, 34, 35
Challenger space shuttle disaster 28
Champeyrache, C. 117
Chappelet, J.L. 128
China 78–96, 165
civil society 43
'Clean Hands' 126, 137
Clinard, M.B. 9, 24, 25
'codes of silence' 28, 31
Cohen, D.V. 26
Collington, R. 52
command-and-control measures 90
competition 25, 43–4, 50, 80, 104, 141, 146, 155
compliance industry 51
compliance structures 62, 67, 88–9, 90, 92
conflicts of interest 43, 155
connecting organizations 47, 48
consultancy firms 42, 44, 47, 48, 49, 51–2
contamination 154, 156, 157, 161
cooperative regulation 91, 160–1
'core scripts' 131, 132–5
corporate abuse 16
corporate crime 2, 8–22
corporate culture 14, 23–40
Corporate Ethical Virtues Model 27

INDEX

corporate life-stages 11
corporate violence 16
Council of Europe Convention on the Manipulation of Sports Competitions *see* Macolin Convention (Council of Europe, 2020)
counter-terrorist financing (CTF) 41, 59
court transcripts as data source 64, 131
Cox, R. 102, 105
criminal prosecutions 59–60, 65, 82, 91, 141
criminogenic cultures 30, 32, 104
criminogenic normative codes 114
criminology
  and agency 67
  case study methods 28
  corporate criminology 24, 33, 35
  critical realism 63
  inclusion of policing 29
  traditional focus of 5, 9
  visual senses 97
critical realism 3, 58–77
critical skills gaps 70
cross-cultural studies 93
culture 14, 23–40, 62, 68, 69, 70, 104
  see also organizational culture
cycling 125, 137, 142, 144

D

Dalla Chiesa, N. 113
Danermark, B. 58, 61, 63, 64
data coding 44–5, 65–7, 158
de Pagter-de Witte, L. 164–5
decentralization of control 41, 43
decision-making, criminal 86–9, 104, 106, 141
definitions
  corporate crime 9, 113
  corporation 18n1
  fraud 128, 129
  fraud in sports 129–30
  harm 130
  infiltration 114–15
  organized crime 120n4
  white-collar crime 1–2
demi-regularities 66, 67, 68–9, 70
detection 90–1, 136, 165
deterrence 49–50, 90–1, 165
deviant cultures 26
Dickel, P. 88, 90
differential association 35, 48
diversity and occurence framework 12–15
diversity of crime 8–22
doping 125, 128, 134, 138, 141, 142, 144, 145
dramatization of risks 51–2
dual taxonomy (Moffitt) 10
due diligence 59
Duff, C. 99, 100
Duncan, C. 102–3

E

economic environments 80, 114, 119
economic stakeholders 42–3
economics 112, 113
education (intervention) 17
elites 2, 103, 113, 137, 145
embezzlement 126, 138
emotions and criminal intentions/decision-making 89, 97–110
employee norms and practices 62
enforcement 53, 118, 162–3
entrepreneurial crime 115, 117, 118, 154, 156, 157
ethics
  Corporate Ethical Virtues Model 27
  ethical codes 92
  ethical cultures 27, 93
  ethics training 89
  experimental research designs 90
ethnography 35, 101
EUROC (European Society of Criminology's Working Group on Organizational Crime) 5, 6
experimental research designs 79, 81, 82, 90

F

factorial survey method 3, 78–96
Fantò, E. 113
FC Seraing/Doyen case 142
fear of arrest 89, 91
fear of falling hypothesis 89
FIFA 126, 142
Financial Conduct Authority (FCA) 59, 60, 65
financial fair play regulations 126, 141
financial loss, avoidance of 89
Fincoeur, B. 144
Fine, A. 26, 28, 33
fines 50, 141, 142, 165
Fletcher, A.J. 67
focus groups 155, 157, 158
food fraud 156, 161, 165
food safety regulations 153–4, 159, 160, 161–2, 163–4, 165
football 125–6, 128, 137, 140, 141, 143
'Football Leaks' 126, 142
forgery 138
Fowler Oldfield 59–60, 65, 66, 67, 68, 70, 72, 73
Franklin, A. 98
Fraser, A. 100, 101
fraud 125–52
Friedrichs, D.O. 16
frontmen 117–18
functional integrity, harm to 130, 139, 140, 144

G

gambling industry 125, 143
Geis, G. 26
generative mechanisms 3

goal-seeking 33, 104
good practice sharing 45–6, 49, 51
Good Regulatory Intervention Design 15
Gotelaere, S. 126, 131, 137, 146
Gottfredson, M.R. 8, 9, 10, 24
governance structures
  banking systems 67–8, 70
  sports sector 129, 130, 138, 141, 142, 144, 146
Graeff, P. 88, 90
Greenfield, V. 127, 129, 130, 138, 146, 147
Greve, H.R. 24
Gunningham, N. 42, 43, 53

H

harm assessment frameworks 127, 129, 130–1, 146, 147
Harvey, A. 144–5
Hastings, C. 63, 65
Herrity, K. 100, 101
hidden dynamics 3–4
Hinz, T. 79, 80, 81, 84, 85, 86
Hirschi, T. 8, 9, 10, 24
Hochstetler, A. 26, 28, 30, 63, 104
Hoffmann, V. 164
Hofstede, G. 23, 25, 26
horizontal versus vertical fraud 129, 138, 140
Hudson, C. 104, 105
Huisman, W. 24, 26, 28, 104

I

identity theft 135, 138
'illegal markets' 156, 164
image transfer 139–40
incompetence 16–17
indirect influences 43, 45, 50
individual-level diversity 11–12
informal markets 157, 158–9, 161
informal sanctions 91
information systems 66–7, 68, 70
information-sharing practices 45–6, 49, 51, 91
informative objectives 50
ING Bank 41, 45, 51
Ingram, J.R. 30
inspections 15
intentions 86–9, 104
  see also decision-making, criminal
interdisciplinary approaches 6, 64, 65, 165, 166
intermediaries 136, 137, 161
internal compliance structures 90
interview methods 30, 44–5, 54, 101, 131, 155, 157, 158
intrinsically motivated change 46
invisibilization of the law 104
Italy 111, 112, 114, 116–17, 141

J

Jung, T. 27
Juventus 141

K

Kagan, R.A. 16–17, 18
Kaplan, P.J. 29
Kaptein, M. 27
Katz, J. 104, 106
Keane, C. 26
Kenyan agri-food sector 4, 153–69
Kihl, L.A. 128
Kindynis, T. 100
Kleemans, E.R. 118
know your customer procedures 68

L

labour laws 137, 147
law enforcement 118, 162–3
  see also police
Lawrence, P.R. 26
Lawson, T. 66
Layder, D. 126, 131
leadership 2, 63
learning circles 48, 50
legal economy, criminal infiltration in 111–24
legal personhood 8
legislation
  industry-wide problems 14
  specialized-generalized behaviour continuum 15–16
leverage 43, 44–53
Levi, M. 1, 2, 3, 4, 5, 63, 72, 118, 128–9, 130
licence fraud 133, 136, 137–8, 140
local residents 43
longitudinal studies 11
Lord, N. 1, 2, 3, 4, 5, 63, 72, 128, 156, 164
Los Angeles Police Department (LAPD) 29
lure 104

M

Mackenzie, S. 99
Macolin Convention (Council of Europe, 2020) 143, 144
Maennig, W. 128, 141
'Maestro' investigation 143
mafia-type organized crime 111–24
management 87, 88, 90, 91
Manoli, A.E. 128
markets 155–6, 158–9, 164–5
match-fixing 125, 126, 128, 135, 139, 141, 143
Matthews, D. 100, 101
Mazzucato, M. 52
Mbemba Mangulu, Chancel 143
McClanahan, B. 97, 98, 100
McNamee, M. 144–5
'mechanical doping' 144
media reports as data source 64
Merz, A. 41, 42, 45, 50, 53
meta-theories 63–4, 72–3

INDEX

Miller, J.C. 100
mixed-method research designs 131
Moffitt, T.E. 10
money, concepts of 61
money laundering
   mafia-type organized crime 117, 118
   peer social control 41–2, 45–8
   sports sector 126, 128, 138
Money Laundering Regulations (2017) 60
MONI (Manchester Organisational Non-Compliance Initiative) 5–6
monopoly 112
moral beliefs 91, 114
moral messages 49
moral norm internalization 88
moral rule breaches 8
Moser, C. 164
motivations 2, 3
   see also decision-making, criminal
multidisciplinary studies 35, 63, 119, 154
multi-layered theorizing 99
multi-level analysis 2, 64, 85
museums 102–3

N

NatWest Bank 58–77
Nazzari, M. 117
negative publicity 43
   see also reputational damage
Netherlands 41–57
neutralization techniques 26, 31
NGOs (non-governmental organizations) 43
non-profits 18n1, 138
norm internalization 88
normalized deviance 68, 70, 106
normative objectives 49
norms 62, 68, 98, 103, 106, 114, 160

O

Oakland Police Department 32–3
observational experiential fieldwork 101
occupational fraud 128, 133, 136, 138, 140
occurence spectrum 12–15
offence-based understandings 2, 16
offender-based understandings 2, 16
Oll, J. 82, 84, 87, 93
Olympics 142
Organizational Cultural Assessment Instrument 27
organizational culture
   affective atmospheres 98, 100
   banking systems 62, 67, 68, 69, 70
   and corporate criminology 23–40
   criminogenic cultures 30, 32, 104
   ethics 92, 93
   information-sharing 91–2
   rule-violating behaviours 24–5
   safety cultures 15

sensory cues 98, 104, 105–6
socialization into culture 25, 26
'tone at the top' 2–3
organizational misconduct 23–6, 29–30
organizational nature of white-collar crime 4
organizational studies 24, 25, 28
organizational theory 88, 89
organized crime 111–24, 138, 157
Other Art Fair 103
Ott, J.S. 25, 27
outsiders' fraud 134, 136, 140
oversight 15

P

Paoli, L. 125, 127, 129, 130, 131, 137, 138, 141, 146, 147
Paralympics 143
parliamentary debates 45, 48
participation in legal economy, criminal 115, 116–20
Paternoster, R. 87, 89, 98
peer learning 48
peer social control 3, 41–57
penalties, adjusting severity of 16
performance-enhancing drugs *see* doping
persistence of criminal careers 10
personal information fraud 135, 141, 143
persuasion (intervention) 17, 42
Philippopoulos-Mihalopoulos, A. 98, 103, 104, 106
phishing 134, 138
Pickett, J.T. 89, 90–1
pilot studies 84, 85, 93
Pink, S. 101
Piquero, N.L. 10, 11, 14, 78, 79, 81, 82, 83, 84, 85, 87, 88, 89, 91
place, effect of 99, 100–1, 104–5
playing surfaces and equipment fraud 135, 141, 144
Pogarsky, G. 84, 90
Pol, R.F. 51–2
police
   misuse of force 29–30, 32–3, 34
   and NatWest 60, 65
   sports sector 136
policy makers 48, 52
political citizens 16, 17
positivism 61
power analyses 86
prevention measures 15, 89–92, 106
price-fixing 26
probability of detection 90–1
'problem of many hands' 52
process tracing method 31–2, 33, 34, 35
profit motives 25, 42, 49–52, 114, 155
psychology 25
psychosocial deficits 10
public interests 43

public pressure 43
publicly available data 64
punishment
  corporate crime 9, 113
  criminal prosecutions 59–60, 65, 82, 91, 136, 141, 142
  and deterrence 49–50
  food fraud 165
  organizational culture 25
  perceived risk of 67, 90
  punitive objectives 49–50
  rational choice theory 67, 90
  regulatory approaches 44, 48, 49
  typological theories of crime 15
  see also sanctions

Q

Quetelet, A. 10
Quinn, R.E. 27

R

R (FCA) v National Westminster Bank Plc Agreed Statement of Facts, 2021 (NatWest Agreed Statement) 59, 60, 68
R (FCA) v National Westminster Bank Plc Sentencing Remarks, 2021 (NatWest Sentencing Remarks) 60, 72
Rabobank 41
Rampart Division Scandal of the LAPD 29
rational choice theory 4–5, 17, 67, 88, 89, 90, 104, 118, 157
Ravenda, D. 121n7
recurring trends/patterns 66
regulatory systems
  administrative law 136
  agri-food sector 153, 154, 155, 157, 158–9
  amoral calculators 17
  cooperative regulation 91, 160–1
  cultural assessments 23–40
  diversity of crime 17
  diversity of enforcement 18
  financial fair play regulations 126, 141
  food safety regulations 153–4, 159, 160, 161–2, 163–4, 165
  good practice sharing 46
  non-punitive regulatory measures 91–2
  peer social control stakeholders 41–2
  punishment 44, 48, 49
  regulatory capture 43
  regulatory pluralism 43
  remediation support by consultancy firms 51
  responsive regulation 15, 54
  risk-based approaches 51
  self-regulation 52–3, 90, 161
  specialized-generalized behaviour continuum 15–16
  sports sector 126, 129, 134, 141, 142, 146
  surrogate regulatory functions 43
  typological theories of crime 9, 14
reintegrative shaming 53
relationship managers 3, 60, 65, 66, 67–8, 69, 70, 72
repeat offending 16
reputational damage 45, 46, 49–50, 88, 89, 139, 140, 144
responsibilization 52–3
responsive regulation 15, 54
retroduction 69–70
Reuter, P. 112, 116, 117, 118
Rhys-Taylor, A. 105
Riccardi, M. 117, 118
risk behaviours 28
risk dramatization 51–2
risk-based approaches 51
risks of taking part in research 99
ritual sites 102–3
rogue law enforcers 162–3, 165
rogue traders 161, 164
Rorie, M. 2, 78, 79, 80, 81, 82, 83, 86, 87, 90, 91, 93
Rossi, P.H. 79
Ruggiero, V. 111, 112, 113, 114, 115, 116
rule-based approaches (versus risk-based) 51

S

'safe rebellions' 99
safety cultures 15
  see also food safety regulations
sample sizes 44, 82, 85, 86
sanctions
  anti-money laundering (AML) 59
  criminal prosecutions 59–60, 65, 82, 91, 141
  criminal sanctions for fraud 136, 142
  deterrence 49–50, 90
  direct influence 45
  fines 50, 141, 142, 165
  informal sanctions 91–2
  peer social control 53
  penalties, adjusting severity of 16
  perceptions of sanction risk 90–1
  sanctionability 8–9, 42
  severity of 91
  threatening 46
  see also punishment; reputational damage
Savona, E.U. 111, 112, 113, 120n1
Schein, E.H. 23, 26, 27–8, 30, 33, 101
Schelling, T.C. 120n2
Schoepfer, A. 88
Scholz, J.T. 16–17, 18
Schrager, L.S. 18n1
'scripts' 131, 132–5
secondary data analysis 45, 89, 131, 158

secondary victims 129, 130, 131, 139–40
security-efficiency trade-off 117–18
self-control 88
self-image 106
self-interest 8, 17
self-regulation 52, 90, 161
self-reporting (compliance) 65
self-reporting (research method) 28, 60, 84
senior management 2
  see also leadership
sensory cues 3, 97–110
sensory ethnography 101
Serres, M. 97
setting up new (criminal) companies 115, 118
Shafritz, J.M. 25, 27
shame 89, 165
Short, J.F. 18n1
short-lived criminal careers 10
Shover, N. 26, 28, 30, 63, 104
silencing 28, 31
Simpson, S.S. 25, 80, 82, 83, 87, 88, 89, 90, 91, 92
Smith, R. 157
snowballing participant recruitment 44
social control 41–57
social desirability bias 83, 84–5
social embeddedness theory 118
social fraud 132–3, 137, 138, 139, 147
social learning 118
social security fraud 128
social stakeholders 42–3
social status 89
socialization into culture 25, 26
sociology 25, 63, 113
soft law 53
Sonnenfeld, J. 26
Soudijn, M. 118
South, N. 97, 100
specialized-generalized behaviour continuum 11–12, 13–18
sports dysfunctions 129
sports sector 4, 125–52
staff training 69
stakeholder influence 41–57
Steiner, P.M. 83, 86
strain theory 33, 35, 118
structure and agency 62–3, 65, 67, 70, 72
subcultures 26, 35
subsidy fraud 132, 137, 138, 139, 140, 146
surrogate regulatory functions 43
survey methods 30, 31, 81–2, 83, 87, 89–90, 92
suspicious activity, identifying 69
Sutherland, E. 1, 4, 24, 26, 48, 113, 116, 127
systemic banks 41

T

targets, pressure to achieve 33, 68
tax offences 117, 126, 128, 131, 132, 136–7, 138, 139
Taylor, B.J. 79, 80, 81, 83, 85
technical skills 119
TEFAF (The European Fine Art Fair) 98
temptations 104
thematic analysis 65
third-party investments (TPI) 147n4
third-party ownership (TPO) 142
third-party stakeholders 43
threats, in order to achieve compliance 46, 47, 48
Thrift, N. 97
thrill 104
trafficking 115, 127, 141, 142, 147
Trafficking Transformations 101
Transparency International 129
tripartism 43
trust 3, 51, 52, 68, 70, 139–40, 144
typological theories of crime 10, 16
typology of sports-related frauds 126–47

U

unconscious beliefs 103
unintended consequences 155, 164
unintentional peer effects 45

V

values
  affective atmospheres 104
  banking systems 62, 68, 70
  organizational culture 25, 27–8, 30, 33
  peer social control 48
van De Bunt, H. 28, 31, 118
Van den Driessche, Femke 144
van Erp, J. 24, 43, 44, 49, 58
van Rooij, B. 23, 25, 26, 28, 33
van Ruth, S.M. 164–5
van Wingerde, K. 50, 52
VAT-frauds 127
Vaughan, D. 24, 26, 28
Verhage, A. 42, 46, 50, 51, 53
victims-centric fraud typology 129
vignettes (factorial survey research) 79–80, 81, 83–4, 87, 89
Volkswagen 26

W

Wall, D. 120n6
Wall, I.R. 106
Wallander, L. 80, 83, 86
Walsh, B. 97, 103, 105, 106
Warr, J. 97
wealth accumulation 114
Wehinger, F. 154, 155, 156, 164

Wells Fargo 26
West, M. 91
Wicker, P. 128
Wikström, P-O. 8
Wolf, B. 97
women 118
workloads 68

workplace environments 99–100
World Anti-Doping Agency (WADA) 142, 144, 145

Y

Yeager, P.C. 9, 24, 25
Young, A. 98, 99, 101

www.ingramcontent.com/pod-product-compliance
Lightning Source LLC
Chambersburg PA
CBHW051548020426
42333CB00016B/2159